BLACK
TITAN

BLACK TITAN

A. G. Gaston and the Making of a
Black American Millionaire

Carol Jenkins and Elizabeth Gardner Hines

Best wishes,

ONE WORLD
BALLANTINE BOOKS • NEW YORK

For
Elizabeth Gardner Jenkins
Because we love you so much
and
Minnie Gardner Gaston
Because you loved him so much

A One World Book
Published by The Random House Publishing Group

www.ballantinebooks.com/one

Library of Congress Cataloging-in-Publication Data
can be obtained from the publisher upon request.

ISBN 0-345-45347-6

Manufactured in the United States of America

Book design by Mercedes Everett

First Edition: January 2004

2 4 6 8 10 9 7 5 3 1

CONTENTS

PROLOGUE

The man lying in the hospital bed before me resembled a carving of a wise African elder, the kind of statue you might see perched atop a rickety roadside table in a dusty Caribbean village. His skin, dark as mahogany and just as smooth, was pulled taut over his carefully delineated features; his wiry body, solid and strong despite the passing years. That he was nearly a hundred years old seemed improbable to me. True, his always close-cropped hair had by now turned entirely white. But his eyes still told you that he understood everything you'd said, and what you meant.

Here was the man who had created ten major companies well before anyone thought a black man capable of the job. Here was a man who had amassed considerable wealth at a time when the words *black* and *wealth* still felt antithetical. A man who had been a central force in the civil rights movement, who had made it into the history books. A man who would live to be 103 years old, despite this bump in his otherwise healthy life.

That we were in a hospital room on his account seemed more a minor adjustment to the tenor of his daily life than the result of a life-threatening illness. This was so not because we did not care about his well-being, but precisely because he made it seem as if nothing at all had changed. The man about to have part of his diabetes-compromised leg removed gave no sign whatsoever of the impending alteration. Instead, characteristic of nearly a century of methodical accomplishment, he was rooted in the present. And at that particular moment his niece from New York had arrived to pay a visit. As his wife of fifty years, Minnie, fussed about him, inquiring of his comfort, he leaned closer to me (the visiting niece), giving an indication that he wanted to say something important, something serious. "You know what our people need now, Carol Ann? Their own stock market. I just wish I were ten years younger. Yes, that's what we need now." Hours later, in the recovery unit, he returned to the same discussion of investing and securities, with no mention of his own, very personal loss that day.

My uncle, A. G. Gaston, was the real thing if you wanted to use words like *legend* or *icon*. Beginning with the question *What do our people need now?* Uncle Arthur (as we called him) developed, over the course of his nearly eighty-year career, an amazingly accurate business philosophy that allowed him to create and grow numerous service-based companies for the black community in Birmingham, Alabama. By 1992 *Black Enterprise* (the magazine devoted to tracking the progress of African American businesses and their creators) had designated A. G. Gaston the Entrepreneur of the Century. I doubt there were many entrepreneurs—white or black—who could rival the span (seventy-three years) or the expanse (banking, insurance, motel, restaurant, real estate, construction, funeral homes and cemeteries, radio stations, senior housing, and a business college) of his empire.

For many years A. G. Gaston was referred to casually as the richest black man in America. We, his family, never knew if that was actually true, but we did know for certain that he was very good at what he did, and that he went to work every day of his life until the day he died. At his death, news accounts would put the combined worth of his companies as high as $140,000,000.

None of us really understood, as our uncle's life and legend were unfolding, how accurately his story reflected a century of hopes on the part of African Americans: initiated by the promise of the Civil War, trampled by the failures of the Reconstruction era, to finally become possible a hundred years later. The sweep of his life was nothing other than majestic: from grandparents who were former slaves, to the civil rights riots on the street just outside his office window, A. G. Gaston had seen it all. Not only had he seen it, but he had done it—and in unparalleled company. Over the course of his life Gaston had worked alongside two giants of this century, both considered saviors of the race: Booker T. Washington and Martin Luther King Jr.

Bracketed between these two men of national and world renown, A. G. Gaston played his part on a smaller stage, in the Birmingham he loved and refused to abandon. He often shared that stage with the more brilliant lights passing through, but his legacy, to all who knew and knew of him, offered just as powerful a message as those spelled out by Washington and King.

Uncle Arthur had always been a presence in my life. He married my mother's sister Minnie before I was born. I'm told that when Minnie Gardner married Arthur George Gaston, it was considered a melding of royal dynasties. While my uncle had begun to make his way in the world, the Gardners, a farming family from Montgomery, were considered some of the most beautiful people in Alabama. Thanks to a thoroughly shaken racial cocktail, the girls were, as they would say in the South, "beauty queens," the boys "handsome devils." Thusly united, my cousins and I grew up in a huge, privileged Alabama family: huge because there were so many of us Gardners (thirty siblings and spouses, forty-five first cousins, and so on), privileged because we were the nieces and nephews of A. G. and Minnie Gaston.

Minnie, one of the oldest of the fifteen Gardner children, had helped raise my mother, Elizabeth, when their parents were no longer able. She lived with the Gastons off and on while she was in school, forming a bond with them that might not have been otherwise possible given the practical considerations of being one of fifteen siblings. It was Aunt Minnie, childless in her marriage to A. G., who later chose my name—the name she had been saving for her own, unborn daughter.

By the time I was seven I had moved to New York City with my parents, but the day school closed for the summer I could be found on a plane headed south, a tag on my dress indicating who would pick me up: the Gastons. It was by now the 1950s, and a deeply segregated Alabama of separate schools and water fountains was in full effect. Segregated buses. Rosa Parks and Martin Luther King. The dogs, the bombings, the murders. But little of this returns in the memories I have of my times with Aunt Minnie and Uncle Arthur. My cousins and I loved the summers of luxury that we were afforded by them: the grand city house, the country homes with pools for swimming, lakes for fishing, highly polished floors for sliding across in our socks.

Looking back, of course, I see how much effort went into sequestering us from the ugliness of the time. I was completely oblivious to being discriminated against in any way. It was only years later that I realized I had never been on a bus in Alabama.

Though Uncle Arthur was, arguably, the king of Birmingham, my Aunt Minnie, or simply "Auntie" as we called her, presided over our clan, the Gastons and the Gardners, like a benevolent queen. During the summer she would take charge of perhaps ten of us cousins at a time. Those summers were also very much like boot camp for us: We were educated thoroughly in manners, morality, and essential life skills like typing. Here we were schooled in the best Socratic method, for Auntie hardly ever spoke in sentences. She peppered us, instead, with statements that required us to come up with the key words to complete her phrase. She was not pleased if you failed to supply the correct answer.

Auntie had created her own domain in the business world, centered on the Booker T. Washington Business College, the part of the Gaston empire she ran. She would help create the federal student loan program that allowed millions of black and white students across the country to secure loans to pay their college tuition. But before her attention and influence were global, she had her eye on us. It was our inescapable fate to find ourselves nailed to a chair in typing class on a broiling-hot Birmingham day. Everyone had to type. Everyone cried and complained. But everyone learned. Years later, nailed to my chair before the typewriter in the newsroom of a New

York television station and on a tight deadline, I felt overwhelmingly thankful for the instruction I had received at Auntie's hands.

There was another important lesson we learned from my aunt: the care and feeding of a Very Important Person. She adored her husband, and he adored her, and this was a good thing for children to experience. Not that our own homes were not loving—it's just that most of our families were consumed by the more ordinary daily scramble to keep our heads above water. In the Gaston home, however, we got to see the benefits of undivided attention—and they were many.

People marveled at my uncle's vigor, well past one hundred. Many thought it was my aunt's special dietary ministrations, and they very well may have been right. As children we were expected to help prepare his morning concoction of raw eggs and orange juice (which we scrunched up our noses at) and his evening meal of a mammoth steak, medium rare, which we were delighted to join him in. In an effort to keep Uncle Arthur's skin soft and shining, Auntie created a lotion of a hundred ingredients that she lathered on him daily. He looked so healthy that people began to ask for it for themselves, and by popular demand Auntie began bottling it. Together Aunt Minnie and Uncle Arthur seemed to have figured out the answers to everything: how to become wealthy by doing good, how to have a successful marriage, even how to live a long life.

By the time we were enjoying these idyllic summers, the name *A. G. Gaston* was everywhere in Alabama. We took it for granted that the motel was named for him, the imposing office building, the funeral homes, the senior citizen homes; that he owned the bank, the radio station. He created a world for us; we had an up-close look at limitless possibilities. We simply never thought, *A black person can't do that,* because our uncle had. But there was never any indication from Uncle Arthur, the man, that he was A. G. Gaston, perhaps the richest black man in America. He was not a show-off.

The experiences that he and my aunt shared with us would make us knowing in a way not available to most children, black or white. They traveled early to Africa, bringing back art and artifacts to decorate their homes, to complement other antiques; sailed to England on the *Queen Elizabeth* in the top cabin; spent time with Soviets in their homes; had their pictures taken with, and advice sought by presidents. They had dinner at the White House when that was a rare invitation for blacks, indeed. In my lucky midpoint position in New York, I often got to see them first, as they disembarked from a plane or ship, full of exotic stories and gifts. My aunt, giving a delighted squeal to see us; my uncle, ever-present pipe in hand, greeting me by the more acceptable of the nicknames my family had bestowed on me: "Well, Miss Caldonia!"

———

Money provides much, but not all. For the fact remained that despite his great wealth and accomplishments, there were many places in his own city from which A. G. Gaston was barred because he was black.

Uncle Arthur was already in his seventies and a successful businessman when the civil rights protests came to Birmingham in earnest. (Martin Luther King Jr. was only twenty-six when he began operating in nearby Montgomery a few years earlier.) I wanted, but never got, the chance to be at his side as he negotiated a path from the secure world he had created to the unknown realm of revolt and beyond. I wanted to hear him debate Martin about the value of negotiation versus street protest. Should children participate? Martin said yes; A. G. Gaston said no. He fervently opposed the use of children to stand against the dogs and fire hoses of Bull Connor. Despite the fact that the national outrage King's plan engendered brought a sudden capitulation on the part of white Birmingham, I know my uncle never regretted opposing this action. Only weeks later, four small black girls would pay the price for that agitation with their lives when the Sixteenth Street Baptist Church was bombed.

If A. G. Gaston was labeled too conservative—as he was by many who wished for more radical action from a man of his influence—it was a label that would stick to King himself later, as the young turks of the Black Power movement and Malcolm X rejected his philosophy of nonviolence. Regardless of his image among the better-known civil rights leaders, A. G. Gaston was, without a doubt, involved: In 1963 Gaston was negotiating behind the scenes with the white power elite in Birmingham; he spent upward of $160,000 of his own money to bail protestors out of jail once they had been arrested by Bull Connor's men. Both the A. G. Gaston Motel (Martin's headquarters) and my aunt and uncle's home were bombed. When my uncle died in 1996, surviving participants of the Alabama struggle admitted publicly that without his influence and financial backing, they might not have succeeded in their efforts. It was recognition long overdue.

Though he was an avid supporter of the quest for civil rights in America, Gaston was nonetheless aware that segregation had given him many of his business opportunities. In a separate but equal society, being the one to provide the "equal" (to a captive audience, no less) was something of an advantage. But he did not take advantage. When segregation ended in Birmingham, and blacks could pick and choose from white and black facilities, like most black businessmen he lost some battles. The motel, the first fine establishment for blacks in Alabama, ultimately closed. But the bank and the insurance companies flourished. A. G. Gaston had built loyalty among his customers, many of whom stayed with him. The memory of not being able to get a mortgage to buy a house until Citizens Federal Savings & Loan came along did not fade for some people. The memory of the respect he demanded for his clients remained.

In return for this loyalty—the loyalty of the customers and the loyalty of his employees, many of whom stayed in the Gaston companies for decades—he essentially gave these business over to them. In 1987, in a then unprecedented business move for a black entrepreneur, he sold companies valued at thirty-five million dollars to his staff for a tenth of that. The move ensured that the institutions he built would stand, even after he died.

As an adult I would learn many important lessons from A. G. Gaston. It was a long time before I recognized what it was that made him different from the rest of us: a singular focus. There were many examples of this spread over the course of my adult life—not the least of which was the focus he evidenced that day in the hospital when he lost his leg to diabetes.

I could have learned so much more from my uncle, but inexplicably, I seemed to have no interest in money, in business, in empire building. So we seldom had detailed discussions of the intricacies of corporate branding—which he had accomplished so masterfully long before business schools taught whole courses on it. Nevertheless, by the strength of his personal code he tried to impart some common sense to me. The issue of tipping was one we tussled over regularly. He, of course, was in the best possible position to argue the benefit of frugality. It had made him a wealthy man. But I was by now an established news anchor in New York City and always felt the need to leave a large tip—to create an image of wealth, regardless of the reality.

After one fairly large group dinner, I mentioned that perhaps we should leave more money behind for the waiter, especially since this was my town, and I was known here. On this night, after we had had the same old argument, perhaps for the hundredth time, Uncle Arthur finally announced: "Carol Ann, I just can't do it." We settled the matter by agreeing that I should pay the tip—and the bill—every time they came to visit.

Uncle Arthur always liked to say that building wealth was simple. He even made a list of ten rules to live and work by, which he published in his autobiography *Green Power.* It always seemed to me that rule number seven was the key, the rule by which A. G. Gaston lived his life and amassed his fortunes: "Find a need and fill it. I never made any money trying to make money as such." This was the rule that had governed my childhood summers spent in Alabama, the moral lesson that continues to shape the members of the Gardner-Gaston clan all these years later. It is a lesson as potent now as it was when Uncle Arthur first took the plunge into business, just under a hundred years ago.

A. G. Gaston was the real thing, indeed, and through his life it is possible to see not merely how the deep racial divisions in the United States hindered the advancement of blacks both economically and socially, but also the ways in which triumph over those odds was sometimes possible by way of hard work, determination, and a belief in the very system our white government had put in place to keep its black citizens at the bottom of the heap. I have been lucky enough in my life to see the genius that was A. G. Gaston up close, to learn from him the lessons for success that shaped his own personal history. This book is an attempt to share that wisdom with all of you.

—Carol Jenkins

BLACK
TITAN

A. G. GASTON, *President*

Born in the Black Belt of Alabama the President and Founder of the Smith and Gaston Interest is a living example of what can be done if the heart is right and the spirit is willing. He misses no opportunity to serve his people, his alert mind is ever busy searching for new fields of service that would carry him closer to the hearts of his people. Morning, noon and night find him busy in his affiliation with churches, schools, fraternal, civic, social and patriotic organizations. He feels that he is definitely his brother's keeper.

From A. G. Gaston Enterprises promotional material

MARENGO COUNTY

What I did any man can do—if he
has willpower, determination
and a plan.

THE IRON MINES

Pick any sweltering day in the year 1919. On the outskirts of Birmingham, Alabama, in a small mining village, hundreds of black men are at work, side by side. The old-fashioned broiler that is the Alabama sun beats down hard upon them, and to a man, each is afloat in his own sweat. In the ground beneath their feet, men less lucky than they swim in the blackness of the pits. Thousands of pounds of iron will emerge as a result of their labor; and thousands of men will die in its pursuit.

Some of the men you see and cannot see are convicts, leased out by the state to bring in revenues; some are war veterans, newly returned to face few opportunities and ample disdain. Nevertheless, one of these men, bruised like all the others by the demands of his working life, is on the verge of taking his first step in the direction of becoming a bona fide millionaire—one hundred times over.

Before this man is through, he will serve as an adviser to President John Kennedy. He will play a pivotal role in the American civil rights movement. One day he will even be likened to the great giants of American industry—Rockefeller, Morgan, and Carnegie among them. Like just about every other black man in Alabama in the early part of the twentieth century, A. G. Gaston started with next to nothing: His mother was a cook in the kitchen of a prominent white family; he never had more than a tenth-grade education. After the war he had taken his position in the mines as a means of survival—only to emerge utterly determined that his life was worth more than what the mines were offering.

That determination was a kind of miracle given the context in which Gaston had been raised. And that miracle is the foundation of the story you are about to hear.

The Olive and Vine Company

In order to appreciate A. G. Gaston and his extraordinary success against all odds, we must first understand the world as he knew it.

Gaston was born in the tiny, western Alabama town of Demopolis. Situated halfway between Montgomery, Alabama, and Jackson, Mississippi, Demopolis boasts a long and infamous history. The town is located at the confluence of the Tombigbee and Black Warrior Rivers, used as water highways by Native peoples, early explorers, traders, and settlers. Lodged within the geographic triangle of Tuscaloosa to the north, Mobile to the south, and Montgomery to the east, Demopolis sits dead center in what came to be known as the Black Belt of southern agriculture—as much for the darkness of the soil as for the color of the people who tended it.

President Andrew Jackson, who would launch a meticulous removal of Native American inhabitants from their lands during his administration, had actually started his sweep years before as a militiaman. In the case of Demopolis and its environs, it was the Choctaws who were forced to relocate in 1816. The following year the land was granted by the U.S. Congress to a group of aristocratic exiles who had been banished from France after the revolution for their allegiance to France's fallen dictator Napoléon Bonaparte.

The exiles named their new home Demopolis—"city of the people"—and re-created there a French village called Aingleville. They had come with the intention of coaxing groves of olives and grapes from the region's fertile soil, founding the Olive and Vine Colony to-

ward this end. However, the combination of unsuitable growing conditions for their preferred crops and the inexperience on the part of
the settlers resulted in a magnificent failure in production. According
to legend, the exiles were comically unprepared for rural life; men
and women alike were said to tend to their farming duties in full
court attire. Not a few of the exiles quickly succumbed to the harsh-
ness of the agricultural regime, and many of those who survived fled
back to Paris once amnesty had been granted to them by the new,
more reasonable King Louis Philippe.

Not all who had come to Demopolis from France, however, died
or left immediately, and those who remained—among them
Napoléon's former aide-de-camp, General Lefebvre-Desnouettes—
laid roots deep in the Alabama soil. The area's few remaining Choc-
taw Indians (the very tribe whose families had been displaced by the
arrival of the French) helped educate the settlers as to which crops
would thrive on the land, and shared their own food with the newcomers to protect them from starvation.

As the decade of the 1820s dawned, much of the area's French influence had been amalgamated into the wider culture of the region.
With many exiles departed, the land that made up the newly formed
Marengo County (977 square miles, in which Demopolis is included)
came into the hands of the cotton farmers who had begun to make
their fortunes across the South—in large part through slave labor.
The cotton farmers dug in their heels and accomplished what, by and
large, the French could not: They coaxed riches from the soil, tilling
the canebrakes that surrounded the municipality and producing a viable living out of King Cotton. Of course, the cotton farmers had one
crucial advantage over the French: Most had brought their slaves
with them.

THE COLUMBIAN WORLD'S FAIR
AND THE STATE OF BLACK AMERICA, 1893

If you had asked A. G. Gaston when his birthday was he would have
told you, with pride, that it was the Fourth of July, the date of the signing of the Declaration of Independence. If you'd asked him to prove it,

he couldn't have: Formal records of rural black births were rarely kept before the middle of the twentieth century. But the date, whether by true accident of birth or by choice, reflected Gaston's lifelong identification as a proud American. He was simply unshakable on the subject. And while many other blacks had adopted the Fourth as their own date of birth for its reverberations on the themes of liberty and freedom, few would buy so fully into those ideals as A. G. Gaston did.

At the time of Gaston's birth in 1892, the United States had just witnessed an unprecedented industrial expansion, a true revolution. Machines had been invented that changed the idea of work; transcontinental railroads shrank distances and the time it took to cross them. Partly as a result, great fortunes had been tallied. The American corporation, only recently invented, had been accorded almost human rights by the government, with "robber barons" Rockefeller, Carnegie, and Morgan amassing unprecedented concentrations of wealth and indulging in conspicuous displays of it. Indeed, the country at large seemed to approve of—even glorify as heroic—the self-made man, with "the love of money and success permeat[ing] all ranks of society, not just the top." By 1892 the idea of competition was firmly embedded in the American psyche: social Darwinism, it was called; survival of the fittest.

Survival was indeed in question for many in America. The year of A. G. Gaston's birth saw 165 black men, women, and children lynched in America—the most recorded in a single year. One year later, the country would suffer a serious financial panic, an economic downturn that would last for five years and put three million of the country's fifteen million workers out of jobs. Thousands, known as "the armies of despair," would descend on Washington to protest the state of the nation's economy; six hundred banks, fifty-six railroads, and fifteen thousand companies would eventually go bankrupt.

That same year, a world's fair took place in Chicago that revealed much about the status of blacks in this newly revolutionized America. Organized to celebrate the four hundredth anniversary of Columbus's discovery of the continent, the fair turned out to be so lavish an undertaking that it was forced to open a year later than originally planned. Forty thousand laborers and twenty-eight million dollars later, the crowds poured in to examine more than sixty-five thousand exhibits, each representing one or another of America's great contributions to the world since 1492. It was here that Scott Joplin first played his ragtime; Thomas Edison was on hand to demonstrate the wonders of electricity. In total, more than twenty-seven million people—nearly a quarter of the country's total population at the time—attended the event.

Of the sixty-five thousand exhibits on view, not one had anything to do with black America. Not that ideas hadn't been presented: Anti-lynching activist and journalist Ida B. Wells, along with many other blacks, had appealed—unsuccessfully—to the boards assembling the fair, arguing that at least *one* exhibit celebrating black contributions should be allowed in the showcase. Event organizers were, however, unmoved. Their one concession was to set aside one day, August 25, 1893, as Colored American Day: Blacks would be allowed free admission to the fair and a slice of watermelon each. In protest, Wells organized and distributed hundreds of pamphlets detailing the plethora of black accomplishments that had been left out of the fair's version of American history, including Elijah "the real" McCoy's steam engine lubricators, Norbert Rillieux's sugar refining process, Jan Matzeliger's shoe lasting machine (which enabled soles to be attached to shoes in less than a minute), Granville Woods's steam boiler, electric railway, and telephone transmitter, and Louis Latimer's improvements on both the telephone and the lightbulb. Blacks, Wells proclaimed, had greatly contributed to the very revolution in American life the fair purported to celebrate: transportation, communication, light. Meanwhile, the most enduring black image to surface from the fair itself was a rendering of a woman named Nancy Green—better known to most Americans as Aunt Jemima.

Whatever had changed in America's conception of itself as a capitalist entity, what had not changed was where it figured its black citizens belonged in that equation. Black achievement, the Columbian World's Fair announced, not only didn't matter—it didn't exist.

THE RISE OF KING COTTON

A. G. Gaston's maternal grandparents, Joe and Idella Gaston, had both been slaves in Marengo County. Art, as he was called as a boy, grew up under their watchful eyes. While he had missed being born into legal enslavement by about thirty years, the effects of slavery were still palpable throughout his childhood. In his autobiography, Gaston would intimate that the significance of this past loomed large, shaping his daily life both practically and psychologically. In fact, it was likely as a direct result of slavery—as it was connected to the cotton trade—that Arthur Gaston came to be born in Demopolis at all.

Cotton first began to spread its dominating hand across the southern regions of the United States in and around the decade of the 1790s. Prior to this, throughout the seventeenth and most of the eighteenth centuries, tobacco and rice formed the backbone of commercial agriculture in the U.S., with the production of indigo also playing a small role. But the increasing demand for and profitability of cotton spurred landowners to attempt to push production farther inland and southward, where "the particular combination of soils, temperature patterns, rainfall and growing season . . . [were] uniquely suited for production of the varieties of cotton most in demand."

The development of Eli Whitney's cotton gin in 1793, which revolutionized the cleaning and shucking of the cotton boll, played a pivotal role in the swell of cotton production throughout the South. By mechanically separating the cottonseed from its fiber, the gin was able to increase productivity up to fiftyfold. Whereas before the gin a slave might be expected to clean about a pound of cotton a day, after its invention that figure rose to fifty pounds a day. This increase in salable product in turn amplified the demand for a workforce capable of transferring the raw product out of the field and into the warehouse. In time, this backbreaking work too would come to be carried out by machines. But in the late eighteenth century, it was a job that remained in the hands of black workers ensnared in the system of slavery.

Of course, slavery in America had far preceded the shift of cotton to the role of principal regional resource; nevertheless, the rise of cotton growing farms toward the end of the eighteenth century *did* spur a similar rise in the economic viability of maintaining a slave population. By the 1820s America had become the world's leading cotton producer, and in this ripe economic environment, slaves became wealth in and of themselves. Historian Gavin Wright suggests that by 1850, "The average slave-owner was more than five times as wealthy as the average Northerner, more than ten times as wealthy as the average non-slaveholding Southern farmer. A man who owned two slaves and nothing else was as rich as the average man in the North." Slavery had turned black labor, according to W. E. B. DuBois, into "the foundation stone not only of the southern social structure, but of northern manufacture and commerce, of the English factory system, of European commerce, of buying and selling on a worldwide scale." For all its moral, political, cultural, and racial repercussions, slavery was essentially an economic instrument; more often than not it "followed the market," digging its heels in most firmly where the profit-to-loss ratio was at its highest.

Influenced by the shift in production values in the 1790s, cotton cultivation commenced its creep across the southern states. From Maryland, to Virginia, on down to Georgia and beyond (and aided by their slaves), planters began to take advantage of the ideal growing environment offered by territories south of thirty-seven degrees on the latitudinal axis. Smaller farmers, driven out of developed areas by larger landowners and their economic power, continued to move westward across the South in search of ever more fertile land for cultivation. As they moved, some brought their human chattel along with them. Others would acquire slaves once their new farms had been established.

In the state of Alabama, as much if not more than in its neighboring states, cotton was what determined a life—so much so that the state, originally nicknamed the Heart of Dixie, soon enough came to be known more often as the Cotton State. Cotton cultivation became the heart and soul of this former Indian territory, its growth dictating the lives of well near every person—white or black—who happened to find him- or herself living in Alabama from the time of the discovery of the Black Belt Prairie until the boll weevil infestation of 1915.

For more than forty years the Alabama canebrake would fill the pockets of the white ruling class with gold while soaking up the sweat of the black labor force that made it prosper. It was only the advent of the War Between the States (as many southerners still prefer to call it) that forced this ruling class to make concessions regarding its unmediated economic dominance of the region. Even then, however, those concessions would be modest, at best.

WHAT THE WAR WROUGHT

One of A. G. Gaston's favorite memories of his early childhood involved sitting by the fire with his grandfather Joe. The old man would pull his Confederate money from its hiding place and pass it into Art's hands, mesmerizing the boy with story after story of life on the plantation. Though the details would not stay with Art as the years passed, their tenor would never leave him. *Take joy in the least of things,* Joe seemed to say, *and take nothing for granted.*

The Confederate money that Joe kept as a reminder of his former life dated from a period in the 1860s when Alabama became one of ten southern states to secede from the Union rather than relinquish its right to hold slaves. When Alabama had been admitted to the Union in 1819, its state constitution clearly approved slavery, and during the war Alabamians would fight viciously to retain their property. The southern Confederacy elected its own president, Jefferson Davis, saluted its own flag, and took as its capital the city of Montgomery, Alabama. The new vice president of the Confederacy, Alexander H. Stephens, boasted of this new government: "Its corner stone rests upon the great truth that the Negro is not equal to the white man. This government is the first in the history of the world based on this great physical and moral truth."

The territory in and around Demopolis was spared the task of serving directly in the war; it never saw action in any of the clashes between Confederate and Union troops, although Confederate troops did, eventually, surrender in the town. (It was not until after the war that its citizens saw the faces of Union soldiers for the first time, when they commandeered the city hall for use as a headquarters for their reconstruction efforts.) Nevertheless, the war loomed large for all of the inhabitants of Demopolis. Each and every citizen was intimately aware that whatever the outcome of the hostilities, life as they knew it would be transformed into something heretofore unimaginable. In Marengo County, that meant the delicate balance between its six thousand white and twenty-five thousand black inhabitants would be upset. All they could do was wait and see.

On January 1, 1863, Lincoln's Emancipation Proclamation became effective. That meant that Joe and Idella Gaston, and four million blacks like them, were now theoretically free. It would be another two years, however, before the South finally gave up the fight for its human property. On April 9, 1865, General Robert E. Lee finally surrendered to Union commander Ulysses Grant at Appomattox Court House, officially ending the war. Six days later, on April 14, President Lincoln was shot by John Wilkes Booth. He died the next day.

Once the war had been won and lost, it was finally possible to take stock of what remained. And what remained, in the South, was an unqualified mess. The land was in ruins; the labor system, nonexistent. But there would be more: In the years 1865–1867 there were massive crop failures due to drought and frost. Epidemics swept through white and black populations alike. Though southern blacks were finally free, many were also now starving, sick, and homeless.

––––––––

Perhaps Joe and Idella had heard the promises of freedom: that the government would confiscate plantation landholdings and divide them up among the blacks who'd worked them. The Gastons were no doubt fascinated when the Freedmen's Bureau (the government agency set up to ease blacks' transition into independence) opened one of its major field headquarters right in Demopolis. Though it became clear rather quickly that there would be virtually no land distributed to blacks, buffering that disappointment was the construction of a new school. While the extant records of the Demopolis school do not turn up either Joe's or Idella's name, it is possible that this is where Idella acquired her formidable computational skills. By the time the Freedmen's Bureau left the South, 150 mostly northern, mostly white teachers had taught some ten thousand former slaves to read and count.

Meanwhile, the war's effects on industry in the successfully retained southern states would continue to reveal themselves as disastrous. With the loss of their free slave labor, cotton planters were forced, bit by bit, to diversify their crop production. Even the advent of sharecropping could not make up for the loss in profit suffered by the plantation owners, and they sought out new avenues for increasing their profit margins. Nevertheless, cotton continued to be the primary crop of the region for decades—until the appearance of the boll weevil and then the Great Depression rendered the "one-crop farming system" entirely unsustainable.

For blacks in the South, and perhaps particularly in Alabama, the aftermath of the war would be alternatingly exhilarating and crushing. At least ideologically, the average southern black person was better off after the war; among other things, it had brought about legislation meant to fundamentally change the status of blacks in America. The Thirteenth Amendment abolished slavery in January 1865; the Fourteenth Amendment, passed in June of the same year, granted citizenship to all people born or naturalized in the United States (reversing the famous *Dred Scott* decision of 1857, which specifically decreed that blacks were *not* citizens); the Fifteenth Amendment of 1869 guaranteed that no American would be denied the right to vote because of race.

But while laws were now in place to protect the ideal of "equality," few blacks were able to enjoy the privileges they were legislated to ensure. In the South, "Black Codes" were drafted to regulate the movements of all blacks—and to force them back onto the farmland. As under apartheid in South Africa, American blacks were subject to curfews and were issued passbooks that they were required to present to any law enforcement official demanding to see them. Proof of employment was mandatory; failure to present working papers could result in arrest (which usually entailed being sent to work on a chain gang). These codes, along with intensified brutality against blacks, would continue to shape southern life for another century.

JOE AND IDELLA GASTON

By all accounts, Joe Gaston was a man to be reckoned with. He was a big man—a man whose body was his most valuable tool and weapon in the struggle to survive. The limp that characterized his stride was the mark of an incident he could not bring himself to recount out loud. Like all male slaves, he had been well trained in the profession of farming, accruing skills he would carry with him into freedom. While still a slave, however, his overseer had elevated him to the significant position of groom on a large plantation in the Demopolis area, complete with a formal "big house" where the owners were lodged. Joe's promotion brought him into daily contact with the master and mistress: He prepared the master's and overseer's horses for work in the fields, and he was responsible for suiting up the mistress's carriages for her trips into town. As slave social structure was determined, Joe Gaston held a position of some prestige. His proximity to the wealth of his owners gave him an expanded worldview—one he would eventually impart to his grandson.

Though there was much about his own early life that could have turned Joe into a bitter and unkind person, in his grandson's recollections he was neither. Ill fortune and disappointment had worked instead to turn Joe into a gentle man, a man of inestimable patience and kindness, who struck his grandson only once in his entire life (and that for openly mocking the old man). Rather than viewing his former slave life as one of deprivation, he eagerly shared with his grandson a pool of memories that were often laced with a positive message.

No less so than her husband, Idella Gaston was a person of genuine significance in the social milieu of both ante- and postbellum Demopolis—as well as in her grandson's life. As the primary cook in the kitchen of the well-respected Cornish family for forty-nine years, Idella wielded a power that was both real and palpable in relation to the other servants in the home. In the antebellum South the "master" of the kitchen was the female slave in charge of preparing meals, and these women ruled with fists of iron. Idella Gaston was no different. She took her work seriously, and her devotion to the family who owned her even more so. If Joe felt privileged to be working near the house, Idella's position *inside* it placed her at the very top of the heap. Her proximity to the family had fostered not only familiarity (as in Joe's case) but also a real sense of responsibility toward the people to whom she had tended, day after day. So great was her attachment to the Cornish family that years later A. G. would write in his autobiography that Idella's two greatest devotions in life were to the white family she worked for, and to her church. Where this left her own family in her estimation can only be speculated, but it seems clear enough that if they happened to appear farther on down the list, the Gastons were nevertheless treated with a generally kind, if nononsense, attitude by their matriarch.

A devout Christian and the official treasurer of the region's Christian Aid Society, Idella was often called "Mother" by the congregation of the Morning Star Baptist Church of which she was a member. (To A. G., however, she was always "Grandmama.") She approached her job as treasurer with as much earnest diligence as she did her tasks in the kitchen. Often enough, the jobs were combined. Regularly on Sundays, the membership of Morning Star would follow the Gastons home after services and fill their vast front yard. Idella would dish out plentiful portions of her famous fried chicken, cautioning all those in attendance to save room for the homemade ice cream that would inevitably follow. This was the parishioners' tangible reward for their faithfulness in giving when the lady treasurer came knocking at their doors. Each donation was wrapped carefully in a handkerchief and then stowed away, not to be touched until the next Sunday when the preacher called for the offering. Not once did a penny go missing on Idella's watch.

By the time A. G. came into Joe and Idella's life in 1892, thirty years after they had been freed from slavery, a life was still defined by its relationship to the land—though, critically, the one-dimensional nature of this affiliation had begun to change. The southern United States was struggling to develop a means of maintaining economic growth in a supposedly free-market atmosphere, and the answer, it seemed, was to maintain the subservience of the black population on both social and economic fronts. To a group so accustomed to working for *less* than nothing, the option of working for *almost* nothing was an offer that could not be refused.

The Reconstruction era—a period lasting from approximately 1865 to 1877—ushered in the early rise of an arrangement between (almost without exception, white) landowners and (usually black) sharecroppers, in which "blacks . . . worked a portion of the land owned by whites for a share of the profit from the crops." Sharecropping, as this new system of farm labor was called, became the de facto replacement for the recently outlawed practice of slavery. Though initially the arrangement seemed to be a good deal for the newly released slaves, offering them not only a sense a freedom in their work but also a means of providing for themselves in the cash-poor southern economy of the period following the war, it was not long before it became obvious that the perceived freedoms of sharecropping were little more than fantasy.

Poor blacks and whites alike, who had looked to sharecropping as a new way of life, soon realized that the system in which they had put their faith to escape the constant struggle to survive had done nothing but increase the strain of that burden. The average sharecropping wage turned out to be about fifty cents a day, and was rarely actually seen. Though the system of sharecropping was based on an understanding that the sharecroppers would receive the benefit of land to farm, it takes much more than land alone to produce crops. For all the extras required to make a farm run—seeds, equipment, fertilizers, food—sharecroppers were forced to borrow against their projected profits. Landowners were only too happy to extend this credit to their employees, at rates of interest that were unregulated and thus usually exorbitant. By the time the crops had been harvested and sold, and it was time for the year's tab to be settled with the landowner, most sharecroppers found themselves deep in the hole, and were forced to begin the new year in arrears.

From this never-ending cycle of debt that offered little chance of profit, there was almost no escape—unless other means could be found to secure employment. Joe and Idella Gaston were, in some fashion, particularly well prepared to try to make their way under this new system of wage labor—in part because each possessed skills in addition to their ability to farm. Both were "hard workers" (in the definitive sense of the phrase), people who held "extra jobs with the white people in town" in order to make ends meet. As rare as these opportunities were for blacks, the Gastons took advantage of what they could and were able to buy their land outright over a period of years. They built the log cabin in which A. G. was born here, working at it in the few small hours left to them between tilling the land and doing various chores in the homes of the white denizens of Demopolis. Joe drove his ox-pulled cart into town daily, offering his services to townsfolk in need of assistance beyond farm labor. Idella retained her position as cook and as such was able to contribute to the family finances in a fashion that was not reliant upon sharecropping. They saved and sacrificed and prayed and worked, and the end result was that Joe and Idella Gaston were able to build a life based on revenue rather than on debt. Amid the tensions and frustrations of "readjustment" to a life without the cotton or the slaves that defined the region, the Gastons were lucky enough to fashion a new kind of existence for themselves, one that left a lasting impression of the value of hard work and sacrifice on their grandson.

MARCHING TOWARD INDUSTRY

Whatever the changing nature of Joe and Idella's own relationship to the land, A. G.'s testimony of his early existence in Demopolis reveals the quickly diminishing importance of a connection to the Alabama terrain, ebbing generation by generation, and in his own family. Though he refers early and often to the lucre of the Alabama soil, and spoke longingly of its "rich loamy" quality throughout his autobiography and for the rest of his life, his existence would not hinge on cultivating a relationship to the land as his grandparents' had. A. G. Gaston's life (and his mother's and father's, for that matter) would be defined by something altogether different: the growth of industry.

A. G.'s mother, Rosie Gaston, had spent the majority of her life in Demopolis, watching and learning from her parents' example as she worked alongside them. Like her mother before her, Rosie was destined to become the head cook for a white family. However, the limiting factors in a town the size of Demopolis were wealth and opportunity. Like just about every other plantation town in the former Confederacy, Demopolis had been sent reeling by the effects of the war and, in A. G.'s own words, "struggled to regain [its] economic balance," even forty years later. While black labor had contributed to making America (and the rest of the Western world) great, America in turn had engaged in what historian Manning Marable has called the most striking fact of American economic history: "the brutal and systematic underdevelopment of Black people."

Rosie Gaston had not been immune to this economic imbalance and the "systematic underdevelopment" that resulted from it. The only skills she possessed (as a cook or maid) were ones in excess in Demopolis, forcing her to look elsewhere—a bigger city—for work. Rosie would walk away from rural life, from the land her parents had worked so hard to make their own, for what would turn out to be forever, in the uncertain and unpredictable search for a job that would allow her to support herself and her young son. Art was left behind, in his grandparents' care.

What did Rosie Gaston feel on that first hot day when she peeled her son from her skirts and headed down a road leading to who knew where? It's impossible to know, precisely. Certainly, sadness accompanied her down that road: sadness at leaving her child, her family, the land she had known from the earliest years of her life. But it's not implausible to wonder whether some of what she may have felt as she walked that road was a sense of relief—relief at having a safe place to leave her son when so many women did not. Relief that she could leave that son behind and still imagine that one day she would be able to reclaim him—so different from what her mother had told her about the days on the plantation, when not even the bonds of blood were sacred and mothers lost their children as regularly as the changing of the seasons. And, perhaps, relief as well at the possibility of a new start, a means of parting ways with the pain that accompanied the loss of a man in what should have been the prime of their lives together.

Of this man—A. G. Gaston's father—we know little. A. G. himself made only one direct mention of his father in the entirety of his autobiography, and that declaration was a scant three lines long. "Papa was dead now," he bluntly offered. "The railroads were coming through Alabama, and Papa got a job as a railroad man. Then he died."

One of the handful of facts A. G. was able to recall about his fa-

ther was that the extension of the railroads through the state of Alabama had offered him a means of survival that was not tied to farming the land—and he took it. Demopolis had been chosen to serve as
the crossroads of the St. Louis–San Francisco Railway and the Alabama Great Southern Railroad, a construction project that would
require manual labor on a grand scale. Blacks who were hired by the
railroads had little chance of doing much besides clearing paths, haul-
ing coal, and laying tracks, so we can assume that it was in one or all
of these pursuits that A. G.'s father was employed. His salary would
have been about $124 a year. It was crippling labor, not least of all
because the heat of the Alabama sun made every movement a greater
burden to bear. It was a well accepted fact that thousands of workers
would die or be maimed on the project; railroad work was a dangerous endeavor. But like most black men, A. G.'s father likely saw the
job with the railroads as a chance—an opportunity to ride the wave
of industrialization into an era where his son might one day conduct
the train for which he laid the tracks.

A. G. would watch closely and learn as first one of his parents
and then the other stepped away from a life that was dedicated to the
soil—as his grandparents' had been—and searched out a means of
survival based on increasingly skilled forms of labor. His father
would die for the promise of the industrial age, and, partly as a result
of this, his mother would be forced to leave him behind as she, too,
attempted to build a life away from the land. Both his father's failure
and his mother's success in the newly industrial society would leave
lasting effects on this boy who, by the age of ten, had already learned
enough of the world to inspire his first business idea.

———

Rosie's hunt for employment led her to Greensboro, Alabama,
twenty-five miles northeast of Demopolis. Once there, she found employment in the home of A. B. and Minnie Loveman. The Lovemans
were a prominent and prosperous Jewish family, owners of the regionally famous Loveman, Joseph & Loeb Department Stores, which
would eventually become the state's largest department store chain.
The Lovemans employed dozens of white citizens in their profes-

sional practice, as well as a considerable number of black employees retained to take care of the business of the home. It was as part of the latter group that A. G.'s mother, Rosie, was taken on. Her skills in the kitchen proved themselves unparalleled by Greensboro standards, and she quickly became an indispensable element in the Loveman household—so much so that when the family expanded their business and relocated to the big city a few years later, there was no question about whether Rosie would be coming along.

The "big city" for anyone living in Alabama at the turn of the century was Birmingham. Often called the Magic City for the stores of coal and iron found there, Birmingham held great promise for the population of the entire region—blacks and whites alike. When cotton was king, plantation owners had avoided the area of Jefferson County (of which Birmingham is a part), due to the aridity and rockiness of the terrain. The soil there was anything but right for growing cotton, so the area remained largely undeveloped until the coming of the railroads at the end of the nineteenth century.

Located at the intersection of two major railroad lines, Birmingham was incorporated as a town in 1871, with a population of eight hundred inhabitants. The city quickly grew in size, boasting twenty-six thousand residents by 1890. The vaults of Birmingham's first coal mine opened in 1878, and twelve years later the mining economy had produced an economic boom for the ruling class. For the underclass, things were not nearly so positive, but the area nonetheless provided opportunities for work that were not linked to sharecropping, offering the promise of another chance for blacks to "get ahead."

The tremendous growth of the Birmingham population and the city's status as one of the nation's leading steel-producing centers turned the fast-growing town into a mecca for business. The tax rate in Birmingham proper—the lowest of the thirty-eight American cities with populations in the one-hundred-thousand-to-three-hundred-thousand range—offered extremely advantageous conditions to the building of industry. In addition, assessment figures for the area were substantially undervalued—within the business district they were less than 20 percent.

It may have been just this combination of encouraging factors that led A. B. Loveman to leave Greensboro and set up shop in Birmingham. A shrewd businessman, A. B. must have quickly realized that Birmingham's economy was ripe for the consumerist cause, and he made the bold move of expanding his fast-growing retail empire into this new center of financial activity. With the relocation of the Loveman family, and the purchase and renovation in 1905 of a grand manor house on Rhodes Circle (an area just south of town that would, over time, develop into an affluent residential neighborhood), life began to change not only for the Lovemans, but for their employees as well. Rosie's years of dedication to the family, along with the newly available rooms on the Rhodes Circle property, made it possible for the Lovemans to allow her to bring her son to live with her, finally. Mother and son would reside above the stable, built with a view of the Lovemans' own house.

Button Fares

In the years that Rosie had been gone, Art had grown from a small boy into a young man. Already testing his boundaries in the one-room schoolhouse Demopolis offered to educate young blacks, for a period A. G. found himself in and out of trouble with the principal of the school, Ulysses S. Jones, a man much feared among the student body. Most often, Gaston found himself punished for "shooting cottonseeds at the girls during class" with his slingshot, revealing the first hint, too, of his growing interest in the opposite sex. One girl in particular, Creola Smith ("plump and pretty" and a year younger than A. G.), caught his eye above the others.

However, A. G. was rarely the instigator of these little crusades against adult authority. By his own admission, A. G. Gaston was, as a child, a "square," afraid of falling into disrepute with the adult community for fear of what it might mean to his future—and, in particular, his future in business. The possibility of such a career had been opened up to him by a certain Sebron Edwards, the first black person in Marengo County to be graduated from high school. After his diploma had been conferred, Sebron went to work in Demopolis as a clerk for the local grocery store. His presence behind the counter, pencil stuck smartly behind his ear as he tabulated accounts, made the young A. G. Gaston aware of new possibilities. Here was a black man in a position of power, not just working but *thinking*. A. G. was so deeply impressed by Sebron that he returned to the market again and again, just to catch sight of the spectacle. He quickly made up his mind that one day he, too, would stand behind a counter and think, tabulate, decide.

It was the vision of Sebron and the possibilities he represented that, in some fashion, kept A. G. from the worst of trouble. His most frequent co-conspirator, a boy named Dennis Martin, had found no such model; as an adult A. G. would blame the dismal course the man's life eventually took on precisely this absence of positive inspiration.

A. G., meanwhile, kept Sebron securely in his sights and soon laid off his more ill-behaved endeavors. Though it made him increasingly popular with the adult population of Demopolis, this transformation into a so-called square had its distinct disadvantages when it came to maneuvering within the social milieu of the children's world. Gaston is entirely forthright about his early experiences as an outcast, explaining in aching detail how his shift away from roguishness also represented a shift away from popularity, and how the loss of friends that accompanied that transformation was a painful enough experience to make him desperate to regain that community by any means necessary. "I . . . was nobody's hero," Gaston wrote. "I was a square . . . my old friends did not seek me out. I grew lonesome."

With Sebron in mind (along with a newfound familiarity with the Weiss family, the prominent negro owners of a local funeral parlor), those means revealed themselves in the form of a swing hanging in A. G.'s backyard. It had been hung there, years before, by his parents, and had been eyed with envy by the neighborhood children since the day it first appeared. It was the only such swing in the neighborhood, and its broad and solid construction (from a heavy rope bound to a four-by-six-foot door) made it an oasis of pleasure to which each and every child in the neighborhood hoped to gain access. Faced with the trauma of increasing isolation—not to mention a now ever-present desire to "make something" of himself—A. G. realized in an instant how he might win back his friends: He would turn his swing into a business venture, charging button fares for a ride.

This first endeavor was a resounding success, and it came to form the backbone of what would be Gaston's trademark for business development. He had, as he liked to say, found a need and filled it. He had sensed the children's longing for a commodity that he (and only he) could offer. He had provided them with a product that served their needs (while, admittedly, also serving his own), and they proved ready customers, willing to pay to satisfy their desires. On that day A. G. collected "several cigar boxes full of fares." He won the admiration of the parents in the town for keeping their children out of trouble, and most importantly, he won back his friends.

He learned a simple lesson that day: People will pay for what they need, or for what they perceive themselves as needing. He had found a need and filled it, and, crucially, he had done it all within his own small community of black children. Moreover, he had found that power was his game, that he treasured the control he wielded on this day over his employees (in this case his cousin Gaston Stern and the infamous Dennis Martin) and customers alike. The boy whose friends had abandoned him had found his way back into the inner circle, and he would make it his mission to stay there. Business, he realized, was his way in.

A New Beginning

It was not long after A. G.'s triumphant discovery of the machinations of supply-side economics that Rosie returned to Demopolis to collect her son. The years in Demopolis had done him well, and the young man Rosie escorted off the train platform and onto a train headed straight for Birmingham was one whose vision of the world was already set on achievement.

But neither Rosie nor A. G. himself was naive enough to believe that "success" was something that would come easily—or come at all. He was, after all, a black boy, and the question of whether he would succeed or fail (in business or in any pursuit) was always second to the question of whether he would live or die at the hands of any white man who saw fit to take him out of the world. In Demopolis the rules had been relatively easy:

> Any "nigger" who did not jump off the sidewalk when [the white folks] came by was considered "biggety" by the whole community, and just not well brought up. Most of the civic leaders and professional men were members of the Klan. All white men were honest by definition, and it never occurred to me until years later . . . that there were good and bad humans of all races.

Though this system of belief was a safe one if you happened to be a black person living anywhere in the American South and trying to keep out of harm's way, what it could not account for was the random, chaotic violence that a large urban area such as Birmingham offered up with little warning. Though only 40 percent of the Birmingham population was black at the time A. G. and Rosie moved there, twice as many blacks as whites died there each year. It was a dangerous place for a black person—a black *man*—to be, and it was clear enough to everyone that playing by the "rules" was no real protection from whatever evil came riding by under cover of a white sheet.

The warnings from the family he was leaving behind flew fast and furiously on the day A. G. waved good-bye to Demopolis. There were "killings" to watch out for, his grandmother reminded him as she wept on the platform, alternately pulling her grandson to her and pushing him away, toward his future. His grandfather said nothing; the only hint of his distress was the unusually emotionless aspect of his expression. Keep out of bad company, Idella cautioned as she handed A. G. a still-warm box filled with the last taste of her famous chicken he would savor for a long while.

On the train, Rosie tried to comfort him by rebuffing his fears. "You ain't scared," she said. "You're big now." Though she wanted to reassure her son, it was also her job, she knew, to instill in him an abiding awareness of the dangers that lay ahead. For this reason she quickly added, echoing her own mother's words, "But I tell you one more time. Stay out of bad company." She would be relentless in her counsel, she had decided—as relentless as the threat of violence itself.

A. G. settled in for the ride with fear biting at the back of his throat. He was, without question, scared, no matter what his mother said. He had seen a lynching once when he was a boy in Demopolis, a black man strung up and hanged from a tree whose branches jutted out over a street corner in the middle of town. He had watched the man get hanged and had thought to himself at the time that it was justice that was being served on the limbs of that tree. That man had stepped out of line and was paying the price for it.

Now, though, as the familiar landscape of Marengo County receded and the train cut through a ridge of trees, A. G. pressed his face against the glass of the window, cooling his forehead against the more complex thoughts that had begun to worry him. Things were no longer as clear as they had once been. The pines leapt by, their boughs swaying in the rush of wind. In the shadows of the sunlight—highlighting first a flower, then a bird, then his own dark face—hung the ghostly remains of the many brown boys who had traveled this road before him.

The box of his grandmother's fried chicken sat, cooling, on his lap. A. G. reached in and picked up a crisp golden leg, eager to feel its warmth. He bit in, voraciously. Birmingham was only hours away.

PROVING GROUNDS

How does a poor man become a businessman?
By accumulating money and keeping his eyes
open for the main chance.

BIRMINGHAM, 1905

The brakes of the train sang out as they screeched to a halt at the border of Birmingham proper. Arthur jumped when the conductor's voice cried out the station stop, a mixture of fear and excitement racing through his veins. They had reached the Union Depot, Birmingham's imposing new train station, built to replace the old wooden-frame Relay House that had greeted Birmingham's first immigrants. Now it was the turreted stone structure that welcomed the thousands of transplants flooding into Birmingham, most of whom came for the mines (coal and iron) and the employment that could be found in them.

The cinders that filled the air, which had collected beneath Arthur's collar and stung at his eyes and throat throughout the trip, finally began to dissipate as the passengers disembarked from the train. As a result of the recent (1898) *Plessy v. Ferguson* decision, blacks and whites now lived "separate, but equal" lives. By federal law, whites were not required to integrate any facility if blacks were given their own, separate accommodations. Toward that end, Arthur and Rosie had been forced to ride to Birmingham in the "Negro coach"—separated from the coal engine by only the baggage car.

They were hardly the first black travelers to arrive at their destination covered in soot.

Arthur helped his mother gather up their few things—a sack filled with his worldly belongings, Rosie's purse, the wilted package that had held Idella's long-since-eaten boxed lunch—and sprang from the train in a quick-step, right on Rosie's heels. He was thirteen years old. He'd never seen a city before, but he was too afraid of getting left behind to dawdle and gaze.

His mother's feet cut a well-worn path toward town. It cost five cents to ride the segregated streetcar, so Rosie and Arthur would be walking. Struggling to keep up with his mother's quick pace, Arthur managed to bleat out a single question as she strode along before him. "Is it far?" he asked. Rosie assured him that the distance was relatively short; it would take them straight through the middle of the city. His job, she reminded him, was to stay close by—and out of trouble.

Turn-of-the-century Birmingham had begun its ascent out of the depression of the 1890s, and was fast becoming a boomtown. Shop-keepers crammed block after block with their wares; shoppers streamed up and down Twentieth Street (the central thoroughfare), now bisected by tracks for the steam-driven streetcars. On either side of the tracks, horse-drawn buggies and mule wagons created a traffic jam of past and future. The city's first steel-frame skyscraper, the Woodward building, had already been constructed—it was ten stories high. The Brown-Marx Building, set to double that record, was nearing its completion.

But for all of its modernization, Birmingham was moving backward in time when it came to race, solidifying its discrimination against blacks—who represented 43 percent of the city's residents. Thriving black businesses (some of them catering to a "whites only" clientele) that had once been interspersed among the white businesses in the central downtown area were forced out of their homes and relocated to nearby Fourth Avenue (which would eventually become the black business district). Alabama's 1901 constitution rescinded voting rights from blacks and "within five months of the constitution's ratification, Birmingham's black population of eighteen thousand had only thirty registered voters." Comparatively, in the 1870s, blacks had made up almost half the voting population of the city.

Despite it all, African American migration to the city continued, and by 1930 Birmingham had the largest percentage of black citizens of any major American city. Mostly they came for the work: Almost half of all coal miners and 65 percent of steel- and ironworkers were black. Others, like Rosie, were servants in wealthy white homes.

In her time working for Mr. and Mrs. A. B. Loveman, Rosie had established a stellar reputation in white society—so much so that the Lovemans regularly lent her services out to their friends. She catered luncheons for as many as two hundred people, complete with hired string orchestras. Rosie had made the transition from log cabin to bustling metropolis seamlessly. Just as Joe and Idella had been in Demopolis, Rosie was valued in this bigger city for her skill. Now her son was with her; she would teach him to become invaluable, too.

As they passed building after building, Rosie told Art what she knew of the activities that took place there. Pointing to one and then another newly built vaudeville theater, Rosie explained, "Folks sing, dance and act out plays on the stage every night but Sunday right here in this building. There too." Beyond the buildings, in the distance, the Red Mountain ridge, home of the industrial mines, belched up the huge streams of fire-tinged smoke that settled in a dull haze over the city skyline.

Before Art could fully take in what was in front of him, Rosie tapped him on the shoulder, calling for his attention. "Turn around and look here, Art. There's the store."

Arthur spun around. The Loveman, Joseph & Loeb Department Store rose before him. His eyes locked on the name *Loveman*. He remembered—"Those were our folks."

At the turn of the century Loveman's store was the "largest and most magnificent department store south of the Ohio"—a linchpin in the Birmingham business district. A. B. Loveman, the company's founder, had been born in Hungary of Jewish ancestry and orphaned by age eight. He arrived in America at twenty-one and peddled fabrics in Tennessee and Alabama to support himself. In 1867 he opened his first general store in Greensboro. By 1887 he had taken on partners and moved into his first Birmingham location. There was already a small Jewish enclave there: "prominent storekeepers, clothiers, jobbers, bankers" who, unlike blacks, had been readily accepted into the developing town's matrix.

A. B. was an apt model for the young Gaston in many ways: He was a self-made man who had risen from poverty to create a successful life in business. He worked diligently and methodically, leaving the house before the sun rose, and staying at the store until late at night to accommodate his working customers. Although in his mother and grandparents Art had examples of a solid work ethic, in Loveman, Art would see the potential yield of all that hard work: prestige, a beautiful home, people to serve you.

While Arthur's mother chided him to stop gawking and hurry up, the boy's mind skidded along in excitement. The apprehension that had shadowed him since he stood on the platform in Demopolis dropped away. Plans for his future so occupied him that he barely noticed the funny red lights dancing in the windows at the edge of town as he and his mother passed out of the business district and into the residential area. Rosie seemed in no mood to explain what they might mean.

Berney Loveman

The two-story brick house that rose up along the far curve of Rhodes Circle, down the rim of the carriage road, was bigger than any Arthur had ever seen. "Here's home," his mother announced with a broad smile as they rounded the flank of the building and headed for the back door. As they stepped over the threshold, Rosie proclaimed their arrival once more, causing Mrs. Minnie Loveman to appear in the kitchen to welcome them. She was "small and plump," according to Gaston's later reminiscences, and as she laid eyes on her cook's son for the first time, she smiled affectionately and welcomed him to her home. Behind her stood her son, Berney.

The distance from the big house to the servants' quarters on the

Loveman estate was, in physical terms, just a short walk across a well-manicured lawn. In every other way, though, it was a journey of a thousand miles. Nevertheless, it was a trip that Berney Loveman took daily, despite his mother's admonitions to keep out of the two rooms above the stable where A. B. kept his horse Prince, and where Rosie and Arthur Gaston lived. The boys had shaken hands in the kitchen of the big house on that first day Arthur turned up in Birmingham to stay. They had been inseparable ever since.

Art and Berney spent their evenings developing whole cities out of blocks, their Friday afternoons pulling candy in Rosie's kitchen, and their weekends hiding together in the woods that bordered the Loveman property—or anytime "Miss Minnie" (as the servants called Mrs. Loveman) summoned Berney to practice his violin. On Sundays during the summer months, Gaston recalls that together they would watch baptisms in a nearby creek. Black and white parishioners alike used the spot to wash away their sins, and Arthur and Berney used these sacred occasions as an excuse to catch one another in a dare: in this case to "chunk hickory nuts at the preacher." As far we know, they never got caught.

And then one day their friendship was over, terminated not—as might be expected—by the Lovemans, but by Rosie, whose creeping discomfort with the boys' relationship had finally reached its breaking point. Their playtime began as usual, with the blocks. After their town had been constructed, both boys agreed that it was the best one they'd ever built, and set to wrestling on the floor in an effort to determine who was the better builder of the two (each claiming that the other was better). As Gaston remembered it:

> [Berney] poked me in the ribs with his forefinger. And we were
> tussling, tickling, rolling on the floor. Berney was fast, but I was
> ten pounds heavier and I pinned him, sitting on his chest.
> "All right . . . uncle," I demanded.
> "Uncle . . . uncle . . . uncle," he laughed.

The next thing Arthur heard was Rosie's voice, cold as stone, ordering him to get up and off Berney. Arthur did as he was told. Berney

gathered up his things and hightailed it back to the big house. Rosie
sank down onto her bed, overcome with emotion.

"Art, I been doin' some thinking," she began, and then detailed
her newly hatched plan for sending him away to school. She explained to him the need for an education, the likelihood that without
it he'd end up "swabbing by the flames in the blast furnace and falling
into bad company." She reminded him that he needed to mix with
people of his own kind, needed to meet and mingle with "well-to-do,
educated colored people" early on if he was to succeed. Watching the
white people had its advantages, she implied, but it was becoming a
part of the elite black community that would make a real difference
in the end. To her credit, Rosie never explicitly mentioned how terri-
bly Arthur's relationship with Berney frightened her. This time
around, she spared her son the pain of a direct confrontation with the
vagaries of racial determination. She was well aware that he would
have many opportunities to battle those particular obstacles in the future.

GETTING AN EDUCATION

The privilege of Rosie's employment situation had placed her in a position to observe the best and brightest of white Birmingham society.
She understood more than most blacks did how whites ran their businesses and homes. And from what she had learned, it seemed to her
that the first step on Art's road to success would be securing a good
education.

Outside the South, black Americans had made huge leaps in education by the end of the nineteenth century. The first black to graduate from Harvard University had done so in the 1870s; W. E. B.
DuBois received his doctorate from the same university in 1895.
Alain Locke was named the first black Rhodes Scholar in 1907. The
Freedmen's Bureau had spawned fifty black colleges, and by the turn
of the century there were a hundred in operation around the nation.
Black doctors and lawyers numbered in the thousands, and in cities
like Boston and Philadelphia, wealthy black communities regularly
held literary teas.

But in the South, slavery and the demands of a farming life had hindered educational advancement for both blacks and whites. As recently as 1890 (just two years before Gaston was born), a mere 30 percent of southern blacks age five through twenty had attended school, whereas the number of whites who had done so across the same range of ages hovered at about 48 percent. This meant that even in the best-case scenario (that being that you were white), your chances as a Southerner of having attended school were less than 50 percent.

As in just about every other aspect of southern living, race played a crucial role in educational possibilities. Not only were the percentages of school attendees lower among blacks, but, unsurprisingly, literacy rates were dramatically lower as well. In 1880, when the first data was collected on the topic, 21 percent of southern whites were considered illiterate. Among blacks, 76 percent fit the same profile—a difference of fifty-five percentage points, and a stark indicator of the lingering effects of slavery and the prohibition against providing blacks with reading skills. The significance of this schism is made evident by this final fact: parental illiteracy has, historically, levied a sizable tax on the following generation. Meaning, in short, that children of illiterate parents were less likely to attend school themselves—or (from the other side of the divide) that children whose parents could read were more likely to be encouraged to attend school. The addition of the racial element to this statistical pool underscores the already obvious disadvantage under which black children labored. The literacy gap did narrow as time went by, so that twenty years later, at the turn of the century, "slightly more than half" of blacks were literate as compared to just over 85 percent of whites. But that divide never fully closed, leaving black children (who would, of course, become adults) swimming against the tide of inequality.

Whether Rosie or her parents could read or write, we do not know for certain. It is clear, however, that both Idella and Joe Gaston could count: They knew enough to be able to keep their own financial affairs in order, and Idella's position as treasurer of the Morning Star Baptist Church would have necessitated at least a basic acquaintance with numbers. If the statistics are right, then, based on her parents' level of academic achievement, it's fairly likely that Rosie was literate to some degree—whether numerically, alphabetically, or possibly both.

Arthur, then, was born into a household in which some level of literacy may have been the norm, and in which the expectation of a higher level of achievement was imbued in the next generation early on, and reinforced often. While still in Demopolis, Arthur had attended school on a regular basis. His parents—whether that role happened to be filled by Joe and Idella or Rosie herself—were "particular" about his upbringing, so much so that they saw to it that any misbehavior on Arthur's part was to be met with direct attention by none other than the fearsome principal of the school.

The move to Birmingham, however, marked a disruption in Arthur's schooling, for Birmingham, though an enormous city by the day's standards, offered few opportunities for the education of its black citizens. Between 1891 and 1907 not a single new school was constructed for the area's young black inhabitants—despite the fact that the city was experiencing a population explosion of gigantic proportions. Moreover, one of the most important schools in the town had burned down in the middle of the last decade of the nineteenth century, leaving more than a thousand black students without a source of education.

In 1905 there were approximately three elementary schools in all Birmingham designated for use by black students. Eight elementary schools and one high school existed for the white population. All the schools for blacks were frame houses, the majority of which hardly qualified as more than shacks. For the white schools, brick was the building material of choice. In this same year, the black citizens of Birmingham "petitioned the board of education for improved facilities," citing the lack of light, heat, ventilation, and desks in their schools as a cause for concern. Their proposal was soundly rejected. It was not until 1910 that things would begin to look up—if only the slightest bit—for blacks on the educational front. A high school would find a way to spring up in a rented building, and the Thomas School—the school that had burned down years before—would finally begin its reconstruction process.

In the meantime, however, Rosie Gaston had a son to raise. The question was, where could she send him to school?

THE TUGGLE INSTITUTE

A woman named Carrie Tuggle provided the answer. In 1908 Carrie "Granny" Tuggle—a former slave and domestic, now engaged in welfare work—had appeared before a Birmingham court and requested that custody of a young boy, about to be sentenced to a term in jail, be granted to her instead of to the state. For whatever reasons— among them, perhaps, the fact that Birmingham was at that time without either a juvenile court system or enough room in its jails to deal with the number of prisoners it already had in its remand—the judge granted her wish. Starting with her work with this first boy, Granny Tuggle (as she came to be known) built the foundation of what would become first an orphanage for the rehabilitation of abandoned and truant children and then a "practical institute" to educate Birmingham's Negro children.

Soon enough, all of Granny Tuggle's beds were spoken for. Because there were few options for educating black children, any parents "in the know" were likely to have struggled to find a way to put their children in Granny's care. The institute was formally established and survived through sponsorship by the Order of Calanthe, the "women's auxiliary" of the Knights of Pythias (one of the leading black fraternal organizations), as well as via aid from a number of prominent Birmingham citizens of both races. Future Supreme Court justice Hugo Black, then a judge in the recorder's court in Birmingham, was one supporter of the Tuggle Institute. "Criminals are generally not made by some inherent strain of viciousness," Black believed, "but by poverty and its attendant frustrations," and it was precisely those frustrations the Tuggle Institute was set up to counter.

Mrs. Minnie Loveman (along with Mrs. Louis Pizitz, owner of the other leading department store in Birmingham) was one of the primary supporters of the school, lending not only her financial and political clout to the institute but also her time and energy. In Gaston's own words she was "among those working to train these colored children"—she was personally involved with the school's progress. That involvement on Mrs. Loveman's part had a direct effect on Gaston's own life: Arthur always suspected that the reason he became one of Granny Tuggle's favorites was that his mother was so well connected, adored as she was by the ladies of white Birmingham society, and Mrs. Loveman in particular.

Until its closing in 1933, the Tuggle Institute was located in the hilly area of northwest Birmingham, on what was called Enon Ridge. According to Gaston, this area was, at the time, the most prestigious residential area in which blacks could live. Leaving Birmingham proper, what Arthur saw as he approached the institute for the first time was "a one and one-half story building with the dining room and kitchen in the basement, classrooms on the first floor, girls' dormitory on the second floor and attic." On the other side of the street were two additional buildings: One housed the print shop and school office, and the other was Granny Tuggle's own house. As for the boys, "we slept four to a room, two to a bed, and we were assigned duties in turn to keep the room clean. And, we really kept it clean, because we never did know when Granny Tuggle would come for an inspection."

It was, most likely, in the main building that Arthur Gaston first clasped Granny Tuggle's callused hand (toughened by the work she—and all of her students—did on and around the property) and looked into her eyes. She would have called him by name as she pumped his hand up and down, staring straight at him through the thick lenses of her glasses. She instilled in him in an instant both awe and respect, in equal measure. These feelings would stay with him throughout his time at the institute, and stand him in good stead in the eyes of the administration.

Granny Tuggle's mission was to train black children to get along in the world; to invest them with certain, very practical skills that would allow them to make a life for themselves as "colored people" in the South, and elsewhere. Academic subjects were taught, but it was made clear to the pupils who passed through the doors of the Tuggle Institute that life, for them, would not be about Latin and Greek—even if they were proficient in it. Life, they were taught, would be about work, after the model of Booker T. Washington.

The Tuggle Institute (circa 1906), where Gaston was first
introduced to Booker T. Washington and his philosophies

DR. WASHINGTON

The students at the Tuggle Institute did not have to imagine what
Booker T. Washington was like: He showed up regularly at the
school, his long frock coat flapping around his legs, to personally impart his views—and encouragement—to the student body. Arthur remembered him as "tall, lean, dignified. He always wore a high
standing collar, startling white against his skin, and the cleft in his
chin worked as he spoke, his wide set eyes flashing as his oratory
gathered force." Washington's life story, *Up from Slavery,* was the
first book Arthur ever owned.

In the early 1880s Washington had taken what he had learned of
the world as a well-educated former slave and dedicated himself to
the betterment of the black population. After graduating from
Hampton University in Virginia, in 1881 he was asked to head the famous Tuskegee Institute, and would spend the rest of his life building
the school into a training ground for the black community. Tuskegee
offered its students a classical course of training, with classes span-
ning the range from art to botany to chemistry to literature. But

Washington was equally committed to providing his students with qualified vocational training, preparing each to fill a position of employment in "occupations that already existed for black people in the South." Boys trained in agricultural arts and trades such as carpentry and mechanics, while girls learned the nuances of household skills that would prepare them to do the only jobs likely to be offered them: cooking and cleaning in other people's houses.

By the time A. G. Gaston first heard him speak, Washington was arguably the most influential black person in the country. President Roosevelt, admiring Washington's advocacy of "industry, thrift, self-discipline, wholesome family life" (and no doubt influenced by Andrew Carnegie and John Rockefeller, both of whom contributed heavily to Tuskegee and other Washington projects), determined that from time to time he would, "appoint to office . . . Negroes recommended by Washington, or of Washington's kind." Roosevelt invited Washington to the White House in 1901 to discuss his proposed candidates, and America—especially the American South—was stunned. It was the first time a president had sought the counsel of a black American, and certainly the first time a black person had dined in the White House.

It was Washington's 1895 address before the Cotton States and International Exposition in Atlanta, Georgia, that had lifted him to national fame and truly opened up the question of what was "right" regarding socioeconomic policy and black America. Washington offered to white America what would later come to be known as the "Atlanta Compromise," a detailed version of his vision for the economic growth of the South through an acceptance of black social subordination. He encouraged blacks to "cast down their buckets" where they were, to remain in the South and provide the physical labor necessary for agricultural production. The gains, he declared, would be collected by the white business owners first, but would, in time, trickle down to the black worker as well. In return for blacks' labor, Washington suggested, whites would invest in their future, funding further educational opportunities for blacks. He recommended that in return for the white community's help in producing this gradual ascent toward economic parity, blacks should postpone any hold on the dream of social parity they might have had. "In all things that are purely social," Washington famously announced, "we can be as separate as the fingers, yet one as the hand in all things essential to mutual progress."

Not everyone agreed with Washington's sentiments. In 1895, the same year Washington made his Atlanta Compromise speech, W. E. B. DuBois was awarded his doctoral degree by Harvard University (making him the first black Ph.D. in the nation). By 1903 DuBois had crafted his response to Washington's theories, published under the title *The Souls of Black Folk*. Therein, DuBois took Washington to task for his "Gospel of Work and Money" and his derision of higher academic pursuits for blacks. Contrary to what Washington had argued, DuBois believed the salvation of the race rested not in the hands of the working class but in the so-called Talented Tenth—those members of the race who would rise to the "top" by way of their intellect. "Was there ever a nation on God's fair earth civilized from the bottom upward?" DuBois asked, in direct challenge to Washington's assertions. "Never," was his own answer. "It is, ever was, and ever will be from the top downward that culture filters."

The furor of debate that erupted from the Atlanta Compromise was massive, and nationwide, and forever after Washington's name would be one that sparked contest between liberal- and conservative-minded blacks and whites. Regardless, in Tuskegee Washington had created a model of education that would be replicated across the southern states. Granny Tuggle and her pupils were a few among many who viewed Washington's model as the road out of perdition.

ENON RIDGE

At the Tuggle Institute, Arthur Gaston set to work trying to make not only his mother but also Granny Tuggle proud. He attacked his studies in government (which he loved), Latin (which he hated), and religious studies with equal passion, so as to retain his prime position. Granny was not afraid to reprimand a student fiercely and in public if she believed the child was not measuring up to the high standards she had set. Gaston recalls being pulled aside by Granny Tuggle many

times and seemingly for no reason at all other than to remind him
that he must strive ever further, he must work harder. There was no
room for error in Granny Tuggle's house.

In time, there was little call for anyone to remind Arthur of the
need to succeed—he became quite adept at putting pressure upon himself. The world of Enon Ridge (the site of the Tuggle Institute) was different from the one he had known either in Demopolis or with the
Lovemans in Birmingham. Unlike any other blacks he had ever known,
the residents here "lived in the two and three story homes . . . with
shiny floors and fine bathrooms such as my mother cleaned in the
homes of white people." Here, a new world of black potential was to
be witnessed, and A. G. Gaston wanted to measure up.

Beginning in 1890, a distinct black middle class began to flourish
in Birmingham. There were black doctors and lawyers, contractors and
architects living and working in the city. By the turn of the century,
blacks had founded their own bank, as well as construction companies,
and began to take an interest in living among other middle-class blacks
who conceivably shared their values and interests. The largest residential community for the black middle class was known as Smithfield,
and Enon Ridge was its smaller neighbor.

Like its larger counterpart, Enon Ridge was a community built to
foster the "independence" and "interpersonal relationships" of a
class of blacks who believed in Booker T. Washington's precepts of
racial solidarity. Residents belonged to elite social clubs and fraternal
orders created to help inculcate core social and economic values.
They were also philanthropically minded, particularly when it came
to the welfare of the students of the Tuggle Institute.

The realities of life on Enon Ridge opened up new possibilities to
Gaston, just as his mother had hoped. It made him aware in a deep
sense, and for the first time, that a black person could aspire to even
more than what Sebron Edwards (the Demopolis clerk whom Arthur
had idolized) had achieved. It allowed him to believe that not only
could he work in a store—he might be able to own it. Not only could
he live in Berney Loveman's house as a servant, but he might own one
just like it himself someday. It began to "disturb" him, Gaston would
write, to see how hard his mother was forced to work to keep their

family afloat. What had once simply been "the way things were" was thrown into sharp relief by the new world revealed by Tuggle. Arthur promised himself that with the skills he learned at the institute, he would make a better life for his mother. He would buy her the best house on Enon Ridge and end her days in the kitchen at the Lovemans'. Perhaps they would even have Berney to dinner.

THE WORKING LIFE BEGINS

Making all this happen, Arthur quickly realized, would require more than just skills. It would require the application of those skills. So Arthur Gaston decided to get a job—or, rather, a number of jobs. He was close enough to Granny Tuggle that he went to her directly to beg permission to go on the job hunt. She had watched him closely from his first days at the institute, taking him with her on her fundraising efforts on behalf of the school and showing him off as an example of the fruits of her good work. And she had watched him watching her as she cultivated these churches and fraternal organizations for the few coins they could spare. She knew that he was coming to understand the value of dedication to task—not to mention the value of money. So she granted his wish and allowed him to enter the workforce while still a student at the institute.

Before long, Arthur had more jobs than he knew what to do with. He accepted every job that was offered to him, no matter how menial the task. And he truly relished his work. Of this first working experience, he wrote:

> I mowed and raked lawns, washed windows, cleaned floors,
> worked as a bellhop at hotels, and anything else that earned me
> an honest dime. I found joy in each job and worked at it until
> it was perfect, even though others working with me teased me
> for it. . . . I would often remain behind to polish a window I
> discovered was streaked, when I thought I had finished.

His work ethic was apparently unparalleled, and soon enough word of Arthur's competence made him a sought-after man. Perhaps part of what kept him in such high demand was his graciousness: Arthur was aware that impressions were lasting and so made a point of distinguishing himself as a polite worker. Each of his employers received a personal thank-you from Arthur after the day's work was done, along with gentle encouragement to call on him again if more work was required. Though these tactics made him hugely popular with the employing population, his coworkers were less impressed. At this point, however, that seemed to matter little. If he wasn't exactly making friends, he *was* making money.

Over the next year Arthur continued collecting and fulfilling job posts until he had to face up to an unanticipated effect: His studies had begun to suffer. He predicted that Granny Tuggle would be displeased, and so set out to disengage himself from several of his commitments. He apologized to his employers for the inconvenience he was causing them in quitting and encouraged them to stay in touch so that, in the event his schedule lightened, he might be of service again. He burned no bridges as he walked away, and promised himself that he would "never leave a job in such a manner that [his] reemployment would not at least be considered." To his relief, nearly all of his mostly white employers were as gracious in their response to him as he had always been in his relations with them. Thereafter, Arthur settled into a period of relative balance, attacking both school and work with equal ardor.

A Big Decision

In 1909 Arthur Gaston was an eighteen-year-old man with a tenth-grade education, and there were decisions to be made about his future. The meager savings he had accumulated while working his odd jobs had seemed like a great deal at first (so much, compared to buttons!), but he soon realized it would take him two lifetimes to earn a real living at the rate he was currently progressing. It was not enough.

On a certain Sunday afternoon, Arthur began to feel acutely distressed. The night before he had attended a Knights of Pythias convention with Granny Tuggle, and she had given him a bold introduction to the group: "This is Arthur George Gaston, and he is going to be a great man." This was not an uncommon occurrence, according to Gaston, and if it bred in him a certain arrogance about his position at the institute, he never forgot that in the world outside such praise would be a rare event. Moreover, he knew that his time at Tuggle would end soon, and that he needed to find a way to actually achieve what Granny Tuggle seemed to believe was true of him.

That morning Booker T. Washington had spoken at assembly, urging the students to let no opportunity pass them by. As he sat alone on his bed that afternoon, Arthur thought about Washington's words. He could hear his classmates teasing each other in the kitchen, the cheerful exchange of youthful male and female voices floating across his solitude. Still deep in thought, he opened the cigar box in which he stored the money he had earned from his various jobs. He fingered the coins. There was little to show for all his hard work. Dr. Washington had talked of grasping opportunity, but what Arthur couldn't see, for the moment, was where his opportunity was. His well-worn copy of *Up from Slavery* lay at his side. Setting his box of money down, he picked up, once again, Washington's autobiographical tale.

Leafing through the book, Arthur quickly rediscovered what he would later describe as his favorite passage:

> Every persecuted individual and race should get much consolation out of the great human law, which is universal and eternal, that merit, no matter under what skin found, is in the long run recognized and rewarded . . . the whole future of the Negro rest[s] largely upon the question as to whether or not he should make himself, through his skill, intelligence, and character, of such undeniable value to the community in which he lived that the community could not dispense with his presence. . . .

Merit, Arthur realized, was the key. It was the foundation of what Granny Tuggle had taught him. Skill, he had developed under her guidance, right along with character and intelligence. A proving ground was what he lacked.

By Gaston's account, it was at this moment that he spied the daily newspaper that lay beside his bed. Its headlines reported increased hostility in the European region. War looked likely. Gaston put two and two together. He would take Dr. Washington's words to heart and grasp at the opportunity that seemed to be presenting itself to him. He would join the army.

THE ARMY YEARS

In 1910, at the age of eighteen, Arthur Gaston left the Tuggle Institute. Though his intention was to enter the army he was, as yet, too young to enlist without his mother's approval (which he was certain would not be forthcoming). So for the next three years he supported himself first by selling newspapers subscriptions to the *Birmingham Reporter* and then by working as a bellhop at the Battlehouse Inn in Mobile, Alabama. The Battlehouse was a luxurious hotel frequented by Mobile's wealthy visitors. As he had in his previous jobs, Arthur dedicated himself wholeheartedly to "hopping," as he called it. He so impressed one guest that the man offered him a job as his valet. Gaston turned him down. On April 14, 1912, the *Titanic* sank just off the coast of Newfoundland. The man who had asked Gaston to be his valet went down with the ship.

It was during this period in Mobile that Gaston fathered his first and only child. It would be, from the start, an uneasy relationship. The child, Arthur George Gaston Jr., was raised in Detroit by his mother, whose name—as well as any information about her relationship with Gaston Sr.—has seemingly disappeared. There is no mention of this son anywhere in Gaston's autobiography, and there is no record that father and son had much of a relationship throughout the boy's early childhood.

As a man who had suffered the loss of his own father early on, Gaston was certainly sensitive to the effects that growing up fatherless could have on a boy. His own idolization of his grandfather Joe, and his insistent desire for valorization by male authority figures throughout his life can, by a certain logic, be traced back to this early loss. This need for "father figures" in the black community was a concern that Gaston took quite seriously, and one that he would address extensively later in life through his involvement with the Boys' Club of America, where he served as mentor to thousands of boys and young men. But during the early years of his own son's life, Gaston clearly felt ambiguous about his relationship to fatherhood. We can assume that he believed himself unable to care for the young boy in an intimate fashion: He made no plans to marry the child's mother or to relocate himself in order to be a daily part of his son's life. And yet, he never lost touch with the child bearing his name, and would eventually step forward to take custody of the boy as a means of initiating him into the family business.

In any case, not long after the child was born, Gaston was able to take a step further in the direction of fulfilling his goals. After three years in Mobile, Gaston was finally old enough to enlist.

Gaston's introduction to life in the army came in a torturous boot camp experience in Columbus, Ohio. "The summer was unusually hot," he wrote, "and the long forced marches, the interminable drills with heavy packs kept us soaked with sweat. We were busy from sunup 'til bedtime and no sympathy was forthcoming from anybody in that unfamiliar place. I wondered why on earth I had enlisted." He survived the experience, however, and from Ohio was shipped to the Fort Riley army base in Kansas, where he would spend more than three years. There, Gaston served in the mess hall on KP, cleaned the barracks and latrines, and—for an extra five dollars a month—picked up work as a "dog robber," devoting his few off-duty hours to "shining officers' boots . . . [making] fires, and cleaning the windows and floors" of the officers' quarters. He ingratiated himself with a number of the white officers, and also became friendly with a number of men from his own division.

It was at Fort Riley that Gaston learned, in his own words, "to respect authority and discipline as the army defined." His first real lesson in that arena took the form of a direct blow to the face laid upon him by his commanding officer, who had no interest in hearing Gaston's excuses for why the pot of potatoes he had been ordered to peel was only half full. The punch—delivered midsentence—left Gaston "[lying] on the ground, amazed and furious at the inhumanity of such a sudden blow." It occurred to him first to complain, second to go

AWOL; luckily he did neither. Instead he picked himself up off the ground and stood at attention before the officer, offering a simple but firm "Yes, sir" as his response. The lesson was brutal, but as far as Gaston was concerned it "saved his life." There were to be no excuses, in the kitchen or on the field. Authority—in the army, as it had at Granny Tuggle's—counted for everything.

By 1917, after years on the base at Fort Riley, Gaston had, in his own eyes, been transformed into "a real man and a seasoned soldier." His physique had hardened under the strain of physical exertion, and so had his spirit. He was more eager than ever to see the world and prove himself in it. He just needed a chance.

On April 2, 1917, America declared war on the Central Powers of Europe; the first American soldiers touched down on foreign soil in June of that same year. Records indicate that the Ninety-second Division (the all-Negro unit in which Gaston served) was officially organized in November 1917 and shipped out soon thereafter.

Arthur Gaston was finally getting his "chance." He was going abroad to prove something not only to himself but also to the entire nation. Like so many other blacks (then as now), he was going to war because he needed the money (fifteen dollars a month), and because it was the only "opportunity" that seemed even remotely available to him. But also, importantly, he was going to war because he believed wholeheartedly in the very ideals of freedom and democracy on which America had been founded, and claimed to be fighting to protect—even if those ideals had never been fully realized at home. *To die on behalf of a country that denied your right to liberty; to die fighting for a democracy that every experience in your life informed you was a lie:* These were the prospects Gaston and his peers were offered under the rubric of military honor. And overwhelmingly, they seized the ring.

WORLD WAR I

Some 2.3 million black men were drafted during World War I. Four hundred thousand of them served in France. And from the beginning of their involvement, there was controversy.

With America's declaration of war in 1917 came an all-out recruitment drive for able-bodied participants. Though the American government claimed an "overwhelming consensus" among its citizenry in favor of war, the (lack of) turnout among able-bodied men willing to fight contradicted that assertion. Nevertheless, one month after the declaration of this massive conflict, a statement was released by the government allowing that the army would accept "no more Negroes" for enlistment. Thousands of blacks were turned away from recruiting stations across the country. One month later, on May 18, 1917, the War Department reversed its position and instituted the "universal Selective Services Act" (which instated the draft), but the damage had already been done. In declaring the moratorium on black enlistment, the Wilson administration had made a very clear and public statement about the idea of Negroes with guns: It did not want them, and would do all it could to assure the white American public that none would make it to the front.

It is fortunate, then, that Arthur Gaston had enlisted when he did. By the time the War Department determined that blacks would not be necessary to fight this war, Gaston had already spent nearly four years humping the training grounds at Fort Riley. He had signed up for the standard enlistment period of seven years, and the army, despite what it might resolve concerning *new* black enlistees, could not very well shunt its currently enlisted black soldiers onto the street. But neither did it have to use them to fight.

The compromise the government struck with itself was one that had been the de facto policy for years: Black soldiers would (until the very last battles of the war, at any rate) serve primarily as support staff, heading up the supply and ammunition brigades that delivered artillery and provisions to the soldiers on the front lines. In this manner, blacks could be utilized in the war effort without putting white citizens through the additional shock of having to accept the image of a black man with a gun defending their nation. The blacks would deliver the guns, not shoot them, and the "real" heroes would remain the white soldiers who took aim and pulled the triggers.

The outright discrimination that shaped the government's policy regarding black soldiers affected more than just their roles on the battlefield—it affected every element of their experience in the armed services. According to historian Gail Buckley, Camp Lee, Virginia, was a shining example of the disparities allowed by the U.S. government in the treatment of its soldiers. "White troops lived in barracks," she writes, "blacks lived in tents without floors or bedding . . . black draftees had inferior or insufficient sanitary conveniences, medical treatment, chaplain service and clothing." At another camp in Virginia—Camp Alexander—a number of black men died from exposure in the winter of 1917 because "they had no coats" to shield them from the cold. The flu pandemic of 1918, which killed more U.S. soldiers than died in battle in the First World War, can also be assumed to have affected black soldiers disproportionately, since their access to medical care was more proscribed than white soldiers'. Thus, not only were black soldiers relegated to "service positions" (which, pointedly, robbed them of the opportunity to ascend to the rank of officer), but their humanity was flouted publicly and daily by the very country they had pledged to defend.

Like every other black man who fought under the U.S. flag during the First World War, Arthur Gaston was assigned to a service division. His "all Negro" unit—the 317th Ammunition Train of the Ninety-second Rainbow Division—was shipped out to Cherbourg, France, not long after the declaration of war. From Cherbourg they proceeded to Paris, where they were stationed while awaiting deployment to the front lines. It was Paris that Arthur Gaston had dreamed of seeing while back at Granny Tuggle's. He had read in the newspapers of the liberties blacks enjoyed in France's capital, had heard of the egalitarian attitude with which French citizens approached black Americans, and he wanted to experience it for himself. In the years spent at Fort Riley he had often been privy to the officers' animated discussions of their time in "Gay Paree," taking in the details of another "magic city" as he spit-shined leather boots until his face was reflected back at him.

Paris had been Gaston's dream—but his first impression of the place was anything but fantastic. His regiment entered the city, according to Gaston, on a less-than-perfect day. "It had been raining," he recounted, "and we had to trot through mud and slush to our quarters." It was a miserable experience, more reminiscent of boot camp than of what he had expected to find so far from home. For the young man who had spent three years dreaming of the great times awaiting him across the pond, this introduction was, in his own words, crushing. The "anticipation and enthusiasm" that had carried him through the years at Fort Riley drained from his body. Had he had the chance, he might have descended into a depression. Fear, however, would quickly replace his disappointment: His regiment had been called to the front.

Little in his years of training in the army had prepared Gaston for actual war. Low-flying fighter planes—both friend and foe—tore overhead in a constant stream of noise, their panic-inducing quality magnified by the fact that many of the men had never seen or heard anything like them before. The steady "bombardment of mortars and 75's" literally brought the men to their knees in fear and confusion. In the tension, insubordination threatened to erupt in the ranks. The struggle to retain order became nearly as critical as the struggle to contain the enemy.

The generally inferior training and leadership that plagued the all-black Ninety-second Division has been well documented. "Organized and trained in five months," Buckley reports, "the 92nd division and its new lieutenants were sent to seven different training camps in Kansas, Iowa, Illinois, Ohio, Maryland, New York and New Jersey; its units were never joined until they reached France. No other division in the Army was trained in so many different camps. . . . In the case of blacks, however, any overlarge concentration was considered dangerous. . . ." The effect of this disjunction in training was a fundamental lack of order on the battlefield, as "basically untrained individual regiments were thrown into the fray." Without the benefit of unified or in-depth training—the kind of training mandated in white divisions—or the support of their commanding officers (many of whom undermined the division on paper and in person), the soldiers of the Ninety-second were effectively dropped into enemy territory without parachutes. As Gaston said of his time on the battlefield, "My own all Negro unit . . . was a greater danger to me than the constant shelling." The men of the division had been set up for failure—and were accused of cowardice at every turn. That so many members of this division neither shirked their duty nor perished is a testament only to their fortitude. And if the United States refused to reward their valor, the French had no such hesitation, awarding the Croix de Guerre and other honors to numerous members of the Ninety-second. A. G. Gaston himself would come home wearing a medal certifying his bravery.

Gaston, it turns out, was among the most experienced soldiers in his regiment. As a result of time already served before deployment, he had risen to the rank of regimental supply sergeant, and as such was responsible for a "six wagon convoy" of supplies that followed the armed troops to the front. This meant he also was responsible for the men who accompanied the convoy. The anxiety that threatened to overtake the regiment put them all at risk, Gaston knew, and order—the type of order he had first rebelled against and then learned to cherish at Fort Riley—would be their salvation if there was salvation to be had. Soon enough, they all witnessed examples of what came when order fell aside, or when commands were ignored: death—of one, of many. Those who survived quickly learned to live with fear as a companion, rather than as a driving force. The soldiers learned to accept everything about the front: the noise, the smoke, the bombs; the cold, wet trenches that stank of the living and dead alike. They learned to take it in stride and to move on, move forward. They learned to focus on the task at hand while thinking entirely of something else. They learned, in modern parlance, to dissociate.

As part of the 317th Ammunition Train, Gaston saw a good deal of action while delivering supplies to the fighting units on the front (including the Battle of Metz on November 10–11, 1918). In one attack he was moments away from losing his own life. By Gaston's account, he and his crew had been quartered in an abandoned house near the front, not long after their arrival in France. After days without fresh water (their supply was purported to have been poisoned), the men were weak with dehydration, exhaustion, and just plain fear. An order came to evacuate the house—the Germans had a bead on the site. Gaston, in his fatigued and admittedly discouraged state, refused. He curled up instead with a blanket and prepared to sleep the night away. Ten minutes later the house exploded in flames.

By that time, however, Gaston was securely situated in a bomb shelter with the rest of the 317th. It was not self-preservation that saved his life, but the generosity of another man, Captain Joe Thompson. Gaston and Thompson had first met at Fort Riley, but had not bonded until their journey overseas. Thompson was an Alabama boy, too, from Mobile, and each seemed to find in the other a source of comfort and familiarity so far away from home. When the men of the 317th had made their way to the bomb shelter after the warning alarm sounded, Thompson had apparently searched for and not found his new friend. Panicked, he ran back to the building and dragged Gaston, semiconscious, into the shelter only minutes before a German shell pierced the side of the house. Upon rising the next day, Gaston revisited the pile of rubble that was almost his grave, and "thanked the Lord" for sparing him. It was an experience he would talk about often in later life, one that reinforced his lifelong relationship with God.

PARIS, 1919

Moments like these were not daily events during Gaston's time at war, but they were frequent enough, and disturbing enough, to require the development of a certain psychological distance from the physical world in which he existed. While the world blew up around him, Gaston tried to rest his mind on Paris. His initial disappointment with the city was, after a bit of time at the front, replaced by a renewed sense of hope for what the metropolis might have to offer. He was not alone in his optimism: The constant terror of the battlefield compelled most soldiers to appreciate the City of Light more than they would have imagined was possible.

Gaston, for perhaps the first (and last) time in his life, was as eager to take advantage of the carousing Paris afforded as any other soldier. While in Kansas (at Fort Riley) he had steadfastly refused to accompany his comrades on the three-mile walk to Junction City to "hang around a joint that catered to soldiers." His objection, he said, was the expenditure of money. Instead, he had sent his entire paycheck back to Alabama each month, in the care of Mr. B. H. Hudson of the Alabama Penny Savings Bank ("one of three banks owned and operated by Negroes in Birmingham"). Before his departure for the army, Gaston had arranged to buy a lot of land for two hundred dollars, with the bank's help, and his fifteen-dollar monthly paycheck always went directly to the repayment of that loan. The extra five dollars he made "dog robbing" was all that he would allow himself access to, and that money was too precious, he felt, to spend wilding with the boys.

The war experience, however, seemed to loosen up Gaston's attitude toward the more playful elements of life. Though there is no evidence that he ever missed one of his monthly payments to the bank, he did allow himself to partake more freely of the social components of military life abroad. He attended performances by world-class musicians, visited cafés and clubs, and dined with some of the many French families who invited black American soldiers into their homes (despite the U.S. Army's regulations banning such fraternization). All this while the city took continuous waves of shelling from enemy forces. The French citizens would not be demoralized, it seemed to Gaston, and following their lead offered a reprieve from the unremitting emotional toll of a life lived in constant expectation of death.

Among the first invitations that Gaston received while in Paris was one from a brother and sister named Michelle and Louis Gibert. The pair had introduced themselves to Gaston and his friend Joe Thompson one day as the young soldiers idled in the park, passing time during one of their leaves. The Giberts, like most Parisians, had no interest in heeding the U.S. government's rules about fraternizing with American Negroes. They were interested in learning English, and Arthur and Joe had a hankering to pick up a bit of French, so a deal was struck. Over the course of their relationship, the Giberts fed not only Gaston's body, but his mind and spirit as well. The foursome spoke of life in their respective nations, and of the racial equality so seemingly apparent in France and lacking in the United States. Sitting together in the kitchen of the Giberts' home, speaking on equal terms with Louis and Michelle, Gaston was reminded of a way of life that he had not experienced since he had lain shoulder to shoulder with Berney Loveman in the woods by the creek, tossing nuts at a common target.

In France he was treated like a man. In France he could walk the streets without jumping off the sidewalks when a white person strolled by. In France, it was clear, the white people respected his uniform, regardless of his color; respected his allegiance to democracy and his willingness to fight for it. In France, it seemed, anything was possible for a man like Arthur Gaston. Eventually it was clear that the war would end and the Allies would win. Though he had watched many men fall around him, Gaston himself had survived, and the question that began to plague him was how and where to make a life in the aftermath of so much loss. France was a place a black man could live—this much was certain. So why not stay and make the best of the best situation?

It was a question put to Gaston many times by his comrades in the ammunition train, a question that dogged him in his own quiet thoughts as he drifted to sleep at night. But his answer was always the same in the end, and it always came in the baritone voice that had delivered the speech that led Arthur to join the army five years earlier. *Cast down your bucket,* he could hear Dr. Washington proclaim. *Start at home.* The experience in France had only served to make Gaston more certain of the fact that Dr. Washington had been right to believe that merit, not color, was the fulcrum point on which a successful life was balanced. Hadn't they all, each and every one of these black soldiers, proved to America their valor, their worthiness, their simple equality in serving in the fields of war? Wouldn't white Americans now realize that the democracy they had fought and died for abroad must be implemented back home? Even a man as smart as A. G. Gaston could believe that things were about to change in the United States. Hadn't they won, after all?

THE COMPANY MAN

A young man should keep his eyes open.
He should study the people around him.
How do they live? What makes them tick?
What do they need?

THE AFTERMATH

In the early months of 1919, A. G. Gaston returned to the United States after nearly two years spent in the bloodiest, deadliest war our nation had yet witnessed. More than ten million men died on the battlefield and more than twenty million more—men, women, and children living in Europe—would eventually succumb to the disease and starvation brought about by the conflict. No published record of this "great" war can help but remark on the horrific physical and emotional environment in which our soldiers (and theirs) lived and fought. On more than one occasion, battles were waged in which upward of half a million men were lost in one day—per side.

While the war raged on, there was little to no official communication from the commanders of the Allied forces to the public regarding the heavy losses that were being incurred. In fact, a full-scale repudiation of those losses was taking place across Europe and, especially, in the United States. Though the U.S. had resisted joining the war effort for nearly three years before plunging ahead in 1917, it was no secret among the governing powers of the nation that U.S. involvement in a war of this scale would prove helpful to a stumbling national economy. Indeed, the year 1914 marked a descent into true recession for the United States, culminating in depressed pricing of farm products and high unemployment rates, with heavy industry and banking interests suffering as well. The war effort, however— even before the United States officially engaged—was an obvious means of bringing economic security back to the land. Within the first two years of the conflict, "more than $2 billion worth of goods had been sold to the Allies," pushing America out of recession and back on the road to financial well-being.

With the war invigorating the pecuniary state of the Union, maintaining public support for the endeavor was crucial, and the government did its best to keep the truth of the massive casualties from the public. Rank-and-file Americans were not, however, foolish, and there is little evidence that points to any broad-based support of the war effort among Americans at home. In fact, the evidence points starkly in the other direction: The institution of the draft, due to the overwhelming lack of turnout for voluntary enlistment by eligible candidates, is only one of a host of indications that Americans were aware that this (much-propagandized) war offered them the chance to *lose* much more than they would gain.

Nevertheless, when war was declared by the United States, its men boarded its ships, willingly and unwillingly, and gave their lives in large numbers for what their government had labeled the defense of democracy (never mind that the Allies were as interested in empire building as the Axis powers were). And perhaps no group had been more ready to fight under this banner of democracy than African Americans. As Lieutenant Colonel David A. Lane of the U.S. Army observed of the black soldiers' determination to serve, "We really believed that it was going to be a war to end oppression of all kinds and to make the world—of course the United States—safe for democracy. We felt that we were embarking on a genuine crusade. . . ." For the colored soldiers of World War I, the principles of democracy were hardly theoretical, as they may have been for their white compatriots. The absence of these ideals at work in American society was borne out every day, in every interaction, for the black American; it was the missing butter on the bread of their daily lives.

The period preceding the U.S. entry into World War I was a categorically difficult one for blacks, with racial tensions running high and spreading across the country. In going to war, here is the America the black soldier was leaving behind: Between 1914 and 1917, 161 blacks were lynched across the U.S.; starting in 1915 the Ku Klux Klan—an organization whose influence and membership had significantly diminished since its peak during Reconstruction—experienced a dramatic revival, spreading through not only the southern states but also the North and Midwest (as a result of the social and economic threat of "industrialization and immigration"); in the same year, Oklahoma became the first state to segregate telephone booths; and D. W. Griffith's film *Birth of a Nation* was released, promulgating offensive racial stereotypes of blacks. In 1917 race riots erupted in East St. Louis, Illinois, and in Houston, Texas, where whites killed anywhere from 60 to 220 black people, and 100 black soldiers were charged with rioting—13 of whom would eventually be executed. Others remained imprisoned for more than twenty years, until released by President Franklin Roosevelt in 1938.

And yet, despite what history had taught them about the machinations of American society, the general (though by no means unanimous) belief among black soldiers, as Lieutenant Colonel Lane expressed so well, was that life would be different on the other side of this war. That was certainly what A. G. Gaston believed; it is what his superiors commanded him to believe. It had been his reason for entering the war. Black leaders who could agree on little else agreed that blacks should be involved in the war effort. In 1918 W. E. B. DuBois wrote that an Allied victory would result in "an American Negro with the right to vote and the right to work and the right to live without insult." So when Gaston's boat docked in Hoboken, New Jersey, in 1919, returning him to the home whose founding doctrine of "democracy" had won the war overseas, he was as certain as the man standing next to him that what awaited him was honor and opportunity.

For many black soldiers, the early experiences that accompanied their return home did much to reinforce their expectant visions. Disembarking from their boats, many soldiers were greeted affectionately by their fellow black Americans—and in some cases, gloriously. Indeed, in at least one well-documented instance, the return of black

American troops was commemorated with what historian Gail Buckley calls "the greatest black American celebration since Emancipation." When the famous 369th Regiment (one of only two combat regiments of black soldiers) returned, victorious, to New York Harbor on February 17, 1919, crowds jammed the streets to welcome them home. The parade of soldiers, which stretched from Fifth Avenue and Twenty-fifth Street in Manhattan all the way to Harlem one hundred blocks away, was, by all accounts, a dramatic event for everyone involved, and one that inspired full-throttle euphoria in witnesses and participants alike. It was a moment to be savored, and one that many soldiers of the era would cling to as the darker realities of return revealed themselves.

COMING HOME

By Gaston's account, crowds of cheering citizens greeted his ship, too, when it dropped anchor in Hoboken, giving him immediate assurance regarding the stories of a changed America that had bounced from soldier to soldier belowdecks. He was admittedly swept up in this warm welcome, certain that his dreams of success would be realized in this new America. He parted from his fellow soldiers with some sadness, but plump with the stories of their heroism that had been stirred up over the course of the Atlantic crossing, his optimism remained intact. In his own words, "The world seemed fresh and wonderful."

It would not take long for this view to change. The general disregard that had accompanied blacks throughout the war had turned, in a number of cases, to true brutality with the arrival of the Armistice. In one instance a member of the military police attacked a private in the 369th, "his head split open . . . for taking the wrong direction to the latrine." Black soldiers were given the job of cleaning up Europe's battlefields, burying and reburying the dead, work that was sickening at best; at worst, noxious. What the war had hidden from view, peace exposed. Black soldiers were still subordinates, and the white officers who remained behind to supervise their work made them painfully aware of it.

Perhaps most damaging of all were the slights to the spirit black soldiers suffered as a group in the days and months after the war ended. In what has often been considered the most glaring public display of prejudice on the part of the U.S. government in the aftermath of the war, the black soldiers of the 369th Regiment—who had been cited for their bravery in battle eleven times and had been awarded the Croix de Guerre by the French government—were forbidden to march in the international victory parade that took place in Paris on July 14, 1919. Though they had their own parade waiting for them in New York, the message the government was sending was once again clear: The United States would not be represented to the world community by Negro soldiers, no matter what the European forces were willing to do.

The accretion of such humiliating events began to tear at the optimism of the black soldiers who remained behind in Europe on cleanup duty. One black private wrote a letter to W. E. B. DuBois in late 1919 in which he wondered what the purpose had been in black men dying for democracy, when it seemed that only white men had benefited by it. It was a question that was beginning to be asked by those black soldiers who were already home, as well.

The America that greeted Gaston and his compatriots once the flag waving had ended was a place where things had changed—for the worse. The year 1919 saw a rise in the recorded lynching of blacks: eighty-three in total, up from sixty-four the year before; ten of the victims were black men in uniform. More than twenty-five race riots would take place in the summer of this year (nicknamed "Red Summer" for the blood that ran in the streets), including one in Chicago that began on July 27 and lasted more than a week, killing thirty-eight people and injuring over five hundred. The Ku Klux Klan, which had begun its reemergence just before the war, continued its growth, claiming four and a half million members across the country by 1924. The hatred and fear that black soldiers thought they were leaving behind had only become more deeply entrenched in their absence, and reinvigorated upon their return. The defeat on the Senate floor of such measures as the Dyer Anti-Lynching Bill in 1921—which would have made lynching a federal crime—and a general indifference on the part of the government to improving the treatment of blacks as a class, made it clear to Negro citizens that no comprehensive commitment to protecting or bettering their lives would be forthcoming.

None of this, however, could have been immediately apparent to Gaston, even if he had wanted to see it (and it seems unlikely he did). The initial comfort of being home was enough to lull him into a false sense of security during the early period after his return. From New Jersey, Gaston was sent south, to Camp Bowie, Texas, where he served out a portion of the remainder of his seven-year enlistment on inactive duty. Once his tour was finished, less than a year later, he would complete the last leg of his journey back to Alabama. On the way he would reunite with family and friends as he traveled east across the southern states.

CREOLA AND "DAD" SMITH

Among the stops Gaston made on his way from Camp Bowie back to Birmingham was in the town of Meridian, Mississippi. There he was to reconnect with the Smith family, old friends of his mother's from back in Demopolis.

Abraham Lincoln Smith was a black man on the model of what Arthur dreamed of becoming. Smith had left Demopolis twelve years earlier to found his own blacksmith shop in Meridian (he had previously been a carpenter)—and his business had been a success since its inception. Smith owned his home and was well respected by the local community, both black and white. He had established himself as a man of great influence in the town, and he looked, dressed, and acted the part. Light-skinned and handsome (in the days when both of these traits facilitated success), Smith donned a formal frock coat everywhere he went to signal his authority, and he spoke eloquently and intelligently, despite the lack of any evidence of formal schooling.

It was Rosie Gaston who had given Arthur his directive to stop the night in Meridian, with the alleged purpose of procuring a report on how her good friend "Mom" Smith was surviving over in Mississippi. But Rosie knew that Arthur's time with the Smiths could prove

A. L. "Dad" Smith

productive on two fronts. On the one hand, "Dad" Smith was a man to know, and Arthur could only be helped by their connection; and on the other, the Smiths had an unmarried daughter, Creola, who was just a little younger than Arthur. The last time Arthur and Creola had seen one another, she had passed button after button into the palm of his small hand to pay her way for a ride on his backyard swing. He had taken joy in watching her plump figure soar above him back then, and he was just as happy to see her, all these years later, grown up into a "pretty and vivacious" woman. During his time in Meridian they would get to know each other again, and Gaston—who had had few real friends in his life—found himself truly happy to have the company of another person.

Interested as he was in Creola, Gaston was even more compelled by Dad Smith. During his visit in Meridian, it appears that the bulk of his time was spent with the father, not the daughter. The two passed hours in quiet conversation, talking over business and the question of the younger man's future. Arthur was optimistic: He had paid off his plot of land by this time, and he was interested in investing in another piece of real estate. To do so, however, would require money, and getting money would require a job—an issue Arthur didn't perceive as a problem in his anticipated "new" society. His time in Camp Bowie had kept him isolated from much of what was happening in America, and in any case he thought himself a better bet than your average Joe. He was dedicated, he was smart (hadn't everyone always told him so?), and he was a soldier. What difference would it make now that he was black?

Dad Smith knew enough to wonder. The world had changed little for the black man in his lifetime, and he had little reason to believe it would. Things would still be tough for any black person looking to make his or her way. There were many things Smith could have said to Arthur; any number of ways he could have burst the young man's bubble on the spot. Instead, what he said was this: "Don't give up your dreams, Art . . . Just don't give up your dreams." It was the gentlest nudge in the direction of caution, though at the time Arthur could appreciate it only as full-fledged encouragement. In retrospect he would realize that Smith had been trying to warn him. But for now, it felt like exactly the reassurance he needed to begin chasing after his desires.

KNOCKING ON DOORS, LOOKING FOR WORK

Arthur left the Smiths full of promise. He landed back in Birmingham soon after, and relished the warm response he received from both his mother and Granny Tuggle. In his absence his mother had taken leave of her place in the Lovemans' kitchen and started up her own "freelance" catering business, counting a number of the city's wealthiest families among her new clients. It had been a big step, leaving the Lovemans, but Rosie—given her generally risk-averse demeanor—must have felt secure enough in her prospects and her savings to make the leap. She rented herself a house on Eighth Avenue North with the money she had accumulated, and upon his return Arthur moved in, once again under his mother's roof. He was twenty-seven years old.

Gaston, however, had no desire to be supported by his mother. He had been taken care of all of his life by one woman or another—

Idella, Rosie, Granny Tuggle—and now, he determined, it was time to return the favor. "After all," he wrote, "I was a young war hero and expected to take care of my mother in proper style." The morning after his arrival home, he woke early and dressed in the dark. Closing the door to his mother's house firmly behind him, he set out about town, knocking on doors, looking for work.

That first day was a failure. As was the one that followed it. And the one after that, as well. Nobody in Birmingham had the kind of job that Arthur was looking for, something other than the "menial and dull" tasks that he, with his limited education and dark skin, was qualified for. Day after day saw him offered only the lowliest form of labor, "poorly paid odd jobs," which he took to keep himself from showing up on his mother's doorstep with pockets turned inside out. Days turned into weeks, and still no one would hire him on a full-time basis. He wasn't starving, or without shelter—Rosie had seen to that. He was, he knew, luckier than most men with whom he had traveled home. But his spirit was sagging. He remembered how Dad Smith had told him to hold on to his dreams, and he began to wonder just how to do that when the way to success seemed blocked at every turn. It finally occurred to him that Dad had known what was coming. But that realization hardly helped. It only made him feel thick for not having grasped it on his own.

The O.K. Dry Cleaning Plant offered a small salvation, just in the nick of time. The addition of Art, small as he was, to her home accounts was eating up Rosie's profits. In order to maintain their household, mother and son had been forced to draw from Arthur's savings—and the money was running out more quickly than Arthur liked to see. Selling his plot of land in Birmingham was simply not an option. He was determined, he wrote, not to jeopardize any chance they had of a future by relinquishing that safety net. So he began to seriously consider taking one of the most menial and dull jobs around: a position in the mines. It was a fate he did not like to contemplate. Growing up in Birmingham, he had seen the ugliness of mine life first-hand, and it was nothing he wanted any part of. The offer from the dry-cleaning plant, though less remunerative than minework, was also less demeaning, and when it came, Arthur snatched it up in an instant. It paid five dollars per week—a paltry figure, even in 1920.

The O.K. Dry Cleaning Company

The dry-cleaning plant was run by a man named Mr. Williams, whom Gaston claims to have both liked and respected. The hours there were steady and allowed for Arthur to moonlight in those various odd jobs around town. While next to nothing, the pay was indeed something, and it kept the coffers of his savings account from being stripped entirely. Most importantly, it kept him from having to sell that cherished plot of land. And it kept him out of the mines.

Arthur was put in charge of driving the plant's delivery wagon. Much to his own surprise, it was a task he enjoyed. Even better was the time he spent between deliveries with Mr. Williams. Williams had been educated at Oberlin College and liked to talk to Art about his time there. They were discussions Arthur prized. Williams's talk about his experiences in college reminded the younger man of his time at Granny Tuggle's: how he'd done well there, how he'd relished the approval, how the knowledge he'd been imparted had changed his understanding of what the world *could* be—even if it wasn't that way yet. Gaston began to dream of going back to school, maybe even to college. There were black men who had done it, many of them.

Yet even in his most hopeful moments, bringing that plan to fruition seemed near impossible. There were too many things to get done, right there in Birmingham; he had his mother to take care of, and challenges enough in his own backyard. Like making sufficient money to keep them afloat from week to week. Further education, if was to come at all, would have to remain part of the landscape of his dreams a while longer. Years later Gaston would write vividly of his anger and frustration during this time. In a 1977 interview, he remarked, "I wanted to go to Tuskegee so bad. I just thought it would be the greatest thing in the world! All I had to do was get there. I wanted to go, but I couldn't make it." It would become one of the few dreams of Gaston's that would never come true.

The disappointments continued to accumulate. Though he had found a job and had enough money to eat, the life he was leading was nothing like the one he had dreamed of at Granny Tuggle's, or during his long sojourn in the army. Life was not better than he had left it—

it wasn't even the same. It was worse. In his growth from schoolboy to man, he had traversed the line from citizen to soldier and back again, and he had expected the world to grow right along with him. What he was finding, however, was that world—to the extent that Birmingham *was* the world—had grown not at all. The world had no place for a black man—not even (or perhaps especially) a black war hero.

Rain or shine found Arthur inside the delivery truck, winding his way through the Birmingham neighborhoods that the plant served. The time spent alone on the truck was time spent contemplating the apparent hopelessness of his future, and during this period Arthur's attitude shifted sharply. The optimism of his youth and early manhood vanished under the cloak of a creeping depression that had come to infect many former soldiers returned from the war. World War I had "changed the psychological profile of a generation," and for blacks the dissonance between what the world had been for them in Europe and what they found upon their return was nearly impossible to reconcile. Where the French had honored them, their own nation had dismissed them; what France embraced, America reviled. How to come to terms with the reality of this situation? How to fashion a life having made an acquaintance with equality abroad, but with no chance of owning it at home?

They were, in large part, irreconcilable issues, questions whose only possible answer is in the negative. The more Arthur thought about his life, the deeper his melancholy. The more he thought about what he didn't have, the angrier he became. The longer he sat on that wagon, the more he hated his situation. His discontent was stewing, looking for an excuse to spill over. It found that excuse in a labor strike proposed by his coworkers at the plant.

Arthur had never been the most popular of boys; he had always been too "straight" to be cool. He talked business, not women, books instead of booze, and none of this made him likely to be invited for a night out with the guys. In any case, when the offers came, he almost always declined—he had better things to do with his money than try to keep up. Nevertheless, it is clear that the approbation of his peers was something Art strongly desired, even if he could never quite bring himself to go along on their exploits in the end. It was the reason he had leased out that big swing in the backyard of his grandparents' house: It had bought him instant friendship.

Things hadn't changed much since his return to Alabama. Most of Art's time continued to be spent alone, or with his family (particularly his mother). At work and afterward, his coworkers socialized with one another, but Arthur was apparently on the outside of that group as well. His disappointment regarding his daily life alienated him from the rank-and-file employees, most of whom seemed to him to be happy to have any job at all. The single friendship Gaston would recall from this period of his life was his bond with Mr. Williams, a man whom he felt he could respect.

It's rarely difficult for any group to identify its most vulnerable member, and of the workers at the plant Arthur Gaston was that man. He was weak because he was not liked—or at least, he was less worth protecting than any other worker there. The plant workers had banded together (without including Art in the debate) and decided to ask Mr. Williams for a salary increase. For his coworkers, Art's friendship with Mr. Williams offered a distinct advantage: If Williams was going to say yes to anyone, it was going to be Art. If not, the only person who stood to lose in the bargain was Gaston himself.

The men approached Art and asked him to be their representative, urging him on by playing into his obvious disappointment and already simmering anger. They reminded him of the many wet days he had spent atop the rig delivering clothes, of the injustice of him doing so much work for so little money. They played their cards exactly right. It had been a string of bad days for Arthur, and the combination of this attention from his peers and the accumulating malice in his heart vis-à-vis his work situation was enough to push him to action before considering the consequences. He went straight to Mr. Williams and delivered his complaint.

GETTING FIRED: THE FIRST AND LAST TIME

Needless to say, things didn't turn out well. For Gaston, the scene became a blur in his mind: "I am not sure whether I quit or was

fired. I remember the astonishment in Mr. Williams' eyes and knowing that it was over, and that something was bad wrong." The only
people who knew the details of what transpired between the two
men that day were Gaston and Williams, and neither is around to
flesh out the tale. What Gaston would say, when he was alive, was
that the worst part of the scenario was not the actual loss of his job,
but the realization that he had let Mr. Williams down. He had "be-
trayed [Williams's] confidence" to impress a group of men who, it
turned out, had sold him down the river. He had let fury guide him,
rather than common sense. The job was not one that Arthur liked,
but it was one that he needed, and in his own estimation Williams
had been kind to him when he hadn't had to be. Whatever we may
think of Williams's treatment of his workers (he was almost certainly
taking advantage of them), it is clear that Arthur had truly respected
the man. And now, for the first time in his life, Gaston found himself
in the unfamiliar position of being a disappointment to somebody he
held in esteem. Though he had never sought out friendships, his
mentors formed the nucleus of his self-esteem. The loss of Mr.
Williams from this group was a serious blow, and it taught him a lesson he would never forget regarding loyalty.

All theoretical lessons aside, the one practical outcome of Gaston's behavior was that he was, in his own words, "flat out of a job."
There would be no plum recommendation coming his way from Mr.
Williams, and not much had changed on the employment scene since
Arthur had taken the job at the plant. There were no brighter opportunities waiting for him, and the rent still had to be paid. His mother,
he knew, would be willing to help out as best she could, but it was not
a position he liked to put her in. There was only one option left.

The next morning he woke before dawn. The ride out to the
Westfield mines was a long one, and he wanted to be first in line
when the hiring office opened its doors.

THE TENNESSEE COAL AND IRON COMPANY

Founded in 1852 near Sewanee, Tennessee, the Tennessee Coal, Iron
and Railroad Company—which would eventually become simply the

Tennessee Coal and Iron Company—was the nation's largest coal and iron manufacturer by the close of the nineteenth century. By 1874 it had switched its focus to coke and iron production to keep up with the times; in 1895, with the acquisition of a number of its competitors, the company held the distinction of being the South's largest furnace operation. During the same year, the company moved its headquarters from Sewanee to Birmingham, in order to take advantage of the mineral riches that lay beneath Red Mountain, Jefferson County's greatest hope for prosperity.

Four years after the company settled in Birmingham, it made a critical shift in its production, turning the manufacture of steel into its primary focus. After a financial crisis threatened to topple the company in the early years of the new century, its owners took a bid of thirty-five million dollars from U.S. Steel, the world's first billion-dollar corporation, owned by millionaire financier J. P. Morgan (to whom Gaston would be compared later in life). TCI was officially sold into northern hands on November 5, 1907.

The shift of company control from southern to northern interests was not insignificant. The growth of Birmingham as a municipality had relied heavily on southerners' interest in southern industrialization (and the money brought into the area by such advances). The absence of that concern on the part of U.S. Steel would impact not only the operation of the mines themselves, but also the quality of life in the general Birmingham area. As historian Lynne Feldman suggests, during this period "U.S. Steel's discriminatory pricing policies of Alabama steel, combined with less-advanced technology, an unstable work force, and inferior resources . . . contributed to Birmingham's slow and disappointing growth as an industrial city." Each of the elements Feldman points to as missing from the strange brew of industrialization in Birmingham represents a critical aspect of life in the Alabama mines during the early part of the twentieth century. Each warrants a closer look.

In the first place, though Jefferson County offered much in the way of mineral resources, it was hardly the richest trove of natural resources on the national geologic landscape. Places such as Pittsburgh, Cleveland, and the Mesabi Range in Minnesota held much deeper stores of iron ore. The hunt for iron in the Alabama hills was thus, to some degree, harder and more desperate than it was in other regions, and by the time U.S. Steel came into the picture, it was resulting in smaller financial rewards than could be found in the North.

The lack of comparable output from the Alabama mines had a stark effect on the daily life of miners once the northern investors took control. When the mines were owned by the smaller, regionally immersed TCI, there had been no need to fight for attention from the powers that be: They had only had one interest to keep in mind. Now the mines were being run by a corporate structure that had little need to try to save the city of Birmingham or its workers. Its focus was making money, and its attention—and all that attended it—went first and foremost to the operations that were making the most money. Birmingham was not one of them.

The result was that for years after they were acquired by U.S. Steel, the Birmingham mines operated without any of the technological advances that had become commonplace in mines elsewhere in the country. Workers continued to break iron into manageable pieces by hand, with sledgehammers and crowbars, long after new methods of handling the material had been developed. They hauled hundred-pound ingots on their backs for excruciating distances, when other forms of transportation had long been in place elsewhere.

It was lost on no one—least of all the miners themselves—that race may have played a crucial element in determining where costs were cut and who received the better equipment. In Birmingham a staggering 65 percent of iron and steel laborers were black, well above the national average for this particular labor pool. Salaries in the Birmingham mines were between 25 and 40 percent lower than what was offered in Pittsburgh. In 1912 that meant $1.55 per day to the Birmingham man, rather than the $2.10 offered up north.

In either case, work in the mines offered not a lot of money for a great deal of (very dangerous) labor. Men generally worked in twelve-hour shifts, six days a week. Furnace men were called on to work double shifts of twenty-four hours every other Sunday. Typically, each miner shoveled an average of eight to twelve thousand pounds of dead weight per day (a figure sometimes put at the even higher estimate of fifteen to twenty thousand pounds), often while immersed in water up to his neck. And the men died—in the mines and in their beds—at an astounding rate. Working in the mines was as close to working in hell as a living human being could get.

For all of these reasons, becoming a miner rarely landed at the top of anyone's list of chosen professions. In Birmingham the peculiarity of the convict-lease system made the job even less appealing. The mines were a de facto prison system: They "leased" prisoners from the county jails to fill jobs at a discount rate. Eighty percent of the convicts who ended up in the mines were "indigent, illiterate blacks who had been arrested for vagrancy and other Jim Crow offenses." Under the Black Codes it was still illegal for blacks to be unemployed. Any Negro found in violation of this statute was liable to be arrested and farmed out to the mines. Sharecroppers who defaulted on their payments often suffered the same fate. Not only did this system behoove the mine owners, it behooved the state: In the year 1914 twelve hundred convicts leased out to the mines were responsible for producing 20 percent of the state's revenues. For black Alabamians, the line between "employment" and "punishment" was one whose delineations were blurred by the frequent sight of chain gangs shuffling to work in the mines.

Becoming a Company Man

After the war, however, many blacks were desperate for any employment at all. Even college graduates found themselves jobless. Arthur Gaston didn't even have a high school diploma. It was clear to him, after the debacle at the O.K. Dry Cleaning Plant, that the mines were all that was left.

The trolley line from Birmingham ended in Fairfield. From there it was a three-mile walk north to the town of Westfield, the location of the newest mining village. Built in 1918, Westfield was the best of what any Alabama miner could hope for. The village was constructed in response to the increased need for workers as a result of the war effort. It featured four-room and six-room houses that could be rented by employees, all of which offered indoor plumbing and frame structures. Additionally, the town included a company store, churches, and schools. For any black person considering life in the village, Westfield seemed to offer security and opportunity—all in the guise of freshly painted homes. If the Great War had done few things to actually better the lives of black Americans, it had at least made Westfield possible.

The fact that everything that made Westfield desirable was owned by the managing corporation and rented—at a premium—to its workers was one that, while noted by employees, was of relatively little practical import. The living situation in Westfield was nearly impossible to beat if you had few options, even if it meant facing the possibility of death on a daily basis. That somebody would rent them their house, sell them their food (albeit at a 10 to 20 percent markup over independent markets), clothe and school their children—and let them do it all on *credit*—was a boon to people who had struggled daily to feed and clothe themselves for generations. Did they know it was a trap? That close to none of them would ever make their way clear of the debt that the mining life entailed? Perhaps. But the luxury of opting out is rarely afforded to people living on the margins of society.

By the time Arthur set out from Fairfield, the sun was already blistering overhead. He was sweating, his shirt soaked. His careful eavesdropping on the conversations of his coworkers at the dry-cleaning plant had given him the tip on the job openings at Westfield. He knew that the mines were offering wages of $3.10 a day, which meant that, if he lasted, he could be bringing home more than three times as much as he had been making at O.K. It meant that he could start saving again, and replenish what he and his mother had had to take from his account.

As he wound his way through the well-kept, tree-lined streets of Westfield, pausing to glimpse home after well-appointed home, the grief that had not left him since the moment Mr. Williams's face had dissolved into shock melted away. The scent of barbecue wafted by; brightly colored flowers danced in window boxes. He watched a house being raised in a newly tilled lot and couldn't help but think, *That one would do just fine for Mama and me.* It wasn't exactly Enon

Ridge or Smithfield, but it was, he realized, as much as he could possibly hope for under the circumstances.

What Gaston could not know at the time was that, much like industrial giant Andrew Carnegie before him, he would find the beginnings of his wealth in the steel mill. Carnegie, like Gaston, was born poor: He came to America from Scotland in 1848 and worked upon his arrival in a series of low-paying jobs, earning as little as $1.20 a week as a bobbin boy in a cotton factory. He started in business small, by investing his savings in railroads. Believing that steel would replace iron as the leading industrial metal, he then invested himself in the mines—and by 1890 his Pittsburgh-based Carnegie Company was producing four million tons of steel per year. In 1901 Carnegie sold this company to J. P. Morgan for almost half a billion dollars.

Believing that "the man who dies rich, dies disgraced," Carnegie spent the rest of his life giving his money away, through the creation of, among other philanthropic interests, public libraries and foundations, and he gave at least a million dollars to Booker T. Washington's Tuskegee Institute. Despite his company's use of tens of thousands of black gang workers to lay railroad tracks, in 1889 Carnegie wrote in *The Gospel of Wealth:* "We cannot afford to lose the Negro. We have urgent need of all and more. Let us therefore turn our efforts to making the best of him."

Having found, however, that "the best of him" was not in high demand, Arthur Gaston determined to make the best, at least, of the only option left. At the Westfield employment office he was automatically accepted into the mining corps (finally, a job a war hero was qualified for) and just as quickly approved for housing. By the end of the week, Gaston wrote, he, his mother, and his grandmother (who had come to Birmingham not long before, following the death of his grandfather) were Westfield residents.

————

The joy that accompanied having a house with electricity and indoor facilities didn't last long. As the realities of life in the mines set in, Arthur found himself descending once again into hopelessness and depression, this time accompanied by the bone exhaustion that was mining's special gift. For more than a year Arthur's life experience was confined to the activities of working, sleeping, and eating. An ache set into his muscles that never seemed to subside, even waking him from sleep. Black mine workers were banned from operating machinery, so the most backbreaking labor was usually theirs. The luckiest among them got the opportunity to work in the "Wood Car Shop" where the railroad cars that transported the iron out of the mines were built. Arthur worked there from time to time, but even this reprieve from danger reinforced his despondency. Men who had war stories of their own stood beside him painting car after car, tired as he was.

The endless parade of former soldiers he encountered who were unable to secure any work but this was dispiriting. Every two weeks Art lined up along with them and watched as they opened their slender pay envelopes. Deductions were always made ahead of time for the milk, and the rent, and any other little thing charged at the store, so that when payday finally came, often all that was left were a few nickels—which more often than not dissolved into a few drinks at the local bar. Something was wrong, Art thought, with a system that made it impossible for a man to get ahead. Though he was less of a spender than most men, he still found himself barely able to break even. His life was slipping away from him and he knew it. He tried to bolster his spirits by thinking of Booker T. Washington and how little he had suffered compared to that man. Arthur, at least, had been born free. He thought about Joe and Idella and how they had liberated themselves from debt in a time when debt was the order of the day. Thinking of his grandparents and their industriousness made him realize that it was credit, no less than the mines themselves, that was killing him. The question was, how to escape it?

An Appetite for Business

The answer came in the form of a lunch box. Though Rosie had left her freelance catering days behind her in Birmingham, she still made it her job to send Art off to work with a full lunch every day. Baked sweet potatoes and large flaky biscuits were sent along to supplement a healthy serving of chicken. Art's coworkers never failed to inspect his lunch box once the noon whistle rang. Many of the men had no families, according to Gaston, and the care that had been taken to provide Art with a meal impressed them almost as much as the food itself. Art felt no hesitation in sharing what he had, in part because he realized he was sharing his mother's love in sharing her food. These men deserved that much.

One particular day, Arthur found himself feeling especially lost. The morning had been spent painting railcars, and the fumes from the paint had nauseated him. When the noon whistle sounded, he sat with his coworkers but didn't touch his food. It didn't take long for someone to notice. A fellow named Junior who had stood not far down the line from him all day glanced in Art's direction and asked after his lunch. Raising his head to answer the question, Arthur caught sight of a dark stripe of paint running from Junior's cheek to his neck. The image chilled him. The paint, it seemed to Arthur, was a symbol, "the mark of a laborer who would always be a laborer." For well over a year, Arthur had been plagued with doubt and confusion. He had, he wrote, "vacillated between renewing my pledge to become somebody and thinking I should forget it." What he realized, looking at Junior, was that nothing would change unless he took the initiative to change it. You didn't get successful by thinking about whether you were going to be successful or not; you got successful by *doing something* to make yourself successful. What Arthur saw reflected in the other man's face was the mark of his own future if he didn't take action.

Arthur held his lunch box out before him and Junior reached for it, happily. He watched as the man tucked into the meal, sighing with satisfaction at the taste of Rosie's food. Junior looked at Art and smiled. Art smiled right back, realizing he had found his business. Men would pay for these meals, he thought. And he was right. Before long, Arthur and his mother—who was excited by the prospect of getting back to doing what she loved, cooking—had "drummed up a nice business." Their boxed lunches brought in enough money that Arthur could begin saving again in earnest.

The success of that business venture gave Arthur a taste for industry, and before long he was once again the boy who had taken so many jobs he could barely keep up with demand. He began selling peanuts and popcorn "on the side," sometimes making as much as twenty dollars on a given payday, when the men felt better about letting go of a few coins. Once he had secured a financial foundation, he began lending out money to his coworkers at a rate of twenty-five cents on the dollar, as a way of, in his words, "occupy[ing] my spare time." At 25 percent interest, Arthur's loans were barely deals, but his was the only lending institution that would take a debt-ridden black miner as a client. With little competition for his services, Arthur's wealth took on a snowball effect, compounding biweekly.

Another man might have felt squeamish about lending to the working poor at such exorbitant rates, but for Arthur the equation was a simple one. In the first place, he was poor, too, and this was merely a way of working to better his own situation. Second, while he had sympathy for the men who were trapped in the mine system, they were not, by and large, his friends. As in many of his other experiences, at Westfield Arthur had found little camaraderie among the men. As always, he was too square to fit in. He refused to spend his money on the small luxuries they squandered their salaries on, and as a result they shunned him. He was, as always, bothered by his alienation, but he stuck to his plan. When that plan involved taking their money for his own gain, there was little to make him feel guilty. Besides, to his mind he was doing them a service. Business was business.

Many of the men who borrowed from Arthur used that money to impress the ladies. Fancy clothes and long nights in the bars ate up any money they could have saved. It was behavior Arthur didn't approve of, even if, for a time, he had tried it himself. For a brief period, Arthur had been willing to allot five dollars of his earnings per month to pleasurable activities in the hope of wooing a lady. He was quickly disabused of any notion that he would make the cut. There were too many men out there willing to spend every penny they had, and more, on a pretty face, and Arthur's diminutive pleasure purse didn't make the grade. While other men wore the latest clothes—"peg top pants, sporty knickers [and] handsome derby hats"—Arthur donned the same fashion year after year, his clothes meticulously tended to by his mother. While other men took their ladies to dances and on "outings," Arthur refused, citing the expense. It didn't take long for his reputation for cheapness to spread. Eventually he gave up on trying to compete at all, and decided to put those dollars in the bank instead.

Saving became Arthur's primary habit. As critical to his accumulation of wealth as the money coming in was the money that was not going out. To the day he died, Arthur Gaston was nothing if not frugal. During his early days of business operations at the mines, he was making an average of seventy-five to a hundred dollars per month. Of these earnings, fifty to seventy-five dollars went straight into the bank, leaving him with twenty-five dollars to spend. Of that, fifteen dollars went to rent. This left ten dollars, five of which he would use for living expenses (essentially, food). The remaining five dollars was what he allowed himself for pleasurable activities. This means that Arthur was saving between 66 and 75 percent of his earnings on a monthly basis. Discounting the twenty dollars that he used to pay his rent and feed himself, his budget allowed for him to spend approximately 5 percent of his earnings, per month, on anything that fell outside his most basic needs. Once the ladies rejected him, even that money began to earn interest.

In the absence of any social outlet among his fellow workers, Gaston joined the St. Paul African Methodist Episcopal Church and founded a "civic league" among the members. He took part in a few company activities such as baseball games (he was a decent shortstop), attended (free) dances, and reveled in the singing performances given by visiting entertainers at the local community house. Most of all, however, he watched his money grow.

The high rate of interest that Arthur was charging for cash loans soon made his informal "bank" the best earner of all his many little companies. In fact, the interest was bringing in more money than all of the other businesses combined. Meanwhile, Arthur had continued his work in the mines, realizing that without his job there—and thus his access to the miners—none of his other businesses could operate.

He had no desire to spend the rest of his life working night and day in Westfield, so he began to consider other business opportunities. Nothing seemed workable. Though he had created a nice nest egg for himself and for his mother, what he was searching for was the opportunity to create a self-sustaining business that would provide them with enough security to leave Westfield behind.

Gaston had begun his empire building with an eye to making money, his early businesses originating from the principles of self-benefit: He sold lunches to men not because the men would not eat otherwise, but because he determined that they would pay for a better product; he lent them money at high interest rates not because these men were starving, but because they wanted to participate in frivolities and were willing to pay a premium for an extra dollar here or there. In essence, then, little of his early moneymaking was about need—it was about fulfilling desires for extraneous goods.

The scheme had served him well, and would have continued doing so, perhaps indefinitely. And if Arthur Gaston had been a different man, he might have been satisfied to maintain his market in the mines and retire early. But he wasn't that man, and his dream was not to achieve middling success, but actual greatness. The problem was, he seemed to have reached an impasse: No new markets were opening up. He racked his brain, trying to figure out what would work, what would sell—until he realized that it was his methodology that was tripping him up. Rather than figuring out what he could *sell,* he decided to step back and take a look at what the community he was living in actually *needed.* It was a turn, in his mind, away from self-interest and toward public service, and the change was one that would inform his business endeavors for the rest of his life.

THE BURIAL RACKET

Payday at Westfield was an occasion that brought everybody to the center of town. Workers crowded around the dark blue pay trolley, jostling for position, waiting to claim what was left of their earnings. Wives circled the scene, waiting to grab their men before they headed off to the bars. Other groups of hangers-on also made it a point to show up wherever the pay car stopped, knowing that the men got paid in cash and were more willing on payday than any other to throw a few cents in the direction of the cause of the moment.

One of the most common pleas heard around the pay wagon was a solicitation for money to cover the burial costs of a recently deceased individual. The scheme was one run by missionaries and "slicksters" and it was one with a high rate of return. In the black communities of the 1920s and beyond, funeral rites were both extremely important and rarely provided for financially. They were a person's last link with the world and demanded a certain propriety and effort. But funerals were also expensive, costing a minimum of a hundred dollars—far more than the average (or even above-average) black person made in a month. Almost no one had the financial wherewithal to pay for a proper burial, so the task of raising money fell to the deceased's church, and beyond that to any individual who took it upon him- or herself to go out calling for funds.

On the one hand, this fostered an intense spirit of community giving and responsibility. On the other, it opened the door wide for fraudulent acts to transpire, which indeed they did. As Gaston explained:

> Solicitors carried lists of names of people who allegedly had died leaving families that were unable to provide the funeral. Some of the names on those lists were of people who did not exist. Others were names of people very much alive.
>
> I knew one woman who must have had at least half a dozen different husbands to pass on during the time money was being begged at the pay car. A different husband died every pay day or so, leaving her with several children.

The widespread poverty of the area made blacks all the more susceptible to the ploys of those trying to hustle them out of their money for supposed burials. It was impossible to know who was telling the truth and was in need, and who was just filling their own purse with the proceeds. Furthermore, many of the miners were likely moved by the knowledge that they could just as easily be in a similar situation: With death a persistent threat, a mine worker had to wonder if it wouldn't be his wife (or mother or sister) out there begging for money to bury him by the next payday.

Burial insurance was not unheard of at the time, but it was an unpopular option among blacks due to the bureaucracy involved in dealing with any white-owned corporation and the difficulty blacks had in actually obtaining it. Few insurance companies were willing to cover black clients—not only because of outright racial discrimination, but because they were a bad business risk: Their mortality rate was appreciably higher, in every age group, than among their white counterparts. And black miners died at an even higher rate than the average black. Charity, meanwhile, was "ready money" and spared a person the humiliation of being laughed at by an insurance agent. So solicitations persisted and the donations flowed. To Gaston, however, those solicitations were an affront. "It was a racket," he said, "and I resented it."

It occurred to him, as he watched yet another man part with his money to pay for the funeral of someone who was probably not even dead, that things didn't have to be this way. Black people needed to have a way of burying their own and knowing where their money was going. Insurance was obviously the best alternative, but insurance companies were owned by whites, who had proven they had no interest in helping blacks attain anything in life, much less in death. Here, finally, was something black people needed and Arthur was certain he could provide: a society that would take care of their burial costs, "squelching" the racket that was robbing them of their hard-earned money while guaranteeing a proper funeral. It seemed logical to him that "if people were so willing to contribute for the burials of persons they did not know . . . they should be willing to pay a small, regular sum to a burial society to prepare for their own inevitable demise."

It was sound business thinking, but adjusting people's attitudes regarding what they "need" is never as easy as it might appear. In Gaston's case, converting the masses to his way of thinking would require first a crisis, then an ultimatum.

The Booker T. Washington Burial Society

Granny Tuggle was the first to hear of Arthur's idea. She was enthusiastic, according to Gaston: both about the society itself and about Arthur's initiative to give back to his community. He discussed the plan informally with a few local ministers, who promised to lend their support. He also contacted Dad Smith, who sent encouragement and praise.

Arthur's basic plan was to structure his funeral society on the model of a fraternal organization. Based on a dues system in which each member contributed a specific amount to the society on a monthly or weekly basis, fraternal organizations had achieved huge popularity among members of the black middle class. Besides the prestige and socialization that came with membership, a number of these secret societies also offered their members financial support in times of need, death benefits being one of the covered eventualities. Arthur had spent a great deal of time touring such societies in his time with Granny Tuggle (the fraternities were generous in their contributions to education), and he recognized their model of membership as one that was easily transferable to the burial business. Furthermore, most fraternal organizations were middle-class endeavors, so there was little likelihood that any majority of miners (who rarely qualified as middle class) would already be covered.

Once his business plan solidified in his mind, Arthur called his first fund-raising meeting at St. Paul A.M.E. Five of the area's most influential pastors and church officials turned up. They all agreed that Arthur's proposal was a good one, but none of them was inclined to invest a dime in setting the plan in motion.

Gaston was left with two choices: let the idea go or pursue it on his own. He had saved enough money by this point to cover any losses that might be incurred by the death of a client too soon, however, he was absolutely determined not to touch that money unless he came across a "sure-fire money-making proposition." The burial society was not that—it was a risk.

Nevertheless, he was certain that the idea was solid, and he still needed a big success to establish himself as a serious businessman.

The only option he could see was to take the risk and start up the company on his own. He remembered his mother's stories of how A. B. Loveman had started his company by going door to door, selling "silks and laces" out of a bag he toted over his shoulder. He had earned people's trust and they had learned his name, and when he had saved enough to set up his business in earnest they came flocking. The key was to start small and build from there, Rosie had told Arthur. At the time he hadn't really understood what she meant. Now it became clear.

Each day after work, Arthur traveled from door to door, "writ[ing] people up" for his burial society. His rate was twenty-five cents per week for the head of the family, and ten cents for "any additional family members" who wanted coverage. He met with modest success. If business was not exactly booming initially, he did manage to convince more than a few people of the integrity of his plan.

———

One of the people Gaston managed to convince was a woman named Sara Emmons. Mrs. Emmons signed right up when Arthur Gaston came to her door. She gave him the requisite twenty-five cents to cover her husband and added another ten for herself. Then Mrs. Sara Emmons promptly up and died.

At this point Arthur had collected a grand total of ten dollars in premiums from his clients—about a tenth of what burying Mrs. Emmons was going to cost him. Her death threatened to ruin the company before it had even had a chance to get off the ground. Arthur had the money to make up the difference, but he was too shrewd to go dipping into his own accounts. Besides, he had already sworn to himself that he would do no such thing. It occurred to him that since Mrs. Emmons had been a member of the society for so short a time, and had paid so little toward her policy, perhaps he wasn't to be held accountable for her burial. After a few more thoughts along these lines, he paid a visit to the woman's pastor and told him as much.

The Reverend S. H. Ravizee of Hopewell Baptist Church had been one of the men in attendance at Gaston's initial fund-raising meeting. When Arthur showed up at his church door to suggest that Mrs. Emmons's burial was not his responsibility but the church's, the Reverend Ravizee wasted no time in enlightening the young man about his obligations. In a dull whisper (the result of damage to his vocal cords), the reverend informed Gaston that he would indeed be responsible for raising the money for Mrs. Emmons's burial. Furthermore, he made it clear that if Gaston failed in his duty, the reverend himself would make sure that the burial society was "broken up," immediately.

There was no way out and Arthur knew it. From the church he caught the streetcar to Fairfield and went directly to the offices of Mr. James Payne, manager of one of the few black funeral homes in the area. Arthur apprised Payne of his situation and, after a great debate, Payne agreed to bury the body for seventy-five dollars rather than the standard hundred, with the agreement that Gaston would reimburse him through collection at the service and, if that didn't cover it, premiums garnered from the rest of his clients over time. It was a dangerous proposition for Gaston because it put him dramatically in debt. Given his limited options, however, he had no choice but to take the deal Payne was offering.

Arthur approached Mrs. Emmons's funeral that Sunday full of trepidation. This was the first funeral his newly founded company had been responsible for, and he had floundered. He was going to be forced to go before the congregation himself and beg for money—a humiliation. Arthur entered the church and sat through the service in a haze, waiting at every turn for the Reverend Ravizee to lash out against him. Finally the time came when, traditionally, donations had been solicited from the congregation. Arthur's stomach seized. He had imagined that the reverend would simply skip over this part of the service, so when Ravizee stepped forward to address the crowd, Arthur froze in his spot.

The reverend announced: "You may view the body and put your coins of comfort on the collection table." Without hesitation the congregation rose and "filed into the sanctuary, circling the casket, then dropping money on the little wooden washstand." Though he was relieved, Arthur knew he was not yet out of the woods. The reverend was prepared to say more. He informed the congregation that this was the last funeral that the church would be taking up a collection for. "The deceased," he said,

> had paid only thirty-five cents into Brother Gaston's Burial Society, and she will get a decent burial as a result of joining. Now, Brothers and Sisters, if you can't spare twenty-five or thirty-five cents a week for a decent burial, you need not look to the church to do it for you. This is the last time for such.

The church filled with sounds of surprise and shock, the loudest of which came from Brother Gaston himself. By placing a moratorium on church collections, the reverend had effectively driven Arthur's primary competitor out of business. Better still, he had pointed customers directly to Arthur's door. The reverend called Arthur forward and gave him the chance to explain the nature of his operation to a captive audience. Two ladies of the church were assigned to be Arthur's assistants, and they stationed themselves at the door of the church to write people up on their way out. Before the day was done they had collected more than fifty dollars in premiums from new clients. Added to the donations that had been set forth during the service, more than enough money was available to pay for Mrs. Emmons's burial.

James Payne was so impressed by Arthur's prompt repayment that he offered a standing arrangement to the young man: He would continue to charge a discount rate of seventy-five dollars per burial if Gaston agreed to make Payne's the sole funeral home for burial procedures. The sheer size of Gaston's clientele, and the quickness with which he had secured it, convinced Payne that he would make up for the discount in volume. Gaston agreed, and the Booker T. Washington Burial Society was born in earnest.

In one day Arthur Gaston's business had gone from the brink of collapse to establishing itself as a force to be reckoned with in the black community. It was a roller-coaster ride that reflected the tenor of Gaston's new life. In the three years he had been home from the war, he had sunk lower than he ever would have imagined possible.

The United States, he learned upon his return, had not changed: It still denied blacks the most basic of opportunities. What *had* changed, he finally realized, was him. He had returned from fighting the world, and now, in the words of W. E. B. DuBois, he was ready to fight at home. From here, he promised himself, there was no looking back.

DEATH BECOMES HIM

*Money, in the years to come, will be the heart
of the matter. A great many of us are going to wake up with
a shock and discover that there is no such thing as
a first class "broke man."*

THE BUSINESS OF BURYING THE DEAD

As it has become increasingly easy to admit, we are a nation obsessed with dying—more so today than ever before. What happens to us *just* after we die tickles our national conscience—the question of *How* (quite literally) *will I leave this world?* having moved in recent years from a place of private debate to one of public consideration. This has not, however, always been the case.

When Jessica Mitford's seminal work on the growth of the American funeral industry, *The American Way of Death,* was published in 1963, the book was met with cries of outrage from every side of the fence imaginable. Funeral directors felt vilified by Mitford's unsentimental treatment of their trade; laypeople were incensed by the newly revealed truths of the burial business; and the guardians at the gates of propriety took Mitford to task for her unflinchingly detailed descriptions of the art of mortuary science—leaking orifices, lip stitching, and all. Mitford's book was a work of social critique of the highest order: It revealed the facts (such as that "the cost of the funeral is the third largest expenditure, after a house and a car, in the life of an ordinary American family"), while utilizing those facts to underscore the social impact of the growth of a monetarily based death culture.

Until approximately the second decade of the twentieth century, death was, to varying degrees, an untouchable concept in the United States. Dead bodies were accorded their due respect and dispensed with—very quickly and with relatively little fanfare. Church and family were responsible for the preservation and disposal of the corpse, the body set to cool on blocks of ice in the parlor to aid in conservation for the short period between death and interment. In many communities (the African American community first among them) touching the deceased was forbidden; the fear was that whatever spiritual evil had brought death to one body was easily communicable to another.

The American approach to death remained determined by superstition and widespread poverty through the end of the nineteenth century. But with the dawning of the modern age in the early 1920s, both attitudes and practices began to shift. The 1920s ushered in an apparent postwar boom in the American standard of living. Unemployment rates fell, real wages rose modestly, and in 1923 the federal government lowered the tax rate as part of the Mellon Plan. The concepts of industrialization, urbanization, immigration, and western expansion dominated both political and cultural discourse. The 1920s seemed, at least, to be a time of good fortune and economic growth in which every citizen could participate. It was the Jazz Age, the time of the Harlem Renaissance, the period in which flappers and anti-Prohibitionists flaunted the legal codes. "America" was reborn during this first decade after the war, and whatever else might be in question, patriotism—"100 percent Americanism," in the words of President Theodore Roosevelt—was a requirement, not a choice.

As is often the case in economic boom times, however, a relatively small portion of the population enjoyed the vast majority of the prosperity. Though it is true that wages rose across the board, it is also true that they rose much more steeply for the wealthy than they did for the poor. From 1922 to 1929 wages in manufacturing rose 1.4 percent per capita per year; stockholders, however, saw a rise of 16.4 percent in the same period. While the middle class continued to grow, with a marked increase in available "white-collar and service industry jobs" developing around the world, the gap between the rich and the poor was widening as well. Critically, one-tenth of 1 percent of the richest families in the nation earned as much in a given year as 42 percent of the poorest families' combined incomes. These numbers are staggering, yet few people at the time felt the need to protest the mounting inequalities produced by an overinflated system. The creation of a burgeoning, economically "secure" middle class made it possible for a growing number of individuals to ignore the poverty that refused to disappear even as the markets spiked upward.

The arrival of these "good times" for a widening swath of the population allowed for the spread of certain ideologies—not least those regarding death rites. For those in the middle, modernization provided an increase not only in money but in time as well, and the confluence of these two elements allowed for deliberation on issues theretofore relegated to the back corners of the mind. Buoyed by the comfort of change in their pockets, and the time to reflect on their options, more and more individuals were able to consider new ways of burying their dead—just as they were considering new ways of buying homes and cars—methods suggested and developed by the newly modernized service industry of funeral homes.

Funeral homes and service directors were not twentieth-century developments; the word *undertaker* had come into popular usage as early as the seventeenth century. What *was* new about the twentieth-century funeral services industry was its shift from the not-for-profit or charity-based organization to a full-blown business venture. As Mitford points out, in 1880 funeral directors were charging their clients a bare minimum of fees for their services beyond cost of materials. But as the market widened and proved that it could and would bear seemingly limitless increases in the costs of funereal care, so the undertakers raised their fees and propelled the trade into its status as one of the most profitable sectors of industry in U.S. history.

Were economic forces alone to be held accountable for the rapid inflation of funeral services? Do we chalk the industry's exponential growth up simply to what the market would bear? It's possible. What is more important, in some sense, is to understand that this market also expanded as a result of a changed relationship between death and the living. At the very heart of this "new" sensibility lay the concept of "memorialization," in which the burial act became a performance of sentimentality and memory making. The shift to this newly emotionalized attitude toward the corpse (incorporating as it did greater interaction between the living and the dead—for example, extended viewing periods) attached "value" to the funeral service, and in turn created a new realm of issues with which the relatives of the deceased were forced to deal. Funerals were no longer thought of as necessary evils; they were to be considered the final means of paying respect to a life.

> Memorialization is love. It records a love so strong, so happy, so enduring that it can never die. It is the recognition of the immortality of the human spirit, the rightful reverence earned by the good life. It is the final testimony to the dignity of man.

It was the funeral itself—that is, the quality of it—that came to confer value upon the recently ended life. And because those faced with planning a funeral for the deceased were more often than not buying in an extremely vulnerable state, the growth of this notion of memorialization as love had a distinct effect on the corporatization of funeral services. In short, when people began to believe that a fancy funeral was the only way to say good-bye to their loved ones, undertakers began making money hand over fist.

Economic Power; or, the One Thing Washington and DuBois Agreed On

A. G. Gaston's entrée into the world of funeral industry is usually represented as a fortuitous accident: He happened to hit on the right idea at the right time. This is certainly true—as it is true of any successful business idea—but it is also critical to recognize that Gaston picked an area of business that had a proven potential for growth and in which he had a bead on an untapped population of prospective customers. Initially, as a provider of burial insurance but not burial services, Gaston was able to keep his overhead extremely low and fix his prices at levels that were high enough to cover his negotiated cost with James Payne (the director of the local funeral parlor), but low enough to lure customers. The difference between these two sums became the money that went into Gaston's own pocket.

The burial society as concept fulfilled the two major conditions Gaston required before he would invest in any business: It met a genuine need in the community, and it offered a real opportunity for him to accumulate wealth. The latter of these forces was reflected in the very name of the company that would launch Gaston's business career. Though the Booker T. Washington Burial Society was christened as such to honor a friend of Gaston's from his Westfield days, the echoes the name evoked of the spirit of Gaston's childhood hero were not coincidental. Booker T. Washington had preached early and often of the necessity of economic independence for the black community. Washington believed that it was through industry that blacks could hope to ameliorate their position in the United States. And he was not alone in his encouragement of business initiatives. Much has been made of the antipathy that existed between Washington and scholar W. E. B. DuBois, and quite rightly. DuBois disdained Washington's tendency to eschew the relevance of social issues, and for his part Washington felt that DuBois's theories were both impractical and elitist in tone. Nevertheless, on some issues DuBois and Washington stood closer ideologically than their furious opposition on others would lead us to believe.

The development of business interests within the black community was one such subject—a topic upon which the men obliquely concurred. The cultivation of "material prosperity" lay at the center of Washington's address before the Atlanta Exposition; the manipulation of markets was, to his mind, the key to advancement. Washington's statement that "no race that has anything to contribute to the markets of the world is long . . . ostracized" epitomizes both his deep-seated optimism and his belief in the ability of economic forces to right the wrongs of social inequalities. DuBois, while deeply at odds with Washington's theories of social moderation, held his own faith in the opportunities that black-owned business offered the race. In 1899, under the auspices of Atlanta University, DuBois published a full-length report on the state of Negro enterprise, highlighting the various functions (economic, social, and psychological) that black-run businesses fulfilled within communities. His dedication to compiling the report is indicative of his conviction that the topic was one of import, and one that deserved further attention from the larger Negro community. It was DuBois who first came up with the idea of creating an association of black business owners, and Washington who saw the idea to fruition in creating the National Negro Business League.

The correlation between business and success (the one as the path to the other) would have been particularly acute for a man like Arthur Gaston in the early part of the twentieth century—a man with less than a high school education. While DuBois spoke of the responsibilities of the "Talented Tenth," Gaston had little access to life on that stratum. What he did have, by the time 1923 rolled around, was an emergent business interest, the faith of a sizable (and growing) clientele, and an unflagging desire to succeed. His endless thumbing through his copy of Washington's *Up from Slavery* had inspired him to action and taught him a crucial lesson: When opportunity knocks, open the door and invite him to tea. It had also instilled in him a genuine sense of self-reliance. Hanging Washington's name on his business was a not-so-subtle reminder—to himself and everyone else who saw or heard it—of what dedication to task might accomplish.

Washington's influence on Gaston was significant, but his was not the singular example of success to spur Gaston into action. Washington was an educator, not a businessman. His greatest strengths were in theorizing a movement and in training young black men and women to embody the accompanying values in their lifework. The Tuskegee Institute was a business of a sort, but its business was education. And though not initially certain where his fortunes awaited, at this point in his life Gaston felt clear that his future was primarily as a businessman, not as an educator. He would have to look elsewhere for mentors in industry. Charles M. Harris and William R. Pettiford may have been precisely what he was looking for.

BIRMINGHAM'S BLACK PIONEERS

Charles M. "Boss" Harris, was, like Gaston, a born and raised Alabamian. After moving from Montgomery to Birmingham in 1899, he opened (with a loan from the Alabama Penny Savings Bank—the same bank that gave Arthur Gaston a mortgage on his first plot of land) what would become the first undertaking company in the city of Birmingham to handle black bodies. Over time, Harris expanded his undertaking business into an insurance business, first as a burial association (Gaston's burial society was not much different) and then as a full-fledged life insurance company. Though when he started in the business he was one of a few black morticians nationwide, by 1927 that number had risen to more than three thousand—thanks in large part to the demonstrated achievements of Harris's enterprise. Harris's success in business was a bona fide example of "finding a need and filling it," and though Gaston makes no direct reference to any association with Harris, it is unimaginable that his influence would not have been felt by the younger man.

Though Gaston and Harris shared a common interest in the development of funerary services for the black community, William Pettiford embodied the type of businessman Gaston would strive to be. Pettiford was an intimate of Booker T. Washington's, and an outspoken proponent of economic development as the means to improving the plight of the black American. He was, to be sure, a more overtly political man than Gaston would ever choose to be, speaking on issues of race and industry at conferences around the country. But it is in his exceptional business acumen and, most notably, his public relations expertise that we see intimations of the man Gaston would become.

Pettiford was not born in Alabama. He was an immigrant of sorts, a transplant from North Carolina. Pettiford had come to Alabama in search of work, and—though he was an ordained minister—he found employment as a construction worker for the railroads. In due course he would find work outside hard labor: first as a teacher and fundraiser at a private university in Selma and eventually, in 1883, as a leader of Birmingham's famous Sixteenth Street Baptist Church. He proved a master at both eradicating liabilities (the church had acquired a sizable debt prior to his arrival) and nurturing the congregation (it nearly tripled in size over a period four years). Soon he was propelled into positions of church leadership throughout the city and state, and was widely considered among the most influential and well-known citizens of Birmingham.

Though a dedicated worshiper, a number of Pettiford's interests (and the ones for which he was perhaps most famous) lay outside the bounds of the church. In particular, his role as a founder and director of the Alabama Penny Savings and Loan Company (which would come to be known as the Alabama Penny Savings Bank) situated him squarely at the center of life in black Birmingham at the dawn of the twentieth century. The idea for building a black-owned bank came to Pettiford as an outgrowth of his alliance with Washington on the topic of economic independence, and, as Lynne Feldman argues, as a means of protecting a class of people untrained in financial planning from "frittering away what little money they had." Formed in 1890 as a public company, and helped along by Pettiford's emergent ecumenical career, by 1913 the bank had accumulated assets of $540,955.63, with branches across the state, and had secured the trust and devotion of a majority of the black citizens of Alabama. Through the bank, Pettiford encouraged blacks to invest in local real estate. He reduced the size of both down payments and monthly payments (because most blacks simply had less money than whites) by stringing policies out for longer periods of time than other banks offered.

The Alabama Penny Savings Bank was willing to take risks on black clients (whose profiles rarely if ever measured up to the mark in white-owned banks) when few others would. It was this openness toward risk, buffered by a faith in the ability of blacks to earn if given the chance, that ultimately brought the bank such success. Though it closed its doors in 1915 (just over a year after Pettiford's death) under a swirl of controversy and an as-yet-unsolved mystery, the bank's positive impact on the black community—both in Birmingham and beyond—was unquestionable. As a result of Pettiford's efforts, the National Negro Bankers Association was formed; a school savings program was initiated to encourage children to become lifelong depositors; and thousands of black citizens became property owners and began to take an interest in their financial well-being. One of them was A. G. Gaston.

In both Harris and Pettiford, Gaston had examples of what he could be as well as actual models of empire building in the very specific context of Birmingham, Alabama; it was (and remains) impossible to consider this context without taking account of the race factor. In a town like Birmingham, as in towns across the entire country, the power structure remained firmly in the hands of the white establishment. In order to succeed in business, it was simply a fact that a black man needed one of two things (if not both) from the surrounding white community: their support, and/or their willingness to disregard his efforts. In Harris, Gaston was given an illustration of achievement as a result of the latter: Harris was doing work no white man wanted—at least not until they saw his profit margin (at which point the market quickly diversified). Pettiford, on the other hand, cultivated white support and relied heavily on it. In the mode of his friend Booker T. Washington, he viewed accommodation as the necessary route to achieving equality, and as a result of his deference he won the "cordial" respect of many of white Birmingham's business elite. Accordingly, his business was allowed to prosper, especially as white shareholders were brought into the fold.

Gaston's early life had been shaped by his deference to white authority. In Demopolis and during his days with the Lovemans, he appears to have inculcated a nearly unswerving dedication to playing the role of the "good nigger": stepping off the sidewalk to let a white person pass, dog robbing in the army—a general *Yes, sir* attitude toward any request from a white person, known or unknown, that came his way. Pointedly, this was not an act. Arthur's appeasement of whites had been indoctrinated since youth, and was complicated by a profound conviction on his part that a white person had never actually mistreated him. Though his experiences before and after the war had sensitized him to the prejudices of racism, he believed that "because I had been industrious and honest, I had felt no wrath from the whites . . . only kindness, or at the least indifference." As a result, his attitude toward whites varied from squarely moderate to what has been perceived as blatantly accommodationist. In any case, it is true that Gaston would go to great lengths over the course of his life to secure and foster relationships with white businessman (and politicians) throughout the state of Alabama. If those are difficult deeds to rationalize, it is nevertheless fortunate that he was able to stomach them. Arthur came into the business world too late to take advantage of "indifference," as Charles Harris had. His basic respect for the power of white-owned industry and whites themselves served him well in the construction of an empire that could not have been realized as a large-scale endeavor without their support (whatever our own analysis of his actions may be).

THE FIRST MARRIAGE: "IT'S A DEAL"

Winning the support of the black community was, however, Arthur's first goal. Initially uncertain of the burial society's soundness, he held on to his job at the Westfield plant while trying to extend membership in the society and increase his financial base. To do so he began to hire insurance agents to take over some of the solicitation calls, paying them at a rate of twenty-five cents per dollar of insurance sold. The addition of these employees resulted in the exponential growth of the company, and soon service calls were being made in surrounding towns. Such growth served to augment not only Arthur's actual savings but also his reputation in the community. The very same women who had called him cheap and refused to date him now turned out to have a soft spot in their hearts for Arthur; the men who had denied him their friendship now took a new interest in his comings and goings. Arthur was quick enough to connect the change in their behavior to the change in his finances, but he was less troubled by it than he could have been. By his own account, he was just happy to have friends, whatever kind they might be.

Gaston was, however, troubled enough by the newfound attention from his neighbors in Westfield—particularly the women—that he concluded he would never find a wife among them. This was a problem. A businessman, he realized, needed a wife. He was almost thirty, and time was slipping away. But meeting and courting a wife required more social finesse than Arthur had demonstrated himself capable of to this point. He was a deliberate man, and he didn't mean to just pick his wife out of a hat. There was only one woman he knew who fit the part, whom he liked and could talk to and who, it should be said, offered him more than just herself in the package: She had a businesman father. Her name was Creola Smith.

The figure of Creola appeared early in Gaston's account of his life: Of the many children who showed up to ride the swing in his grandparents' backyard, Creola was the only one Gaston called by name. Though there is little evidence that they stayed in touch after Arthur left Demopolis as a child, the relationship between their mothers appears to have sustained the connection. Their reintroduction after Art's return from war was a friendly one, and it seems that from that point forward Art may have toyed with the idea of marriage. But even if he had been solid in his commitment from the moment they were reunited, turning such a commitment into a marriage would have been impossible at the time. Creola was the only child of a successful and influential man. At the end of the war Arthur Gaston had nothing to offer her, and those first few years of work in the mines would provide little more. Regardless of what his feelings might have been, he would have to wait until the tides had turned in his direction to make any sort of proposal to Cre or her father.

The early success of the burial society had gone a long way toward establishing Arthur as an up-and-coming entrepreneur in the black community. He knew that he had made a name for himself in Westfield, and that he was on the path to building bigger enterprises. That was something a man like Dad Smith could respect. The year 1923 held the promise of being even better for the business than the last, if things continued to progress. Though Art knew there was a good chance that Dad Smith would refuse him entirely (Smith was outspoken about his disinclination to let his only progeny marry), he nevertheless arranged to take a few days off work to travel to Meridian and make his proposal.

It would have been entirely permissible for Arthur to go straight to Dad Smith to ask for his daughter's hand in marriage, but Arthur wanted Creola to be the first person to hear of his intentions. Their childhood friendship seemed to allow for a level of comfort that Arthur struggled to find in other relationships, so his directness with her is less surprising than it otherwise might have been, given his general character and concern with propriety. What Creola Smith actually felt when she received Art's proposal we have no precise way of knowing. What we can assume, however, is that whatever combination of emotions cropped up for her, they filtered out to a generally positive resolution: She said yes. With Creola hiding behind a door, Arthur then approached Dad Smith to finalize the arrangement.

Smith was, Gaston admitted, at first unconvinced of the merits of the union. He had no interest in securing a marriage for his daughter, not only because it represented the end of his family name, but also because it did not serve him in any way to do so. A. L. Smith was a businessman, and he perceived his daughter marrying as a definitive mark in the "loss" column. Without Smith's approval it was impossible for the union to take place. Negotiations continued, with Gaston offering up his various successes as symbols of his worthiness and Smith acknowledging them and yet declining. Finally Gaston hit upon a proposition Dad Smith knew better than to refuse: a business interest, bearing the name *Smith & Gaston*. It would serve as the all-important continuation of the Smith name, while offering Dad some potential profitability to soothe the emptiness left by Creola's departure. The couple were married a few days later. Dad Smith's only stipulation was that Creola finish her college degree before leaving town. Arthur went back to Alabama alone, but returned to collect her from Meridian in June of that same year.

The addition of Creola to Gaston's life was significant. It allowed him to create a life independent of his mother for the first time since returning from the army, and it provided him with the social sphere that he had always been lacking but deeply desired. Creola was as much of a social being as Arthur was not. She had, in Gaston's words, "never known a stranger," and the house they rented a stone's throw from the one he had lived in with his mother (and where she continued to reside) was "promptly filled with her hearty laughter and new friends." Moreover, her interests leaned toward community service, a field in which many acquaintances were made and relationships built—all of which would prove useful to the growth of business, as Gaston would quickly learn.

The first few years after Gaston and Creola's marriage were, by his record, both happy and basically uneventful. He continued to build the society while she fulfilled her duties as his wife and aide. But then, in swift succession, two events occurred that would alter the course of their lives: Rosie Gaston died and Arthur was laid off from the Westfield plant.

LOSSES

Rosie's death, as expected, hit Arthur hard. With the deaths of Joe and Idella in recent years, and now the loss of Rosie, Gaston had essentially lost his entire family base. Furthermore, in Rosie's death he lost not only a mother, but also his closest confidante and business adviser. Nothing Arthur did, from a business perspective, happened without Rosie's approval. He was painfully aware that any success he had found in life had been a direct product of her sacrifices and prescience, and in her absence he spent months adrift, grieving.

Not long after this blow came the layoffs at the plant. Though the burial society had continued to thrive, Gaston was smart enough to realize that the same economic slowdown that had cost him his job would certainly affect his clients' ability to pay their premiums. The time still wasn't right, then, for Arthur to rely solely on income from the society. He would need another job, and one was waiting for him in the coal mines of a neighboring municipality. The pay was $4.10 a day—even more than he had been making in Westfield.

The trade-off for this higher wage was one, it turned out, that Arthur wasn't willing to make. As terrible as the work in iron and steel had been, coal mining was worse. Arthur had had the good fortune to have spent a substantial part of his working life at Westfield aboveground, in the wood shop and other plant facilities. In the Edgewater coal mines, he had no such luck. He was assigned to work in "the ring" of the open-pit mine (the second of three levels below ground) "push[ing] the buggies" filled with coal up a slender ledge to the top of the pit. Six months into his tenure at Edgewater, after a day in which an overhanging rock shifted its position in the earth and trapped Arthur and his coworkers underground—necessitating that each man cling to the body of the rock and traverse his way around it while dangling over the pit below in order to escape—he resigned from his position. The physical danger of the job was more than he could take. Creola reassured him that his decision was the right one, and pushed him to concentrate his efforts on the burial society instead.

Without diminishing Creola's importance to the evolution of the Gaston empire, it is essential to consider the value that Dad Smith added to this business matrix. In the years since the couple had been married, Gaston had tried numerous times to entice Smith to make the move from Meridian and set up shop in or around Birmingham. But happy as Smith was to hold a potential interest in Gaston's business, he was unwilling to relinquish his own thriving interests in Meridian for an as-yet-unproven venture with Gaston. For what it was, the Booker T. Washington Burial Society was respectable, but it had yet to make the leap from one man's side interest to a formally established, collectively administrated organization. Arthur's skittishness about taking the next step may have been the result of his mother's insistence on measured foundation building; it may have been a result of the relative security that life in Westfield offered. But in any case, both of those pressures had disappeared, leaving him free to proceed at his own inclination. And if pursuing the business wholeheartedly could convince Dad Smith to lend himself to the project, then the risk would be worth it.

Growing the Business

After leaving Edgewater, Arthur threw himself furiously into trying to expand his business. He worked fifteen-hour days, going door to door to solicit clients. As a result, business grew exponentially, and Arthur and Creola began to see this growth reflected in their bank statements. It was only then that Gaston claimed to have begun to think of the insurance business as a truly lucrative industry. Previously he had considered the society a step on the ladder that led to bigger things. But with his undivided attention, it seemed possible that the company might actually be able to support them while giving rise to new business opportunities.

Dad Smith watched the growth of the burial society with a critical eye, and was pleased enough with what he saw developing that he finally agreed to come on board full time. When Arthur left his job in the mines, he and Creola had also left their home in Westfield and set up residence in nearby Fairfield, on the outskirts of Birmingham proper. Leaving Meridian, Mom and Dad Smith moved into the same neighborhood, to be close to their daughter and son-in-law-*cum*-business-associate.

Though business was the center of Smith's life, it may not have been business alone that led Creola's parents to relocate to Fairfield. The Smiths were getting older, and Dad in particular—a diabetic—had begun to suffer from the strain of the disease. More critical, however, was the state of Creola's health. As a young girl she had been vibrant and fit, but the move back to Alabama following her marriage had not served her well. Though her physical condition was stable in the first years after the move, when she and Arthur were forced to relocate to Fairfield she suffered from an exhaustion that became chronic and debilitating and put an end to any question of whether the couple would have children. Creola also gained a great deal of weight during that time, only worsening her general state. Though Gaston claims her spirits were high throughout this period, he also admits to having harbored "grave concern" regarding his wife's health. Her parents would have been aware of her worsening condition, and it is likely—given the closeness of the family—to have influenced their decision to move nearer by.

With the Smiths' arrival in Fairfield, Gaston decided to formally organize his burial society, naming himself as president, Dad Smith as vice president, and Creola as secretary. The group also established a board of trustees that included a number of powerful pastors in the Fairfield area (including Gaston's old friend and supporter, the Reverend Ravizee) and a few other men of influence in the local communities. It was important to Arthur that the people associated with the company were men who were accorded respect in the community; he was very clear on the fact that as their reputations went, so did his business. It was this idea in particular that led him to his devotion to Dad Smith. Smith had succeeded not merely in creating a successful business back in Meridian, but also in creating a mystique—one so powerful it preceded him in the greater Birmingham area. The frock coat that he wore and the "aura of wealth, dignity and responsibility" that apparently radiated from him were precisely the elements that Gaston wanted people to associate with his business. He was never shy about voicing his belief that "prestige" drew customers; as he would come to say later, "Once you . . . get a reputation for having money, people will give you money." Having Dad Smith to dress the part and emanate the attitude was his first lesson in the power of said reputation.

With Smith's help in the public relations department, and Gaston's ceaseless drive, the company continued to expand, spreading its agents farther and farther afield within the state. However, by the time it had managed to accumulate a modest profit, the society was dealt a series of blows that threatened its survival. The first of these crises came at the hands of James Payne, the black funeral director whose negotiations with Gaston regarding the price of burial had made it possible for the society to succeed initially. Payne was a good businessman, but also, it turned out, a bad drunk. After being caught "transporting moonshine whiskey in the funeral hearse," for which act he was arrested, Payne was dismissed by the (white) owners of the funeral home. With Payne's ouster, the deal the men had struck for discount funerals was null and void. In an effort to prevent his company from sinking under the weight of newly inflated prices, Gaston made the owner of the establishment, a Mr. Bell, a bold offer: He would buy the funeral home from him, lock, stock, and barrel.

If you had tried to predict, before Mr. Bell made his decision on Gaston's offer, what this white businessman would have said to surrendering his interest to a black man, you would have been hard pressed to come up with a definitive answer. When it came to undertaking, white sentiment about who ought to have been burying black people was honestly split. In some parts of the country and even the South, white undertakers fiercely defended their right to bury blacks—though, it must be said, purely out of financial concern: The vast majority of white-run funeral homes had very different standards of care for their black bodies and families than they did for their white clientele. Blacks who dared to enter the business were often run out of town at the end of a gun. Other white morticians, however, were just as happy to let those black bodies go, maintaining segregation in death as in life.

Though the reasons that Mr. Bell let Gaston have his business are unknown, he did in the end acquiesce. The selling price of the company and its buildings stood at fifteen thousand dollars. Gaston agreed to provide Bell with a down payment of $500, and to continue to pay off the debt at a rate of $150 per month. Though Gaston had been saving aggressively since returning from the war, it is unlikely that he would have had the financial wherewithal to produce five hundred dollars on the spot. Dad Smith's pockets, however, were much deeper. Together the men produced the requisite sum, and before long they were operating not merely on the insurance side of the business (through the Booker T. Washington Burial Society), but also on the funeral services end. They called the company, simply and as promised, Smith & Gaston.

In attempting to save his business from destruction, Gaston had—wittingly or unwittingly—secured for himself a situation that virtually guaranteed a greater influx of money into his own hands. Because he now owned the mortuary that performed the services for which his insured customers would be paying, he held all the tools necessary for affecting profit-and-loss margins. With the purchase of the mortuary interest it was possible for him to cut costs, thus increasing his profits. His only real constraint was what the market would bear, which essentially meant figuring out how much he could ask people to pay for funerals before they would be forced to turn away. Gaston had, essentially, done what every great American businessman has done to succeed: He eliminated the middleman and freed up a greater share of net gains for himself.

DISSOLVING THE COMPANIES—AND STARTING AGAIN

All of this would have been perfect for Gaston if Mr. Bell hadn't met his own fateful end not long after their agreement was made. The heir to his estate was his son, a Mr. George Bell, who had nowhere near the good feeling toward Dad Smith and A. G. Gaston that his father had had. Perhaps he saw the potential for financial gain in the merged companies. Perhaps he just didn't like the idea of black people having control of that much wealth. Whatever his reasons, he had no intention of letting the agreement between his father and Smith and Gaston stand. The two men were informed that the younger Bell was prepared not only to reclaim his rights to the funeral home, but also to assert his rights of ownership over the burial society.

Smith and Gaston were forced to employ an attorney to defend them in the suit when civil negotiations failed. The chief of police was brought into the fray and showed up to demand the company's records. A forceful female member of Gaston's staff, who had hidden the records in her house, dissuaded him from claiming them. It was a crises of major proportions. As a result of the younger Bell's actions, Smith and Gaston were forced to dissolve the two companies entirely. They withdrew all the money saved in the companies' accounts and hid it in the homes of their partners, along with the premiums they continued to collect from their customers.

With the dissolution of the companies, Bell's claims against the men faded out. Gaston oversaw the incorporation of a new company, and the money that had been hidden in homes around Fairfield gradually made its way back into the bank. Gaston was also able to raise the necessary funds to complete the purchase of the mortuary building from the elder Bell's estate. Throughout the legal finagling, he had managed to hold on to the two cars—a Studebaker hearse and a Ford motorcar—that had come as part of the original deal for the funeral home. With the younger Bell out of the way, Smith & Gaston launched back into business, this time undertaking a "strong promotional program" as a means of luring business. The Smith & Gaston Funeral Home became the corporate sponsors of gospel singers statewide; it became a concert promoter as well, importing and exporting musical talent throughout the state of Alabama. Under its auspices the "first regular Negro radio program" was initiated, and it wasn't long before *Smith & Gaston* became household words throughout the black community.

Though Gaston never explicitly admitted as much in his autobiography, it was around this time that money literally began to roll through the door. Before the creation of Smith & Gaston, Arthur was always careful, in writing the narrative of his life, to mention how little money he actually had, despite all his hard work. From this point on, however, no such remarks were made. In part, this may have been an effect of his closer relationship to Dad Smith, whose investments in the companies were significant (and may have given Arthur, for the first time in his life, a sense of a buffer between himself and poverty). But operating at both ends of the business also afforded him extensive freedom in pricing. Government regulation of the funeral industry didn't begin until 1984; prior to this, funeral homes were known to mark up their caskets as much as 700 percent over base price. Even if Gaston had raised his prices at a comparably modest rate, he would still have been set to accumulate capital at a rapid clip—and expenditures such as corporate sponsorship and paid radio ads prove the point.

———————

Though things were getting better financially for the Gastons, Creola's health was worsening. As the 1920s came to a close, her physical condition continued to deteriorate. Soon she was forced to spend longer and longer periods of time in bed. No diagnosis was offered, but suffering she was, whatever the cause. To make matters worse, Dad Smith's health was on the wane as well. His diabetes had necessitated the removal of one of his legs, right around the time that the business had been threatened by Bell's suit. Gaston was careful to point out that the loss never slowed Dad Smith down. "He did not spare himself," Gaston wrote. "He was always beside me, working to save the business. And out among our people urging them to save money to buy their own homes, to register to vote." Though the amputation of his leg had bought Smith some time and relief, it was a clear he didn't have much of either left. But Smith's number one priority—the business—never shifted. It was a lesson Gaston internalized quickly—a way of being he made his own.

Gaston was clearly concerned about the conundrum of Creola's health, and perhaps even more so about Dad Smith's deterioration. Yet his treatment of their illnesses in his autobiography often feels cursory—as if these particular incidents were tertiary narratives in the story of his life, rather than pieces of the whole. Gaston was not unmoved by the medical predicaments of his wife and father-in-law, but his inability to help them recover created a psychological block in his treatment of them (on paper, if not in person). Now a man in his midthirties, Gaston had built a life on the ideal of "taking action": His life, to his own eyes at least, had been saved by *doing*. But for both Creola and Dad Smith there was, increasingly, nothing to be done. Though Gaston pitied them, he could not help them, and so (though he cared for them both), he could not truly focus on them. What inspired his deepest consideration were the things that could be changed. And there were plenty of obstacles in the business world to keep him from having to think too closely about the problems he could not solve.

The one nonbusiness related problem Gaston could take a stab at resolving, however, was his relationship with his son, who was quickly becoming a young man. It may have been the growth of his own father-son bond with Dad Smith, or the reduced pressure associated with parenting a teenager rather than a child, or the simple expansion of his financial security that made him do it, but whatever the impetus, when his son turned sixteen, A. G. Gaston Sr. determined to bring the boy to Birmingham to oversee his future.

In the very best-case scenario (that being that the child who arrived in Birmingham had suffered no ill effects from the lack of fathering he had received throughout his lifetime and bore no resentments toward his father for his absence), the adjustment—for both father and son—would have been a difficult one. For a man like Gaston Sr., who for all his growing acumen in business would never be described as "emotionally open," brokering that adjustment would be all the more complex. His intentions regarding his son were based on a deep sense of responsibility owed to the boy, as well as love, but his expression of those sentiments was most likely born out in action rather than emotion. To wit: Upon A. G. Gaston Jr.'s arrival in the city he was quickly put to work in the family business, which Gaston Sr. hoped would instill in the son the kind of drive and dedication that had made the father a success.

What the quality of A. G. Gaston Jr.'s life had been before his arrival in Birmingham, we do not know. What is clear, however, is that somewhere in the transition to Birmingham, somewhere in the shift from being an essentially fatherless child (in terms of day-to-day activities) to coming under the control of an increasingly powerful and influential father, A. G. Gaston Jr. began to struggle under the weight of that heavy burden. Nevertheless, he and his father would remain close over the years, and Gaston Jr. would maintain employment in one or another of the Gaston companies throughout his life. But in the end, Gaston Jr. would never come to play the role of heir apparent that Gaston Sr. plainly hoped he would. The story is not an unfamiliar one: Sons throughout history (particularly first or only sons) have crumpled under the pressures associated with besting the expectations of their successful fathers. The situation, in the case of the Gaston men, was apparently no different.

Whether Gaston initially had the sense that his son would not grow into precisely the same kind of businessman he himself had become is unknown. Regardless, it is unlikely that such foreknowledge would have made any difference. Gaston's sense of duty toward his son, which early on had been tentative at best, had grown enormously as Gaston aged. Fatherhood (in the terms in which he understood it: mentorship) was a responsibility that Gaston Sr. had no intention of shirking again. And yet, as with the deterioration of Creola and Dad Smith, any concern Gaston might have had for the state of affairs on the home front (that is, the relative happiness of his son) was severely tempered by his near tunnel vision when it came to prioritizing his interests. Business, as always, came first.

THE CRASH

Though the 1920s began as a decade of economic prosperity, they ended with an explosion heard, and experienced, around the world. The apparent buoyancy of the decade's middle years, during which unemployment rates were cut in half (dropping from 4.27 million in 1921 to 2 million in 1927), altogether disappeared with the infamous crash of the stock market in 1929. Most economists agree that the bursting of the economic bubble of the first quarter of the twentieth century was inevitable, brought about by the "fundamentally unsound" nature of the nation's economy. According to economist John Kenneth Galbraith, the crash was a result of a combination of "very unhealthy corporate and banking structures, an unsound foreign trade, much economic misinformation and the 'bad distribution of income.' " The last in that list of ills had perhaps the most direct impact on the average workingman (though they all would have affected his life prospects): It describes the allocation of one-third of "all personal income" to the top 5 percent of the earning population. The result of such a wholly unbalanced economic system was (along the lines of a socialist critique as offered by Howard Zinn) the creation of a "permanent depression" for those in the underclass; in this mode of thinking, it was capitalism itself, with its blind adherence to the goal of corporate profits at any cost, that caused the markets to crash.

The less radical view, of course, is that it was the uncontrolled speculation occurring in the world markets that brought the economy to its knees. Regardless, the effects of the crash were, as has been well documented elsewhere, devastating. Thousands of banks and other business shut their doors for good. Furthermore:

> Those [businesses] that continued laid off employees and cut the wages of those who remained, again and again. Industrial production fell by 50 percent, and by 1933 perhaps 15 million . . . —one-fourth to one-third of the labor force—were out of work. The Ford Motor Company, which in the spring of 1929 had employed 128,000 workers, was down to 37,000 by August of 1931. By the end of 1930, almost half the 280,000 textile mill workers in New England were out of work.

Poverty, homelessness, and despair—elements that had long been part of the lives of the poorest and darkest of American citizens—now became a reality to broad swaths of the population. Whatever insulation had muffled the agony of the lower classes was now stripped away, and breadlines lengthened in cities around the country.

Perhaps more than any other element, it was the outstanding rate of unemployment produced by the Great Depression that distinguished it from other, relatively normal cycles of economic downturn. The available examples seem infinite: In 1933 Cleveland, Ohio, was suffering from a 50 percent unemployment rate. In Toledo in the same year, the rate of unemployment was 80 percent. Nationally, the rates rose from 3.3 percent in 1929, to 8.7 percent in 1930, to 15.9 percent in 1931, to 23.6 percent in 1932; in a period of fours years the unemployed segment of the nation had grown from three million to twelve and a half million individuals. Though unemployment had begun to rise well in advance of the crash, the exponential increase in joblessness, coupled with the extended period of time the average individual remained out of work once a job had been lost (about a year for a third of the unemployed), had its own crippling effect on both the economy and the national psyche. Fewer jobs meant less spending, particularly on the part of the newly impoverished middle class, nine million of whose savings were decimated by the failure of one-fifth of the nation's banks. Those who had been spared this particular indignity quickly ran through the (usually meager) funds they had managed to accumulate and before long found themselves in a similarly ruined state.

Malnutrition and the threat of starvation became the order of the day. In 1934 in New York City, 110 deaths due to starvation were recorded, up from 29 the year before, despite President Hoover's proclamations to the contrary. Acutely hard hit were the inhabitants of mining towns and the farming populations of the midwestern and southern states, many of whom—sharecroppers and landowners alike—were driven off their land and into the western states in the hope of securing better opportunities. What people found on the other side of the country was rarely any better than what they had left: It was not uncommon for families to be found living in caves and sewer pipes across the American West.

The early prosperity of the 1920s had also had a distinct impact on issues not exclusively economic. Specifically, waves of immigrants flooded the nation's shores in the wake of the First World War—both a cause and effect of America's industrialization. They helped stir an already roiling pot of racial and ethnic strife, and the backlash that arose—in the public and private sectors alike—was significant. The increased economic security of the period had brought with it the affiliated impulse to exclude those situated on the lower rungs of American society from access to the benefits of this newly industrialized world. The immigrant threat—newcomers willing to work for lower wages—brought a certain brand of racism to a peak, and work and money became both racialized and nationalized (as they always had been, if less volubly so). The revival and expansion of the Ku Klux Klan is but one indication of the era's discontents. Now not only blacks, but also Jews, Catholics, and Slavic and Bolshevik immigrants were feeling the group's wrath. And it was not the Klan alone that was setting limits: The federal government weighed in with the National Origins Act of 1924, which "gave preference to immigrants from northern and western Europe . . . [while] it severely limited immigration from the rest of the continent, and virtually barred Asians." Americanism, it became obvious, was about money: who could have it, and who should not.

BLACK AMERICA DURING THE DEPRESSION

If things had been bad from a racial standpoint when the economy was stable, it doesn't take much to imagine what happened when the markets collapsed. Though rarely referenced as a separate class when the sufferings of the depression years are parsed out, the experience of blacks during this period was, with little exception, even worse than that of the average white worker. If the old maxim *When the rich get richer, the poor get poorer* holds, it is nevertheless just as true that when the rich get poorer, the poor get poorer still. And blacks were, in almost every instance, the poorest of the poor. Moreover, discrimination on racial bases in no way disappeared as a result of economic agonies. In fact, the lack of resources made these demarcations even more evident.

To begin with, blacks as a class were obviously at a disadvantage long before the depression ever dawned. As historians Steven Mintz and Susan Kellogg report of life in the 1920s:

In Macon County, Alabama, the site of Booker T. Washington's
famous Tuskegee Institute, thirty miles east of Montgomery, black
families lived in abysmal conditions of poverty. . . . Most dwellings
had dirt floors, no windows or screens, and almost no furniture.
A fifth of the homes had no water; three-quarters no sewage
disposal. . . . Black income in Macon County averaged less than
a dollar a day.

These were the living conditions of millions of southern black families when times were "good"—and when the markets hit bottom,
blacks were among the first to feel its effects. They were first to lose
their jobs in any situation where a choice could be made about who to
lay off. Only a year after the crash, when overall jobless rates had yet to
feel the full impact of the sagging economy and hovered well below the
double digits, black unemployment rates had already climbed as high as
70 and 75 percent in some cities (Charleston, South Carolina, and
Memphis, Tennessee, respectively). Nationally, joblessness in the black
community stood at a rate one and a half times higher than that of
white unemployment throughout the depression era. The already inad-
equate diet of salt pork, hominy grits, corn bread, and molasses upon
which most southern blacks had subsisted for generations became even
more limited when even that average dollar a day stopped coming in.

The disproportionate suffering of poor blacks was met by a near-
total lack of response on the part of state and local governments.
Some cities (New York among them) paid out no relief at all to as
much as three-quarters of the unemployed black population. Nationally, approximately one-quarter of jobless blacks were refused aid.
And even in places where aid was given, it was paid out to black families at a fraction of the rate at which it was disbursed to whites. The
situation in Texas provides one example of the inequalities of aid provisions: For every dollar of aid a white family received, a black family received 75 cents.

BIRMINGHAM—THE WORST-HIT CITY IN THE NATION

Though the effects of the depression were to be felt in every corner
of the country, Birmingham and its environs suffered particularly

profoundly. It was this municipality that the Roosevelt administration designated the "worst hit city in the nation." In one day in June, four Birmingham banks shut their doors, leaving the average depositing wage earner high and dry in regard to his or her savings. By 1932 the city's situation had grown so dire that it was estimated that a mere 8,000 of Birmingham's 108,000 potential wage earners were gainfully employed at a level of pay comparable to their predepression wages. This left a hundred thousand people either not earning at all, earning at a greatly reduced rate, or working part time. By 1934 more than half of all mortgage holders in the city had defaulted on their loans. Demands on the Community Chest—established by the city in 1923 to help the poor where other social programs had failed—increased exponentially; the organization was forced to attempt to double its fund-raising goal in 1931 (almost none of this aid would wind up going to black charities). The financial crisis completely crippled city government, resulting in the cancellation of any municipal projects that might have created jobs for the unemployed.

As elsewhere in the nation, the position of blacks in Birmingham worsened drastically and quantifiably throughout this period. In 1930 the total black population of the Birmingham metropolitan area was 99,077. Before the crash, the city boasted two hundred black-owned retail stores, with $601,916 in total annual sales. Five years later the number of black retail establishments had sunk to 132, with sales hovering at a stagnant $193,000—signifying, among other things, a dire lack of money in the black community. Birmingham had once been the center of black business in Alabama, but by the middle of the 1930s there was simply no money to spend. Though the Red Cross organization in Birmingham offered the city's black community more support than was to be seen in many other areas in the nation (62.8 percent of its relief was going to blacks in 1932), the amount of relief offered was rarely enough to cover the expenses of the families touched by the aid, much less allow for discretionary spending.

A Scheme?

A life in business is defined by fluctuation, but it is notable that by Gaston's own account, the depression was hardly a remarkable period in his life; not once in his autobiography does he mention the existence of the economic holocaust blistering the nation. This is clearly an act of willful forgetfulness on his part; no person who lived through the era was unaware of its devastation. But, like Creola and Dad Smith's illnesses, the depression was nothing Arthur Gaston could do anything about. As in those cases, rather than dwelling on what was beyond his power, Arthur once again buried himself in what he could control: his work.

One reason Gaston was able to remain financially buoyant in the midst of the depression had to do with a lending scheme Dad Smith had cooked up to maintain their cash flow. Starting in the late 1920s, cash-strapped municipalities began paying employees in what Gaston called "script": government-issued IOUs that could be redeemed for cash at a specified time. Gaston remembered that the script notes looked just like regular money, though they were plastic rather than paper. The problem for state and city employees was that the script was redeemable only on a yearly basis, leaving many workers with plenty of IOUs but no way to turn them into ready money.

Smith, however, devised a plan that would in his estimation serve the employees and fill his own pockets. As Gaston would later describe it in an interview with a young graduate student,

> My father in law . . . he used to take those scripts from the schoolteachers. They were paying schoolteachers about $30 a month in script. He would buy that script for 50 cents on the dollar. Teachers would get $15 a month and he would have $30 in script. We would just hold that and exchange it.

The depths of Smith's pockets allowed him the opportunity to front the teachers their money at a significant margin of profit. If Gaston had any reservations about the ethics of the exchange, he never mentioned them. Neither, however, did he bother to include the scenario in his autobiography. Silence, in this case, speaks a thousand words.

———

Meanwhile, Smith and Gaston's more legitimate businesses continued to prosper. It has been said that the only guarantee in life is death, and luckily for those in the funeral industry, the dead always need to be buried. Though not entirely untouched by the economic downturn, funeral homes and their owners continued to conduct business throughout the 1930s. While people struggled to put food on the table on a daily basis, paying their last respects to their recently deceased had become a priority for which many were willing to beg, borrow, and steal.

The introduction of embalming practices through the early years of the twentieth century helped to bolster funeral sales when the nation's financials bottomed out. Few families understood that embalming was a choice rather than a necessity, and the perceived need for embalming automatically spelled out a need for professional service. Black families were particularly sensitive to this "requirement," due to long-held traditions of open-casket funerals and wakes. Blacks wanted to see their dead, sometimes, now, to touch them, and embalming made this possible in a way (and for a period of time) that the "cooling board" had never been able to provide. Keeping up appearances has always been radically important in the black community, and the concept of funeral as status symbol did not die simply because of a general lack of money in the depression era. Indeed, the rampant deprivation of the time may have only increased the craving for a valiant farewell: With so little left and grief such a ready part of everyday life, the funeral provided both the rare chance for open expressions of sorrow, and the equally rare opportunity to offer and witness a bit of beauty amid so much chaos.

For all that may be said of the Machiavellian machinations of the funeral industry, it remains true that the job of funeral planning was one in which Arthur Gaston took pride and believed. He may have been making money doing it, but it is clear that money was not his only concern. From his earliest days Gaston had wanted friends, and now—through a combination of his wife and his work—he had them. He had wanted respect, and now he had that, too. In building a business founded on loss, he had made many intimate connections with the families in the Fairfield region. He had built trust into an area of commerce in which blacks had come to expect to be abused, and he and Dad Smith had done their parts to lend an air of prestige and value to the final act of lives that were usually distinguished only by their perceived insignificance. The service that Smith and Gaston offered to Fairfield and its surrounding areas was both real and significant, and Gaston likely would have maintained a strong relationship with the city if he, too, hadn't found himself run out of town at the end of that proverbial gun—pointed by the mayor's hand.

A DELICATE DISENGAGEMENT

There's no trick to making money. It's a rule,
just like the rule of nature. You do certain things
and you get certain results.

Voting Rights in Fairfield

A. L. Smith had never been a man to hold his tongue when it came to the welfare of the black community. He was particularly interested in voting rights, and his deteriorating health through the end of the 1920s and into the 1930s did little to quiet his fervor on the topic. Smith was, it seemed, a true believer in the political system, and in the idea that black votes could change the tenor of life in America. In one particular election, however, his success in getting blacks to turn out to vote would have an unanticipated effect: It would leave the incorporated businesses of Smith and Gaston in a precarious position in the Fairfield community.

As the story goes, the incumbent mayor at the time had paid little attention to his black constituents throughout his term, and continued to ignore them as the time came near for his presupposed reelection. A few weeks prior to Election Day there were only thirteen blacks registered to vote in Fairfield, and the white community appeared unlikely to vote the man out of office. There was, however, another candidate in the running—a man who campaigned heavily in the black community for votes. A. L. Smith continued with his own efforts to bring out black voters, and together the two men served up a victory to the challenger. The incumbent lost the election by a mere three votes, and though it was impossible to know for certain where those three votes came from, it was not hard to guess that the newly registered black voters had played some part in the changing of the guard. However, in the next election four years later, the former mayor beat his challenger and regained his old seat in the mayoralty. He was candid about his belief that Smith had cost him the last election and began what has been referred to as a "campaign of harassment" against Smith and his cohorts.

The political storm that erupted in Fairfield after the second election left Gaston with few choices. His name had become synonymous with Smith's, and it became impossible for either of them to run a business in Fairfield. According to Gaston, "We were constantly plagued with traffic citations and intimidated in a manner perhaps peculiar to small city law enforcement. We couldn't park cars or hearses in front of our building. Our employees could not drive to make a bank deposit without getting a ticket on some pretext." What Gaston does not say overtly but is clear about (in that "manner perhaps *peculiar* to small city law enforcement") is that not only the business, but also their *lives* were at risk. In Alabama, black men and women had been lynched for much less than opposing a sitting mayor—and Klan membership was rampant in the state. As Supreme Court justice Hugo Black—an Alabama man himself—would later tell Gaston, you couldn't get elected dogcatcher in the state of Alabama if you weren't a member of the Klan; membership was truly the rule, not the exception, and a nigger was still a nigger no matter how much money he had. Gaston quickly recognized the danger in the situation and prepared a plan for leaving Fairfield, in order to save both his business and his life.

The first question, of course, was where to go. In some senses the easiest road would have been one that led due north, into the industrial centers of the Northeast or Midwest; many thousand others had given up on the South during the Great Migration. Racism was hardly absent in the North, but it was covert enough to allow for real opportunity. However, Gaston was not inclined to make a change that drastic. He had constructed a life in Alabama, and had built a name and a brand that had brought him the respect and admiration he'd searched for from his earliest days. A move to the North meant leaving much of that behind and starting over, with no guarantees that he'd ever reclaim the success he had worked so hard to bring about. And that was one risk Gaston was unwilling to take.

If not the North, the next most obvious choice was Birmingham. As Smith & Gaston had grown, it had established a reputation that had spread not only throughout western Alabama but into the big city as well. In Birmingham, Gaston would be able to leverage his reputation to full effect. Between Dad Smith's business contacts and the work that Arthur had done to grow the Smith & Gaston empire in Fairfield, Birmingham offered a near-perfect opportunity for expansion into a bigger market, without the risks attendant upon staging a massive relocation. Once again Booker T. Washington's words guided him: Gaston would cast his bucket down in Alabama—back in the metropolis of Birmingham.

THE MANSION ON KELLY INGRAM PARK, BIRMINGHAM, 1938

Once Gaston had made up his mind to make the move, he traveled a number of times to the city—both on his own and in the company of Dad Smith—to survey potential building sites. The building to which he found himself drawn again and again was a palatial structure on the edge of Kelly Ingram Park, in downtown Birmingham. It was a regal white construction in the mode of plantation house revival, formerly the home of a "baron" of the coal industry and, more recently, the city's postmaster. The structure had fallen on hard times during the depression era, and would need a thorough remodeling before it could be occupied. The asking price (which included a lot of brick apartments that sat next door) was twenty-five thousand dollars.

The cost of the building was more cash than Arthur had to spend, and Dad Smith was apparently reluctant to make such a large investment in the company's headquarters. For whatever reason, however, Gaston locked his mind on owning that particular building and refused to let the idea go. Maybe it was the notion of a black man owning the biggest house facing Ingram Park—where blacks were still

The mansion on Kelly Ingram Park—Smith and Gaston's first Birmingham home

forbidden to gather for recreation, and through which they had until only recently been forbidden even to walk. Maybe it was the irony of a man who once worked in the mines owning the home of a man who had benefited so richly from his backbreaking labor. Or perhaps he simply liked the house. Whatever the reason, Gaston determined that the building would be his; the issue yet to be resolved was, how would he afford it?

The solution came in two parts. The first was through Gaston's old friend Percy Benton. Given Dad Smith's refusal to make a loan himself (if indeed he had the means to cover the entire purchase price), Gaston was at first uncertain to whom to turn for such a large amount of money. It was Benton, the attorney who had helped extricate Smith and Gaston from their legal trouble with the Bells, who suggested that Gaston look to sources in Birmingham, rather than Fairfield, to fund his project. Moreover, Benton suggested, borrowing in the city would be an excellent method of Gaston establishing himself there and furthering his connections. Benton was supportive and reassuring about the purchase, pledging both his personal and professional efforts to helping Arthur "work it out."

Though Percy Benton could provide emotional support and counsel, what he could not provide was the hard cash needed to secure the purchase. For that Gaston needed either a willing businessman or a bank. He found the former in the person of John Commons, "a well-to-do Negro who had made money selling coal and ice." In Gaston and his proposal to buy the house on Ingram Park, Commons saw potential for growth, and agreed to help the younger man out. However, he—like Dad Smith—wanted to be cautious with his investment. Rather than agreeing to lend Gaston the entire twenty-five thousand dollars, he pledged ten thousand—the cost of the adjacent apartment buildings, which he planned to rent out as income property. Gaston was pleased to have found a partner, but Commons's plan left fifteen thousand dollars outstanding—a sum that still outstripped Gaston's means.

The final piece came together when Percy Benton secured the aid of Birmingham's largest funeral services firm. Brown-Service (as the company was called) was represented in its dealings by a Mr. Rufus Lackey, who came to Gaston with an offer not of fifteen thousand or even twenty-five, but of fifty thousand dollars—a complete mortgage to cover costs and renovations. The more established funeral home was looking for a way to expand its own business by reaching out to the black community and claiming Negro clientele. Gaston believed that the firm's interest in lending him money stemmed from its belief that doing so "might open the Negro market"—which was a real possibility, and therefore a real threat to the overall success of Smith and Gaston's business.

Despite the risks attendant upon placing oneself under the financial thumb of a competitor, Gaston took what Brown-Service was offering and inked a deal for the fifty-thousand-dollar mortgage. He was, simply put, overjoyed at having been able to make his dream come true. Dad Smith, on the other hand, was much less certain of the judiciousness of encumbering the business with so much debt. He had heavily protested their acceptance of Brown-Service's offer, warning Gaston that the bigger firm was offering "too much money." "That's getting too big, too fast," he warned. Smith's quite rational fear was that their young company would be unable to compete under the kind of financial strain that such a large mortgage would place on them. If they defaulted on their loan, the larger company would be able to claim not just the building, but Smith & Gaston in its entirety.

But the biggest risk of all, for Smith, was what effect a loss of that nature would have on his reputation. He had spent a lifetime building a name for himself—in Demopolis, in Meridian, and then in Fairfield. He had accumulated wealth and reputation in a time when there was no other path for a black man but the one that was labeled *caution*. It had, happily, led him to success. His son-in-law, on the other hand, seemed all too ready to leap off the end of any pier without checking the depth of the water beneath, his only safety net held by white investors who had yet to prove any real interest in seeing blacks succeed. Jumping off the end of that pier with his own name was bad enough; taking Smith's name down with him was a whole other story.

Dad Smith's objections to the scheme might have been passionate in any scenario, but they were certainly intensified by his knowledge that he was dying. Smith's health had been deteriorating for years, and through most of the 1930s he had struggled to recover from debilitating bouts of diabetic crisis. He had already lost a leg to the disease, and his general state of being seemed to be declining daily. Soon, Smith knew, it would be Arthur alone running the business, and the older man felt an obligation to try to ensure that the decisions his son-in-law would make without him would reflect his prudent aversion to risk.

Smith voiced his concerns regarding the Brown-Service offer to Arthur repeatedly, explaining his hesitation in plain terms. But Arthur would not be swayed. His retorts to Smith's fears were typical of any younger man who fancies himself on the cutting edge vis-à-vis his older, more conservative counterpart. While Smith was anxious to preserve what he had already built, Gaston was eager to expand, and he was honest with his father-in-law about his aims. Gaston saw the Brown-Service deal as "a good price and a good opportunity." He entreated the older man to see that "[Smith & Gaston] can't stand still. We have to grow." No final decision could be brokered without

Smith's consent, so Gaston worked incessantly to convince the elder man of the soundness of the proposal. In the end Arthur's fervent confidence won out over Smith's apprehension, and both men signed on the dotted line. The house on Ingram Park was theirs.

FAREWELL

Within days of finalizing the deal, renovations began on the old house. The previous tenants, a group of elderly white schoolteachers, were quickly relocated so that the architectural firm of Miller, Martin & Lewis could begin their work. Both Smith and Gaston took a detailed interest in the plans for shaping the company's new headquarters, and Smith in particular spent great portions of his days on the construction site, micromanaging various details of the project. Having lost the war to keep the company within its perceived bounds, Smith became consumed with ensuring that, if the leap were to be taken, it be taken in precisely the right way. Gaston recalled that as the project got farther off the ground, Dad Smith became more "enthusiastic" about its completion, and began to see not solely the risks, but also the opportunities that the newly revamped house might offer the company. Smith began to see the building as "a showplace" for all they had achieved, rather than the money pit he feared it might become.

In the years since the Smiths had moved to Fairfield, Gaston had grown to rely on Smith's support and guidance in all things business-related. Even when the two men disagreed, Gaston recognized the strength of the partnership. Moreover, in Dad Smith, Gaston was finally able to reclaim the father he had lost as a small child. The men fought like father and son, and loved each other in the same fiercely loyal manner. Which made Dad Smith's death, just a few months after the purchase of the Ingram Park structure, all the more painful.

While Gaston was devastated by Smith's death, nobody took the loss of the man harder than his daughter, Creola. At the time of Smith's death Creola Gaston was still a relatively young woman (she was probably in her forties), but her own failing health had begun to cripple her—emotionally as well as physically—and the loss of her father was a blow from which she would never recover. After his death, her stints in bed lengthened; the happiness and laughter that had drawn people to her vanished. Only two things remained that elicited joy from her: Arthur's descriptions of the progress the builders were making on the new funeral home, and the letters of a student from Tuskegee by the name of Minnie Gardner.

MINNIE GARDNER

Minnie Louise Gardner was the fourth of fifteen children born to Billy and Roberta Carson Gardner, both of whom were the descendants of plantation owners and slaves. The Gardners owned a large, working farm in rural Lowndes County, Alabama, twenty-eight miles from the state capital of Montgomery.

What became known as the Gardner farm was actually a tract comprised of several contiguous forty-acre land grants from the U.S. government in the 1860s—presumably land the Freedmen's Bureau had appropriated and dispensed to three Carson brothers described as mulattoes from Sumpter County: Hugh, Walter, and William. Both Hugh and William served in the Alabama legislature in 1868, during Reconstruction, and Hugh's daughter Roberta (Minnie's mother) was given her farm when she married Billy Gardner near the turn of the century.

Billy Gardner's mother, Susanna, was the daughter of slaves who had come to America on separate ships but were purchased by the same family. This family, the Spanns, owned one of the largest plantations in Alabama. Susanna's father, Tom Gardner, though black, was appointed overseer of the plantation; his wife was called Hannah. Their daughter Susanna had three children by one of the Spann sons, Ransom Davis Spann, and all three of the children—Billy, Marybelle, and Anna—were accepted and reared by their white grandparents. When Ransom Spann died, he left in his will instructions for Susanna to remain on her property in exchange for a "debt" he owed her—presumably his three children. One of these—Billy—was Minnie Gardner's father.

Billy Gardner was a "gentleman farmer" who attended to his

farming duties well dressed and astride a white horse. In a 1946 newspaper clip, Gardner said he had been offered the right to vote in Lowndes County, long before other blacks had any such privilege. The family raised milking cows and self-sustaining crops on the farm and were considered prosperous for their time and place. And like most farming families, Billy and Roberta Gardner had many, many children as a means of securing labor.

From the time of her birth on April 3, 1909, until she left as a teenager to further her education, Minnie lived and worked on the Gardner farm. The division of labor was simple and unchallenged: The boys worked the fields and the girls tended the house. Minnie was, for many years, the oldest female child living at home (her only older sister, Annie, lived with their maternal grandmother), which left her the head of the household. She spent her early years helping to care not only for the children that came after her, but also for their mother, who suffered under the strain of constant pregnancies and an undiagnosed diabetic condition.

Every ounce of energy that anyone in the Gardner family had went into making the farm work, whether their job was milking a cow or ironing a shirt. Of the fifteen children whom Billy and Roberta raised, every single one went on to live exceptional lives by anyone's standards, but particularly for black people in the first half of the twentieth century. Hard work, determination, and a deep belief in the transformative power of education were the cornerstones upon which the Gardners laid their childrearing foundations.

Billy Gardner had six sons and trained each of them carefully in the art of running a successful farm (though only the youngest son, Robert, would make a life of farming). He also, however, had nine daughters, and though they were useful in their own way, some plan had to be made for their futures. The conventional approach would have been to simply prepare them for farm marriages—a task for which they would have been adequately schooled in their early years at home. But it seems as if the Gardners—most especially Roberta—wanted something different for their daughters. Rather than looking to marriage as a way to get the girls out on their own, Billy and Roberta looked to education: Every one of their nine daughters was sent to college.

Minnie, though the second daughter in line, was the first to leave the farm to attend school. By the time she arrived at Tuskegee she had already established a firm sense of herself and her place in the world. Nobody who ever met Minnie Gardner was left unaware of her take-charge attitude, honed by all those years spent keeping her siblings in line. Her sisters Roberta Gardner Shorte and Susie Gardner Lowe recall that Minnie ruled with an iron fist: She was unafraid to use either belt or switch to get the results she demanded of her brothers, but especially her sisters. Though she had no trouble using this kind of force when the need arose, she was also unimpeachably kind, and it was this combination of characteristics that made her a standout addition to the student body at Tuskegee, where she worked three jobs to support herself.

From the time she left Lowndes County, Minnie became the leader-at-large of the Gardner progeny, taking it upon herself to care for them all. Her mother was ill, her father was busy with the farm, and Minnie, although not the oldest, would assume the responsibility for educating her sisters and brothers—and their children after them.

The Next-Door Neighbor

During the time that Minnie was enrolled in college, her eldest brother Hugh had also struck out on his own. He, too, said good-bye to Lowndes County and moved in the direction of Birmingham to try his hand in a trade other than farming. He was able to find work and a good home on the outskirts of the city, in a place called Fairfield, where many other blacks had also found opportunities. Soon after moving into his new home, Hugh Gardner introduced himself to the man who owned the house next door, a man named A. G. Gaston. The Gastons quickly became friendly with Hugh and his young family, which often included his younger sister Minnie, who spent her school recesses vacationing in her brother's home.

Creola Gaston and Minnie Gardner clicked at their first introduction. Both were vivacious women who were unafraid to laugh out loud; warm and welcoming to any soul who passed their door. In the younger woman Creola saw the parts of herself that she had lost to illness: the vitality and hunger for living that had begun to ebb in her own weakening body. For Minnie's part, Creola's combination of generosity and infirmity could not help but remind her of her own mother, who had spent a lifetime struggling against the limitations of her body while trying to nurture her enormous family. In the other each woman found a salve for the pain of memory, and their friendship grew accordingly.

Creola was not the only person in Fairfield who took an interest in Minnie Gardner. Arthur Gaston was unwaveringly honest about his own early attraction to the woman that "all the young men talked constantly about." There is no evidence, however, that his attraction to Minnie ever took the form of anything but admiration while Creola was alive. His interest in her was hardly surprising, for in a number of obvious ways Minnie was a reflection of what Creola once was and could have been. Physically, the women were similarly built: Like Creola, Minnie was small and full-figured; her features were sharp and bore a strong suggestion of her Native American and Caucasian ancestry. Her hair was, like Creola's, what was called "good hair," fine and wavy. The main difference in the women's physicality was their skin color: Unlike Creola, whose skin was extremely fair (much like her father's), Minnie was considered dark-skinned by the standards of the time and place. In an era in which skin tone remained a marker of status within the black community, Minnie's dark complexion could easily have become her Achilles' heel. But it never did. She was the talk of the town; everyone wanted to be near her.

Included in that "everyone," perhaps surprisingly, was Dad Smith. Though he too was sick, he recognized the vigor that Minnie's visits brought to his daughter and took a shine to the younger girl himself. Before long Minnie was paying visits to Smith as often as she was to Creola. While Gaston maintained throughout his life that Minnie and Creola had had the tightest bond, Minnie's sisters claim that Minnie and Dad Smith built an equally close relationship through the years. Though Smith loved Gaston as a son, he had never quite recovered from the loss of his daughter to marriage. It may be that in Minnie, Smith found an opportunity to reclaim that father–daughter bond without interference. For Minnie, Dad Smith (light-skinned to the point of appearing white—just like her own father) may have offered the kind of one-on-one attention that a father with fifteen children could never give to any individual child.

Upon graduation, Minnie was offered a job at a school in Georgia. Her schooling at Tuskegee had been aimed at preparing her for just such a career, and happy as she was to be spending her vacations in Fairfield with her brother and the Gastons and Smiths, turning down the job offer was simply not an option. The disappearance of Minnie from Creola's life, at least, was a real blow; the older woman had truly come to depend upon Minnie's optimism and cheerfulness as a distraction from her physical discomfort. Gaston, too, had come to rely upon Minnie's soothing effect on his wife—and father-in-law—and worried that without her Creola in particular would sink back into the depression she had begun to succumb to before Minnie's arrival.

Not long after Minnie left for Georgia, however, came the Gastons' move to Birmingham. It was a fabulous opportunity for the business to grow, and in any case the newly aggravated climate in Fairfield had forced Gaston's hand. But the move offered hope on another front as well: A. G. prayed that the change of scenery might distract his wife from her condition and raise her spirits once again. He prayed that it might reinvigorate Dad Smith as well, who desperately needed something to keep him going.

For a while, for both Smith and Creola, the relocation to Birmingham worked just this kind of magic. But before long Dad Smith was gone, and any distraction the newness of Birmingham might have provided Creola disappeared under the weight of her grief at losing her father.

Minnie's letters were a godsend during this time, but they could not heal Creola. A. L. Smith's death had claimed a vital piece of his daughter, and it was clear to those around her that she was losing her battle with illness. A. G. did the best he knew how in trying to care for her while overseeing the restoration of the house on Ingram Park, but he was, he admitted, distracted. The building was almost ready—and was turning out even better than he had imagined it would.

———

As Arthur approached the new funeral home from Kelly Ingram Park the morning it was set to open, it gleamed in its newness; it spoke of things to come. But for perhaps the first and only time in his life, A. G. Gaston found himself unable to concentrate on what he stood to gain. All he could think of was what he had lost: Joe, Idella, Rosie, Dad Smith, and now Creola. The night before, she had died in her sleep.

Arthur sat down on the front steps of his new building and stared back into Ingram Park, back in the direction he had come. He was rich, he was powerful, and he was, save for his son, profoundly alone.

———

If Arthur Gaston had been a different man, perhaps he would have told us more about how it felt to lose Dad Smith and Creola, one after the other, in a period of only six months. Perhaps he would have pondered his own alienation more deeply, and left us with some truer understanding of who he was, emotionally speaking, as a human being. But that was not, in fact, the kind of man he was at all. He was a man who recounted events without betraying much sentiment of the negative sort; like his grandfather Joe, his spin on any subject always tended toward the positive, as if regret and dissatisfaction (be it over the cruelties of an impoverished childhood or the loss of a relative) were luxuries he either could not afford or simply refused to brook. Any pain he revealed at the loss of these two seminal influences on his life was always (with the brief exception of his description of the day of Creola's death) filtered through another: When Dad Smith died, it was Creola who expressed the pain of that loss. And when Creola died, it would be the last Smith left standing—her mother—who would play out the agonies of her death in a manner that allowed Arthur to grieve indirectly but intensely.

MOM SMITH

Though she had taken a backseat in the ventures of Smith & Gaston while her husband was still alive, "Mom" Smith was acutely aware of the workings of the businesses, and set out to prove, not long after her husband and daughter were deceased, that the Smith name still had a hand in controlling the company. She had every reason to be concerned: The loss of A. L. and Creola left A. G. with broad powers in the day-to-day aspects of the business, as well as with a 51 percent control of the company's shares. Without the psychological impact of either her husband or her daughter to influence A. G.'s judgment, Mom Smith feared that before long her 49 percent holdings would wield little power in the decision-making process. Though she had supported the marriage of her daughter to this son of her old friend, there is no evidence that she and Arthur had ever been particularly close. The tenderness Arthur evidenced for his wife and father-in-law never spilled into his descriptions of his mother-in-law; more often than not, she was simply left out of the picture when Arthur made reference to his relationship with the Smith family.

A savvy businessperson herself, Mom Smith determined first to shore up her control over A. G. not in the business arena but elsewhere: Rather than endeavoring to challenge Gaston head-on for control of the companies initially, she instead made her power play personal. Creola's death had obviously left A. G. without a wife, and it was clear to everyone that he would marry again. Whoever that new bride turned out to be would have a strong effect on the future of Smith & Gaston. A new woman in the family would mean a new world order in the Smith & Gaston universe, and Mom Smith was smart enough to recognize that her once unchallenged place as head of household now stood threatened. It thus became Mom Smith's plan to make sure that the woman A. G. chose for his wife had close ties to the Smith family, as a means of ensuring A. G.'s continued allegiance to the Smiths—and specifically to Mom Smith herself.

The woman who fulfilled all of Mom Smith's criteria was a young female relative of Creola's, most likely a cousin, who remains nameless in every document and throughout the family lore. All that can be said of her is that she had obvious expectations of marriage (and the apparent wealth that would attend it), and that she was spurred along in her hopes by Mom Smith's desire to maintain her hold over A. G. and the company. Whether she liked A. G. personally—or even knew him well—remains unknown. It was a marionette act in full bloom: Mom Smith held the strings and the young, un-named lady danced, her guide wires visible to all who cared to take in the performance. Nobody was fooled, least of all A. G.

Gaston was not reticent about his feelings for the woman Mom Smith favored. He had little interest in her, and openly described her as both brash and uncompelling. She was, in his estimation, a flighty girl who had no interest in business and no sense about it. If he chose her, he understood, he would merely be possessed of a wife, a de-pendent. That was not what Creola had been to him: Creola had been first his friend and then, truly, his partner. He could not do with less in his new mate.

Though A. G. and Mom Smith disagreed over who his future wife should be, they did so quietly and over a protracted period of time. There were no pitched battles in public places, no threats issued back and forth. In the classic southern tradition, each maintained, for a time, a suitable level of "propriety" in the matter.

Too Much Success

While A. G. struggled to handle his losses at home, problems began to crop up on the business front. The establishment of the funeral home at the corner of Kelly Ingram Park had met with great success, but also inspired suspicion and resentment in some spheres of both the black and white communities. The primary accusation leveled at Gaston was that he was "acting big with white folks' money"—im-plying that he was merely the black face of a white-owned interest, put out front to lure blacks into patronizing the establishment. It was difficult for many blacks to believe that a black man could have accu-mulated so much, accustomed as they were to the general state of poverty that seemed to be the constant companion of blackness in the southern region. Great success was almost always suspect under these conditions; thus came the charge, from blacks and whites alike, that Gaston was simply getting too big for his britches.

A charge of "uppitiness" from the black community was one thing, but from the white community it was another: It was down-right dangerous. The renovation of the funeral parlor had served to rejuvenate black interest in Ingram Park, and blacks had begun flocking back to the spot for recreational purposes. This did not sit well with many in the white community, who had been only too happy with the de facto restriction of the park to whites only. Birmingham was still, in those days, a place where lynchings took place with waning but noticeable regularity, and A. G. quickly realized that expansion of his power brought with it a concomitant growth in his vulnerability. He had little means, however, of deflecting the negative attention. The best option appeared to be waiting out the storm with whatever grace he could muster. A. G. instructed his employees to keep the grounds and buildings in spotless condition, "so it will not appear that the white people have lost the building and the Negroes are letting it go down."

The rumors and distrust surrounding the company were dismaying to Gaston. But he had little choice but to ride out whatever upheavals public sentiment happened to throw his way. Once again Gaston found himself with few "real" friends, though his business ventures kept him flush in acquaintances and partners. He was well into his forties by this time, but personal intimacies remained a difficult realm. The only place Gaston felt he could take comfort was in the letters that continued to arrive from Cedartown, Georgia. Minnie Gardner, still in her teaching post across the state line, offered Gaston her friendship as few others had.

———————

In the months that followed Creola's death, A. G. and Minnie remained friends and devoted pen pals, but nothing more. Mom Smith's plan to get A. G. to marry her niece had kicked into high gear, and A. G. spent the majority of what small energy he had for personal affairs fending off his mother-in-law's requests. Eventually, however, Gaston realized that he wanted more from Minnie Gardner than their weekly missives could provide. Soon he began courting the young teacher, taking weekend trips to Georgia to visit her. These visits, and their relationship as a whole, were kept quiet, so as not to arouse suspicion in Mom Smith. Gaston knew she would be none too pleased by his decision to date someone other than her niece.

Though her death was never officially documented, it is generally accepted that Creola Smith Gaston died in approximately 1938. A few years later Minnie Gardner was once again living in Birmingham, brought back by A. G. Gaston himself to serve as an instructor in his newly founded business college, named, unsurprisingly, for his old idol.

THE BOOKER T. WASHINGTON BUSINESS COLLEGE

The Booker T. Washington Business College was conceived of and founded by Gaston in 1939 to provide training to potential employees of the insurance company and funeral home. The growth of both companies had necessitated the hiring of additional employees, but Gaston was continually dissatisfied with the caliber of applicant who came knocking at his door in response to employment ads. Few had the basic training required to work in an office environment. It didn't take long for Gaston to realize that the only way to ensure that his employees were properly trained was to educate them himself.

Initially, in June 1939, Gaston hired a Mr. Howard L. Turner of Birmingham, Alabama. Mr. Turner's job was to teach typewriting, shorthand, bookkeeping, and English to a small group of employees at the insurance company. Word of the program got out, and by September "eager potential clerical workers from all over the city were seeking admission" to Mr. Turner's classes. By January the demand had gotten so enormous that additional staff were added—thus the beginning of the college. Constructed "in the tradition of the Tuskegee Institute," the business college was designed to provide blacks with practical tools for living and working. Its expanded classes trained blacks in the areas of accounting, business law, and salesmanship, as well as clerical and secretarial work.

The founding of the business college was a triumph in terms both public and personal. For the black public of Birmingham, the creation of the school represented a chance for a better life through the study of applicable skills. If you could type, perhaps you wouldn't have to mop floors for a living; if you knew how to clerk, maybe you could get out of the mines. For blacks in Birmingham, BTW Business College represented hope, and Gaston was more than happy to give it to them.

For Gaston, however, the business college represented a different kind of hope: It was yet another step toward the vertical integration of his companies, and with its establishment, his empire commenced a new wave of growth. Gaston's interests were taking on the distinct shape of a pyramid: He controlled funeral homes that performed burials, the insurance company that paid for those burials, and now the means of training employees in both these companies. And unlike both the insurance company and the funeral home, the business college required relatively little investment of effort and overhead to get it up and running. The people were hungry for education (wherever they decided to take it), and A. G. Gaston was offering it to them as few others had. The college was an instant success in a time when southern blacks in particular were looking for a deal of any kind.

THE NEW DEAL

In 1933 Franklin Delano Roosevelt took office as the thirty-second president of the United States, after running on the reassuring platform that America had "nothing to fear but fear itself." It was a sentiment the nation needed desperately to hear: The country was, at that point, still in depression freefall; some five thousand banks had failed nationwide. In a flurry of action known as the First New Deal, Roosevelt regulated the stock exchange, coordinated the faltering rail system, and sent five hundred million dollars to the states for direct relief. He saved a fifth of homeowners from foreclosures and allowed for the refinancing of farm mortgages. Some two and a half million young men were soon able to find work for a dollar a day in parks and forests, where they planted nearly two billion trees.

Blacks, however, were not a part of this First New Deal. Roosevelt had courted southern segregationists in order to get his New Deal legislation passed, and as a result of his early capitulation, "nearly 400,000 Negro sharecroppers and more than 300,000 black tenant farmers never received their payments from the Agricultural Adjustment Administration" (the arm of the government that compensated farmers for reducing their crops). In Birmingham the chasm between what aid the government was willing to provide and the needs of the local community continued to grow. Direct federal relief to the poor met its end in 1935 under the assumption that those who were able to work would be "absorbed" into Works Progress Administration (WPA) programs, while the truly unemployable could be aided by private local institutions. Unfortunately, a quota system had been attached to the creation of the WPA. With the passage of time, the number of families eligible for aid was reduced at a rate that far outstripped the actual reduction of families in need. Moreover, blacks were routinely and systematically excluded from the few entitlements the programs could offer.

By the end of the 1930s, however, America's tune regarding blacks and poverty had begun to change—if ever so slightly. By the time of his reelection in 1936 President Roosevelt had been convinced of the growing importance of the black vote. In 1934 Eleanor Roosevelt (who would famously resign from the Daughters of the American Revolution when they refused to let Marion Anderson sing in Constitution Hall) and others had prevailed upon FDR to take an interest in black affairs. In response, Roosevelt formed his "Black Cabinet," which included Mrs. Roosevelt's friend Mary McLeod Bethune (head of the National Council of Negro Women) and Robert Weaver (who would later become an official cabinet member of the Johnson administration) among the group of some thirty advisers. The group fought for adjustments such as equal pay in federal programs and encouraged Roosevelt to increase the number of black federal employees.

With the Black Cabinet in place and a new focus on the black vote extended in the 1936 election, blacks saw pathways open up to them in many New Deal programs. Whereas in the past, programs such as the Agricultural Adjustment Act (the legislative aspect of the Agricultural Adjustment Administration) had operated in such a manner as to essentially drive blacks out of business through discriminatory practices, now programs began to welcome blacks as participants. The WPA began to reach out to the black community by developing "educational and cultural programs," employing blacks in artistic endeavors (under the auspices of the Federal Art Project, the Federal Music Project, and the Federal Writers Project—

which employed and trained the likes of Richard Wright, Ralph Ellison, and Zora Neale Hurston) and funneling money into the flagging black educational system. The government undertook to begin training its black citizens—teaching somewhere in the arena of 250,000 blacks to read and write during the 1930s.

While Roosevelt's latter New Deal strategy did make an imprint in the South, the racial animus that defined the region was not quelled by Washington's interest in "racial justice." Though regional leaders were given mandates as to how opportunities were to be meted out in black and white communities alike, southern representatives often ignored or dismissed these directives, denying blacks access to the programs the government attempted to put in place. Adding to southern blacks' alienation was the fact that a relatively large proportion of the South's employment prospects revolved around rural, agricultural, and manual labor—farming, sharecropping, and mining among them. The mechanization of the farm industry, as well as the spread of mining technology to the South, rendered hundreds of thousand of these jobs obsolete—jobs that had previously enabled blacks to scrape together a means of subsistence.

Meanwhile, in the northern half of the nation, employment opportunities blossomed (relatively speaking). Though the North still operated under a racialist system of resource allocation, the growth of factory-based production created a viable (if proportionately small) sector of employment for blacks who needed work. Once the tale of better opportunities in the North was set spinning, little could be done to stop its propagation. So it was that in the years immediately preceding the Second World War, a northern migration sprouted wings, with millions of blacks leaving the shrinking southern market for unskilled labor in pursuit of new blue- and white-collar opportunities in northern cities such as New York, Chicago, and Detroit.

The emigration ran counter to Gaston's personal model of development: Rather than casting their buckets down (as Booker T. Washington had taught, and as Gaston had done himself), blacks were fleeing the southern states to make contributions in other areas of the nation. Gaston knew that many of his students would take the education they had secured at BTW Business College and head straight up the seacoast if they could, but he hoped to induce more than a few to see the situation as he had, making Birmingham their home and "Dr." Gaston (as he came to be called) their employer.

MR. AND MRS. A. G. GASTON, REDUX

The founding of the business college also offered a convenient end to the long-distance courtship between A. G. and Minnie Gardner. Gaston had grown tired of the physical distance between himself and his new romantic interest, but prior to the founding of the business college, no jobs had appeared on the Birmingham horizon to make Minnie's transition back to Alabama a smooth one. Without a marriage proposal, Gaston could not bring Minnie back himself; trying to funnel money to her surreptitiously for her support would have aroused too much suspicion in the community. The business college, however, was a legitimate and ideal solution to their quandary. A. G. needed Minnie in Birmingham, Minnie needed a job, and the college needed a teacher—which Minnie happened to be. At A. G.'s urging, Minnie returned to Birmingham in 1940 and began her work at BTW. Before long she was serving the college not merely as an instructor, but also as head of school operations.

Though their business relationship took the foreground in the early period after Minnie's arrival, the courtship between the two remained a crucial element of their interaction. Their romantic aspirations remained, however, a silent, if open, affair: The threat of Mom Smith's displeasure still hung heavy in the air. Whether it was fear of Mom Smith's wrath or simple concern for her emotional comfort that kept him quiet, A. G. was clearly unwilling to make his feelings for Minnie plain to his former mother-in-law.

Three years passed, during which Minnie and A. G. worked side by side at the school. The young woman applied herself to ensuring the success of the college as though it were her own. She was, A. G. found, tireless in her devotion to her students, and (critically) unwaveringly loyal to him. A. G. Gaston—the man who would have sacrificed nearly everything in his life for financial success—had finally met someone as single-minded as he; in Minnie Gardner he had met his match. He decided to marry her. But in a true twist of fate, A. G.'s choice of Minnie for his wife would land him in a position that threatened to bankrupt him—and in the end would force him to forfeit every liquid asset in his possession, and then some.

Minnie and A. G. Gaston were finally married in 1943, in a private ceremony on the front porch of her sister Roberta Gardner Shorte's home in New York City. A. G. and Minnie had left Birmingham on the pretext of attending to business; they told no one of their plans. The wedding was, in the memories of those in who witnessed the event, a spur-of-the-moment affair. Roberta recalls Minnie arising one morning and nonchalantly requesting that her sister obtain a minister; that same afternoon all the pieces were in place. The entire guest list included perhaps a dozen individuals: Minnie and A. G., Roberta and her husband, Cecil, and few close friends from the New York area were the only people present.

As it was for A. G., this was a second wedding for Minnie (her first marriage to a man named Billy McDaniel had ended in divorce when her mother suspected physical abuse), and while her first nuptials had been an elaborate affair on her parents' farm, replete with flowers, food, and dance, this time around things were simpler. A. G. wore his standard, well-pressed business suit, his crisp wool fedora clutched at his side; Minnie was outfitted in a neat skirt-and-jacket set, her trademark ruffled collar, and a string of colorful beads clustered tightly about her neck.

The minister performed the marriage rites without incident, and at the appropriate time the bride and groom embraced publicly for the first time. Afterward, Roberta served simple sandwiches and iced tea on the porch, while Mr. and Mrs. Gaston talked business with their guests. The business college was blossoming, Mr. Gaston would say, and all thanks to Mrs. Gaston's hard work. New classes were being planned, Mrs. Gaston would report, a new teacher brought in from the country. The business—even on a day like this one—never left their minds. It had served as their Cupid's arrow, and the cultivation of that spark fulfilled both of them, spiritually and professionally.

MOM SMITH'S CHALLENGE

After several more days in New York, the newly minted couple returned to Birmingham to present themselves to the community. They both knew that the first person they owed an explanation to was Mom Smith. Whether Mrs. Smith had been privy to the small bits of gossip that had sprung up in the years between her daughter's death and the present day, or if she was caught completely by surprise by the apparent defection of her former son-in-law, remains unknown. What is clear, however, was her outrage at what she considered A. G.'s betrayal of her family. She wasn't the only one incensed by Gaston's choice. Creola's cousin, who had figured herself the new Mrs. A. G. Gaston, was equally furious at being passed over for the title. Having lost any claim to the Smith & Gaston fortune, the cousin, who had little else to lose, encouraged her aunt not to let A. G. off the hook. With a 49 percent stake in the companies, Mom Smith held enough power to shake the businesses to their foundations if the mood struck her, and at the urging of her outraged niece that is precisely what she determined to do.

The idea hatched by the women was this: to exercise Smith's shareholding power by demanding a thorough and precise accounting of each of the businesses (an audit, so to speak), which would force the business into receivership and, potentially, destruction or sale. It was a bold move, but Mrs. Smith had little to lose in the attempt; she had known A. G. Gaston since he was a boy, and she knew him well enough to know that he would stop at nothing to save his company. She was right.

Upon learning of Smith's challenge, A. G. once again turned to his old friend attorney Percy Benton for help. Benton informed him that his only chance to save the business was to try to make an out-of-court settlement with Mom Smith. Gaston suspected that the price of retribution would be high, and in this case, too, he was correct. The terms that Mom Smith insisted upon were dizzying: The settlement would require him to deed her his home as well as forfeiture of nearly every cent he had and more, in order to negotiate a cash buyout of her interest in the insurance company and funeral home. It was more money than he had, for sure, but the choice was plain: Give up all that he had accumulated thus far or give up his rights to the company. It is fair to say that he hardly hesitated in making his decision. The survival of the business was his central concern, no matter what the immediate personal cost.

How A. G. came up with the money to pay off Mom Smith remains controversial. Some members of the Gardner family believe that it was Billy and Roberta Gardner who gave their new son-in-law the enormous sum of money Smith was demanding (estimated to have been anywhere from ten to fifty thousand dollars), in exchange for the promise from Minnie that she would care for and educate her younger siblings when the time came for them to leave home. Billy and Roberta certainly had the financial means to divest themselves of such a large sum (their farm was their collateral), and it seems plausible that it was indeed their generosity that allowed Gaston to meet Mom Smith's demands.

Gaston would have had other means of securing funds, as well. He had remained, since his early days at the mines, both an avid saver and an unabashed penny-pincher. Extravagances were indulged rarely to never. Moreover, he had built up a name for himself in the community—just about everyone in Birmingham (black and white) knew who A. G. Gaston was by this point, most importantly the banking and other professional institutions where Gaston constantly did business. It is possible (if the looming specter of race makes it impossible to say *likely*), therefore, that loans might have been forthcoming if Gaston had requested them.

Whether he did request such favors from business associates remains undocumented. Regardless, Gaston was indeed able to turn up the appropriate sum of money to satisfy Mom Smith. He signed the requisite papers and gave over to his former mother-in-law (and last link to the Smith family he had once loved so completely) his life's earnings. He did this with sadness but without much regret. Gaston had made a choice—both in marrying Minnie and in forfeiting his assets—for the future. If his decision to agree to Smith's terms appears risk-laden and emotionally driven, that is because to a certain extent, it was. But Gaston had lived too long in the business world to allow his emotions to override all common sense.

Dad Smith had taught him important lessons in the handling of business, and he employed one of them now. The simple lesson was this: "Never borrow anything that, if forced to it, you can't pay back." The amount of money Mom Smith was asking for was vast, but it was, relative to the revenue stream he knew the combined companies were capable of producing, eminently repayable. Though the settlement had relieved him of all his personal wealth, he now had sole control over the entirety of Smith & Gaston enterprises, which by this point also included the business college. Furthermore, the debt he had incurred to achieve this position represented a manageable deficit. He and Minnie would have little else for a time, but they had full rein of the businesses and they had each other. Experience had taught him that he would rise again; all that was required was effort. And between the two of them, Minnie and Arthur Gaston had effort enough to move a mountain.

The Beginnings of an Empire

The period that followed Mom Smith's removal from the company interests was one that Gaston regularly described as the happiest in his life. He and Minnie worked ceaselessly to rebuild their fortune by bettering their businesses and met with great success in doing so. The business college continued to boom: In 1943 (the year that A. G. and Minnie were married) the college had graduated fifty-nine students— and the numbers kept rising. Though the school had been founded to supply Gaston's own interests with employees, soon graduates were being employed all over the state and the nation. The Gastons operated an "open-door policy" in regard to school admission. This meant that any student, white or black, who proved an interest in attending the school was admitted—regardless of his or her ability to pay. The expectation was that once the student obtained employment, he or she would repay the school the cost of tuition.

It was, in Gaston's own words, a business that was run on trust and on the cultivation of a familial culture between the student body and the administration. Unlike most other educational programs, the BTW Business College was able to make these kinds of exceptions because of the foundational support that Gaston's other interests

(Smith & Gaston and the insurance company) provided. If financial crises hit, one or the other of these companies "underwrote teachers' salaries and other expenses." One branch of Gaston's business empire was almost always capable of feeding another. The customer base of the original companies was strong and growing, with loyalty to the Gaston brand the hallmark of their success.

Within a few short years Gaston once again found himself on top of his game. Soon A. G. and Minnie would move into what company literature would call their "palatial" home on Fifth Avenue and First Street North. It was an imposing brick manse, enormous by black Birmingham standards, its front porch always bursting with blooms and elegantly decorated. They knew that Minnie could not have children, but their house would always be full. Gaston's son and his growing family, which would eventually include five children, were frequent visitors. The Gastons informally adopted Dixie and Elizabeth Gardner, Minnie's youngest sisters, and pursuant to the arrangement that had been set up with Minnie's parents (whether they had given the Gastons the money or not), they sent both girls to college at Tuskegee.

Gaston had used the rebuilding process not only to improve the quality of his businesses, but also to develop his own prowess as a businessman. Somewhere along this road to renewed riches, he decided to focus on

> . . . becoming the very best businessman I could be. I studied,
> read, listened attentively to the advice and counsel of auditors,
> lawyers, brokers, bankers and other financial advisors. I learned
> to quickly digest a profit and loss statement. I realized the great
> importance of keeping good records and was scrupulous about
> their detailed accuracy. I saved a part of all I earned, was always
> watchful for sound investments, insisted on the topflight perfor-
> mance of my employees, and learned the hard way not to make
> the same mistake twice.

What is particularly remarkable about this new dedication on Gaston's part to educating himself on the principles of business management is what it reveals of all that he had *not* been doing prior to this time.

The previous successes of Gaston's companies had not been accidental, but neither were they guided by any formal education in good business practice. Gaston had relied, for most of the period during which he had begun accruing wealth, on the guidance of Dad Smith—who himself likely had limited formal education in management. In Dad Smith's time, however, the world had been a different place than it was now becoming. Smith had been ably to rely on his name alone to accomplish his goals, but A. G. was living in a world in which competition for the black dollar was increasing daily, and where the anonymity of private business—black or white—was fast disappearing. If Gaston was going to survive in this new economy, he would have to study and observe—which he did, to spectacular effect.

There is a telling picture of A. G. Gaston from this period in which he is seated in his office, perched expectantly behind his giant mahogany desk. Cast in gold, his nameplate sits before him, a framed photograph of Booker T. Washington hanging on the wall just behind him and to his right. His desk is stacked with books, a telephone, and papers, but what is most visible is a placard sitting immediately to Gaston's left and facing outward, toward the camera. The placard bears just one word in bold letters: THINK. It was Gaston's new directive and his personal imperative. He had begun to climb again.

CAPITAL IDEAS

The bedrock of all financial success is capital accumulation.

THE CADILLAC

As the story goes, one day A. G. decided that after all his years of sacrifice and hard work, he deserved a luxury item—a purchase that would "be a badge of [his] hard-earned prestige" to those around him. What Gaston had his eye on was a brand-new Cadillac, one like his grandfather Joe had owned in Demopolis, making it clear to everybody that Joe Gaston was *somebody*. Armed with the conviction that his name would pave the way to loan approval, A. G. Gaston knocked on the office door of Harris Moriarty, manager of Birmingham's First National Bank. Moriarty and Gaston had known each other since the days of the purchase of the building bordering Ingram Park, and Moriarty was a man whom Gaston believed he could trust when it came to financial matters.

Arthur didn't waste time getting down to business. He outlined his need for a loan to the bank manager and apprised him of the fact that the money he was requesting was for the purchase of a new car. It didn't take Moriarty a minute to reply. "No, A. G. Gaston, I will *not* give you a $5,000 loan for a Cadillac . . . You do not need a fancy car."

Arthur was stunned by Moriarty's refusal—and not merely because it meant he wouldn't be getting his Caddy. Before Gaston had managed to utter more than a few words of polite disbelief, however, he realized that the bank manager was not done. Moriarty had other thoughts for that five-thousand-dollar loan. "I've been watching your business develop, Gaston. It's growing rapidly. You can be proud of yourself." Gaston thanked him for his praise and waited for what would come next. Moriarty laid his cards on the table. "I'll make you a $5,000 loan," he offered, "to buy a bond to deposit with the state."

The bond Moriarty had in mind was one that would help Gaston comply with state insurance regulations. Moriarty even promised to go the extra step of speaking with a state official to approve the purchase. There would be nothing left for Gaston to do but sign on the dotted line and promise to repay the loan at a rate of 10 percent of the gross monthly income of the businesses. It was a wise and forward-thinking plan, without a doubt, and one that would establish Gaston's growing empire as a formally recognized component of state commerce.

However benevolent Moriarty's intentions, there was no way Gaston could miss the patronizing aspect of the proposition. Gaston had entered his friend's office with a particular plan in mind and Moriarty—a white man—had summarily disabused him of the notion that he had any right to determine where he might use the money he was requesting. The bank manager did not *suggest* to Gaston what he should do with the money—he gave him an ultimatum. Either use the money for a bond or walk out the door empty-handed.

For some men, the ultimatum alone would have been a deal breaker. But not for Gaston. He accepted Moriarty's offer with little hesitation, realizing that the manager's proposal would stand him in better stead in the long term than the purchase of a quickly depreciating vehicle. Gaston took Moriarty's deal because he knew it was yet another step on the path to financial strength. It was an offer he knew better than to turn down.

Though the rate that Moriarty had demanded on repayment—10 percent of gross earnings—leveled a blow to Gaston's standard of living, before long business had ramped up to the point that the absence of that 10 percent was less acutely felt. The growth of business in turn enabled Gaston to repay the loan sooner rather than later, and his precise and timely payments helped him to establish a record of good credit at the bank.

So successful was Gaston's bond-buying venture that he quickly made a habit of it. Once Moriarty's loan for the first bond was paid off, Gaston continued to collect 10 percent of his gross profits for investment purposes. This practice of taking 10 percent off the top for savings became Gaston's second signature tenet of moneymaking: "A part of all you earn is yours to keep." Simple as it may now seem, Gaston's new slogan—which he disseminated through the community first by word of mouth among his employees and later by way of advertisements for his bank—became the foundation of his rules for wealth accumulation. It had taken Gaston twenty years of business practice to be introduced to the formal model of investment, and he meant to spread the gospel of return on principal to anyone in the black community who was willing to listen.

THE FINANCIALS

In 1941 A. G. Gaston and his companies released a public accounting of their success. A widely distributed sales brochure proclaimed that the company now had "Over Six Million Dollars Insurance in Force Protecting 33,000 Negroes in Alabama," having collected $154,952.93 in premiums that year. (Comparatively, in 1925, two years after the company started, a total of $2,216.04 in premiums had been collected.) By this point, the company was already the largest black-owned employer of blacks in Birmingham, paying out $67,853.80 in commissions to its army of sales representatives. These representatives still canvassed door to door, collecting weekly sums from clients in amounts ranging from quarters to dollars.

On the funeral end of the business, Smith & Gaston buried seven hundred people in 1941, bolstered by the company's well-known ads that encouraged customers to remember, "In the event of death, always call Smith & Gaston." That year the companies spent almost six thousand dollars with "Negro Newspapers, Printers, Churches and Charity Donations"—by their own account, "More than All Other

Funeral Homes and Insurance Companies in Birmingham Combined." The companies claimed the only daily radio program in the South, and urged people to tune into WSGN at 4:35 P.M. daily and at 9:05 A.M. on Sundays. Branding and advertising were taking on a revitalized role in growing the empire, with newspapers, radio, and churches providing the platform for launching an infiltration of the Gaston name into the daily lives of Birmingham residents.

And in case anyone in Birmingham was still wondering, the publicity was sure to make it clear: All the companies were, as they put it, "Strictly 100 Per Cent Negro."

World War II

Though the tilt of his hat cut a more severe and self-assured angle during this period, what had not changed in Gaston was his support for and belief in America as a democratic ideal, and as a body politic. In fact, the richer Gaston got, the more inclined he became to pledge himself to the "American way"; he began to feel that he was living proof that in America anything was possible. But even for A. G. Gaston, this coming war was a complicated business.

When war was finally declared this time around, it was done in the light of defending the world from a breed of racism that threatened to wipe out an entire ethnic population. The irony of this rationale was not lost on black Americans. "If you haven't got democracy yourself," A. Philip Randolph, head of the Brotherhood of Sleeping Car Porters, wondered, "how can you carry it to somebody else?" Republican presidential candidate Wendell Willkie was outspoken on the matter. "When we talk of freedom and opportunity for all nations," Willkie opined, "the mocking paradoxes of our own society become so clear they can no longer be ignored."

In this new war, America once again positioned itself as big brother to a deeply flawed world, but blacks knew better than most on what slippery ground the nation stood in making such claims to righteousness. The poet Langston Hughes was not alone in his thinking that "the two problems have much in common—Berlin and Birmingham. The Jewish people and the Negro people both know the meaning of Nordic supremacy. We have both looked into the eyes of terror." Furthermore, it was clear to many blacks that the winning of this war would not help their own situation at home. The black soldiers of World War II were the sons and younger brothers of the same World War I veterans who had returned to the United States expecting change and had instead been met with disappointment. Moreover, the same government that had promised so much then couldn't even bring itself to play by the rules on the surface of things now: It patently refused to desegregate the armed forces sent out to battle fascism abroad.

One episode, highlighted in Howard Zinn's study of U.S. history, underscores the alienation felt by some in the black community when it came to the war effort. Speaking before a group of "several thousand" blacks in the Midwest, Walter White, then president of the National Association for the Advancement of Colored People (NAACP), shared the story of a black student speaking to his teacher about his feelings on the war. "The Army jim-crows us," the student had said. "The Navy lets us serve only as messmen. The Red Cross refuses our blood. Employers and labor unions shut us out. Lynchings continue. We are disenfranchised, jim-crowed, spat upon. What more could Hitler do than that?" According to Zinn, White had shared the story assuming the crowd would frown upon the student's comments. Instead, he said, "The audience burst into such applause that it took me some thirty or forty seconds to quiet it."

Nevertheless, patriotism prevailed. In wartime then (as it is today) nationalistic pride was the absolute order of the day. Whatever opposition burbled beneath the surface, this was the era of Victory gardens and Rosie the Riveter; an era in which hundreds of thousands of housewives could be convinced to turn in every piece of cast iron they owned for the supposed creation of weapons. It was an epoch that cultivated the belief that civilian participation in the war effort truly mattered, with points given to ordinary citizens for their dedication to this battle for freedom.

By 1945 more than one million blacks had enlisted in the armed forces; five hundred thousand served overseas, seven thousand of whom were raised to the rank of officer. President Roosevelt had promised that 10 percent of armed services would be black (the same percentage as in the general population). He had set up the Fair Employment Practices Commission in 1941 and issued Executive Order 8802, confirming "the policy of full participation in the defense program by all persons, regardless of race, creed, color, or national origin." Nevertheless, three-quarters of black soldiers remained relegated to posts in service and supply (menial if essential work).

However, in 1941, twelve miles from Booker T. Washington's famous institute in Tuskegee, Alabama (and on land owned by the institute), construction was completed on the Tuskegee Army Air Field—soon to become a training ground for the army's black pilots. For the first time in U.S. history, at Tuskegee blacks would be trained to fly and participate in combat. However, all commanding officers on the base were white. The airfield therefore would be as segregated as the state it was in, featuring separate barracks, restrooms, and drinking fountains for its black and white soldiers. It was a segregation that lasted throughout the war.

Though white Tuskegee residents opposed the project (as did much of the country and the military), overall one thousand airmen were graduated from training at the airfield. The Ninety-ninth Fighter Squadron and the 332nd Fighter Group, formed from Tuskegee Air Field graduates, distinguished themselves in the North African, Sicilian, and European campaigns, "strafing enemy shipping, skip-bombing and fighting serial battles from April 1943 until V-E Day." Six airmen won the Purple Heart; sixty-five, the Distinguished Flying Cross.

Though relegated to the ground like most civilians, the Gastons did their part to aid the war effort. As federal workers were called into service, their jobs were vacated, and in 1943 the government put out a call for secretaries and office workers to be employed in Washington and across the country. Booker T. Washington Business College placed itself at the forefront of the cause, administering civil service examinations to qualified applicants and eventually sending fifty-six graduates to work for Uncle Sam. Each of these students carried with him or her into the workplace the imprimatur of A. G. Gaston's strategy for success, and it was not long before his name became legend in black communities in the North, as well as across the South.

In addition, Gaston chaired the Negro Division of the War Finance Committee, which raised more than one million dollars in war bonds (a sum equal to approximately ten million 2003 dollars) during its existence. The bond drive honored the first Alabamian killed at Pearl Harbor: a black man named Julius Ellsberry. Gaston proudly posed with a group of his fellow fund-raisers in front of the army Hellcat airplane donated to the local black school, Parker High, as a reward for the group's enormous contribution. Gaston was personally awarded a medal for distinguished service from the Department of the Treasury for his work. He hung it in a place of prominence on his office wall.

AGGREGATING CAPITAL

By 1946 Gaston's enterprises were flourishing. More than eleven million dollars' worth of insurance was now in force on a quarter of a million subscribers. The insurance company now offered both burial and straight life insurance policies in the amounts of one to five hundred dollars. Claims were paid in either burial services (conducted, of course, by Smith & Gaston) or cash. More than half a million dollars in premiums was collected in the 1946 calendar year.

By this point there were sixteen branches of the Booker T. Washington Insurance Company in existence, in Alabama cities such as Bessemer, Montgomery, Huntsville, Anniston, and Tuscaloosa, making it possible "for every man, woman and child to secure ample insurance coverage." Taking advantage of the war surplus, the company purchased two jeeps—"at a cost of $2,600.00"—and painted them with the BTW logo. Salesmen (and women) could now travel ever-farther distances to recruit customers. "Negroes living in the most remote sections of Alabama may have the protection of the largest and strongest Company of its kind in the entire South. . . ." promotional materials proclaimed. "Be on the look-out for the man in the Jeep."

The company hierarchy now included an official director of publicity. There were five radio broadcasts to keep track of—not to mention a budget of nearly fifteen thousand dollars spent on newspaper

On a trip to Paris in the 1950s, Minnie and A. G. Gaston take in the Eiffel Tower.

SMITH AND GASTON

Dignity . . .

Beauty . . .

Simplicity . . .

1 and 2. Display rooms, patrons are shown through the display rooms to choose the kind of casket they want for the remains of their loved ones.

3. The men who give you courteous and dignified service in your hour of need. Front row, reading left to right: R. L. Heggins, R. C. Smith, R. L. Lumzy, Adolph Littleton, and Johnnie Collin. Back row: Henry Gibson, Otis People, Rev. E. Hester, Joe Williams and William White, Jr.

4. R. L. Lumzy, Director of the Home Office Funeral Staff, standing before one of the black beauties that transport the bereaved families to and fro.

Part of the success of the funeral interest hinged on the company's ability to provide services from the most basic to the most luxurious.

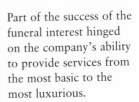

At Home . . .

1. After a busy day it is reclining for Mr. and Mrs. Gaston in the sitting room.

2. Duty calls at the office and it is time to go to work. Mrs. Gaston bids a pleasant day as she gives him his hat.

3. Nine o'clock and the President arrives at his office, ready for the task of operating Smith and Gaston Interest.

A. G. and Minnie Gaston at home on Fifth Avenue and First Street North during the 1940s.

The courtyard of the Gaston Motel. The motel became the Birmingham headquarters of Martin Luther King Jr. (pictured) and his movement for Civil Rights.

On one of his many trips to The White House, Gaston poses with President Lyndon Johnson and a group of visiting economic advisors.

Elizabeth Jenkins, Minnie Gaston, and Carol Jenkins in New York, circa 1984.

Mrs. Gaston with a few of her charges: George Washington, Harold Washington (in arms), and Carol Jenkins, on the porch of the Gaston's Birmingham home, circa 1947.

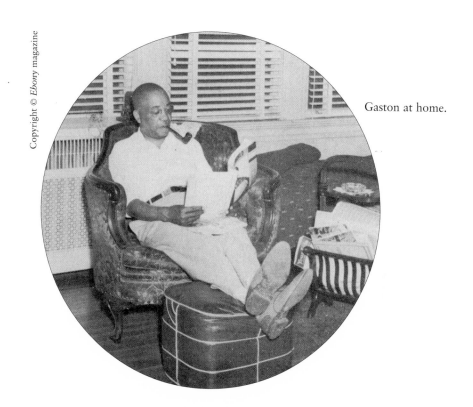

Gaston at home.

Mrs. Gaston visits a typing class at the business college.

Mr. Gaston plays pool with a few members of the A. G. Gaston Boys and Girls Club.

A. G. and Minnie Gaston's home on Fifth Avenue and First Street North, in Birmingham proper. The couple resided here until moving to the suburbs in the 1950s.

An early rendering of young Art with his Grandpa Joe and oxcart.

The Gaston's house in the Birmingham suburbs. It was this residence that would be bombed in 1963 and from which Mr. Gaston would be kidnapped in 1976.

Minnie and A. G. Gaston pose in their suburban home for a profile in
Ebony magazine.

The Booker T. Washington Insurance Company Jeep-fleet
that sold insurance and collected premiums door-to-door

and other ads, including billboards, all bearing the insignia of Smith & Gaston Funeral Directors: an impressive eagle carrying in its beak a ribbon emblazoned with the words SERVING ALABAMA.

Not only the insurance company had expanded in the war years. The funeral business had by now extended beyond Birmingham, as well. Branches of Smith & Gaston were to be found in Montgomery, Jasper, Fayette, and Bessemer, boasting a fleet of hearses and limousines, "coaches ready to serve at a moment's notice." In Birmingham the line of hearses stretched more than a city block, set end to end.

At the business college, now bearing the new motto *Knowledge Is Power and Power Is Success,* the classrooms were packed. More than two hundred "G-I men" were enrolled in the business courses at the school, their tuition paid for by the government under the GI Bill. The Booker T. Washington Employment Agency was formed to accommodate the swell of blacks who would be facing joblessness as a result of the war's end. Many positions that had been created by the war were terminated with the end of the conflict, and countless veterans would also be returning home, in need of work.

Gaston's sponsorship of radio programs also widened its reach during this time. The show *Echoes of Smith and Gaston* (a gospel program) aired Monday through Friday and on Sunday mornings. The singers and actors in Gaston's Kiddie Klub had their own show, broadcast from the Frolic Theatre every Saturday morning. The Smith & Gaston Golden Belle Singers (a group of five male singers) performed with the famous Golden Gate Quartet on a number of the company's radio programs.

The aforementioned Kiddie Klub, sponsored by The Gaston Interests (as Gaston's charitable foundations were now known), had become a special favorite of both Mr. and Mrs. Gaston as a means of giving back to the black community. The club was open to "every Negro boy and girl in Alabama between the ages of four and fourteen . . . for the purpose of developing the better side in Negro Youths." In addition to offering tutoring and "talent development," the club sponsored picnics at Tuxedo Park and an annual Fourth of July swimming party to celebrate Mr. Gaston's birthday, as well as academic scholarships and awards for educational achievement.

In addition to the half-hour weekly radio program produced under the club's auspices—and run, incidentally, by the young club members themselves—the Smith & Gaston Kiddie Klub extended to its members the fine and uncommon pleasure of a free trip to the movies. Every Saturday afternoon the Frolic would fill its seats with the young members of Gaston's club, each of whom—for a few hours at least—would be kept out of the kind of trouble that plagues poor youth of every race. Eleven thousand children throughout the state of Alabama had joined the Kiddie Klub by 1953—the same year that Gaston would initiate his statewide spelling bee, founded to encourage academic excellence and aid in student retention; dropouts were a continuing problem in the Alabama schools for reasons primarily related to poverty. By 1965, "100%" of Birmingham schools were participating in Gaston's spelling bee.

It was also during this postwar period that Gaston began to take on a larger role in national organizations. He joined the National Insurance Association, National Funeral Directors Association, and increased his level of participation in the National Negro Business League (NNBL). Long a member and leader of the local chapter of the NNBL, in 1947 Gaston took over leadership of the national group, which had been founded by Booker T. Washington in 1901 (through a generous grant from Andrew Carnegie). At the league's inaugural meeting held in Boston, Massachusetts, some three hundred black business owners from thirty-four states had gathered with the purpose of sharing information and encouraging other blacks to go into business.

During Gaston's term as president of the league, the *Journal of the NNBL* was founded. In a letter dated September 12, 1947, under the masthead THE NATIONAL NEGRO BUSINESS LEAGUE, OFFICE OF THE PRESIDENT, and addressed to W. D. Morison, head of the National Association of Real Estate Brokers in Detroit, Gaston wrote:

> I am now putting the finishing touches on the September issue . . . I have decided that this would be a good opportunity to give the National Association of Real Estate Brokers a good send-off by dedicating our October issue to the N.A.R.E.B. . . . I would write an article from the President's desk bearing on the real estate business among Negroes. . . .

Morison quickly sent out a letter to his members: "I think this is a very fine gesture on the part of our friend, Mr. Gaston and every real estate broker in the organization should take advantage of this opportunity." The legend of Gaston's power had spread to blacks across the country. His influence was now felt not just in Birmingham, and not just among fellow insurance men, but also across the growing spectrum of black business interests nationwide.

BROWN BELLE BOTTLING COMPANY

Desire is often described as the fundamental element of change; it is just as frequently the fundamental element of failure. Even the smartest of businessmen have been known to undervalue the potential for disaster in a given market—and more often than not it is the most human of drives that trips up these seemingly superhuman success stories.

Wise as Gaston's investment strategies were as a whole, not every venture could be a resounding success—and one in particular was a bona fide failure. The Brown Belle Bottling Company, formed in 1938 by Gaston (in partnership with a few friends from his growing circle of business acquaintants in the Alabama region), was to be the first and only major business failure of Gaston's career. Like any good businessman, Gaston was always on the lookout for opportunities that offered high profit margins and low overhead. Brown Belle— a soda pop manufacturing operation—seemed to fit the bill, even if it was a difficult venture to incorporate into the funeral home– insurance company–business school triumvirate.

Just as with his other companies, Gaston built Brown Belle from the bottom up. Rather than stepping in to buy an already existent but foundering operation, he started from scratch, investing in all his own equipment, facilities, and supplies. Nor did he simply jump into the fray without researching the field: Unlike the days he spent in Westfield going door to door, learning the trade as doors slammed in his face, by now Gaston had the time, resources, and business acumen to conduct a thorough investigation of the workings of the soft drink business before endeavoring to join the competition. He spent months researching viable markets and conducting profit–loss analy- ses to determine the feasibility of this new operation. All the answers seemed to come back in the affirmative. Every inquiry, even account- ing for "maximum overhead expenses" (including, to some degree, theft), seemed to support the belief that the margin of profit on the production of soft drinks would be high. And not marginally high, but astoundingly so. Though there are no hard numbers available for precisely how much Gaston believed he could make in this venture, his own description of his eagerness to be involved, observed in the light of his by-then-sizable financial holdings, makes it clear that the sums in question were not trivial.

Just as appealing to Gaston as the potential for actual profit was the speed at which that profit could seemingly be accrued in this new business. Unlike the insurance and funeral companies, with which it had taken him years to build not only the corporate structure but also a dedicated customer base, Brown Belle could seemingly be up and running—and selling—in no time flat. The company's only "major expenses," as Gaston termed them, were the purchases of the bottling system, delivery trucks, and the product's sweetening agents: sugar and syrup, the most basic of ingredients. It would be set up in a building that Gaston owned on Fourth Avenue between Fifteenth and Sixteenth Streets. Gaston would, he believed, be able to take advantage of his name recognition not only to spur sales, but also to draw the best and the brightest to the ranks of the Brown Belle employee roster. From every side the business looked like it would be a hit, and Gaston had no trouble convincing his friends and acquaintances to become stockholders in the new company by investing their money up front. People had grown to believe in A. G. Gaston, the brand, and jumped at the opportunity to get on board with his newest venture.

Initially, they were not to be disappointed. The regional community, which had also come to believe in the A. G. Gaston brand, greeted the launch of the company with much fanfare. Gaston reported a profit the first year on sales of more than a hundred thousand dollars. He employed a staff of fifteen, including four truck drivers. One of the beverages sold under the Brown Belle label was called "The Joe Louis Punch," named for the popular heavyweight champion. Like the other Gaston enterprises, Brown Belle was a family affair: Arthur Gaston Jr. (who would, over the course of his life, also work in his father's funeral homes and print shop) served as the company's general manager, and Thomas Gardner, one of Minnie's brothers, acted as manager of sales.

Unafraid of using the outlets afforded him by his other business enterprises, Gaston arranged for wide-spanning publicity to accompany the soda's release (one popular slogan: "When it's a cold appetizing beverage, the call is for Brown Belle"). He advertised anyhow and anywhere he could, including "paint[ing] beautiful brown girls on our trucks and sponsor[ing] 'Miss Brown Belle' contests." He launched an all-out campaign to make the Brown Belle name a household word ("Each and every day, 'Make mine, Brown Belle' ") and before long he had achieved his goal. Blacks in Birmingham were, in this case, eager to support a black-owned business, and when it came to soda pop, Gaston's was the only choice. Soon the soda was selling

From A. G. Gaston Enterprises promotional material

Miss Brown Belle: part of a promotion for the Brown
Belle Bottling Company—Gaston's only business failure

respectably all over the state, and Gaston began formulating plans to
expand throughout the country and into South America and Cuba.

In October 1946 Gaston delivered a speech in Washington to the
Second Conference on the Negro in Business. Emmer Lancaster, the
Negro adviser to the U.S. Commerce Department, had convened a
conference of black business leaders (the first of which took place in
1941) and asked Gaston to appear at this, the second convention.
Both A. G. and Minnie Gaston would go on to be frequent participants in the conference over the years. In Gaston's 1946 speech, he
urged young black businessmen to "Go into a new business, not the
regular run-of-the-mill business, but a new type of business and conduct it the same as the other group is conducting it." The encouraging tone of his speech might lead you to conclude that all was well in
his newest endeavor; this, however, was hardly the case.

Though the Brown Belle label had continued to sell well, it eventually became obvious that the company was hemorrhaging money
internally. Sales were high, yet little cash was actually showing up in
the till. The problem, once it was discovered, was clearly multifac-

eted, but at its core was the disappearance of enormous amounts of that basic ingredient that makes soda sweet: sugar. As Gaston put it,

> . . . we had not considered what a conveniently marketable product sugar was. We didn't know the extent to which some people would go to supply the demand for this, our foundation product. We learned that through some unscrupulous personnel, the bulk of our sugar was going into the cupboards—or stills—of our employees and their friends.

Adding to the difficulties was the fact that the problem was systemic: "Route men, office personnel and customers" were apparently in collusion with one another to claim a larger portion of the pie than they were justly due. It was not merely a matter of firing a few bad seeds; in order to save the company, an entire restructuring of the business would have to occur, complete with new accounting methods and enforcement policies. Furthermore, somebody would have to take on the burden of constantly monitoring the business's state of affairs, and that someone would have to be a person with a significant interest in seeing the company succeed. Only a stockholder would take that kind of interest, but the stockholders in Brown Belle had other business interests of their own to attend to.

If there were a likely candidate for providing the close supervision Brown Belle would need to regain its balance, it would have been Gaston himself. But it is clear that he was hesitant to take on this more involved role. For better or worse, Gaston had conceived of this enterprise as a means of making easy money. It was a project he believed in, certainly, but not one that felt close to his heart in the way that his other ventures had. By Gaston's own admission, the Brown Belle concept had nothing to do with his cardinal rule of "finding a need and filling it." The idea had come to him as one that would afford relative ease, but had turned out to be trickier than he had imagined. Now, with the company in disarray, he was forced to make a critical decision: soldier on—which would require him to dedicate himself wholly to revitalizing the company—or pack it in and admit defeat.

For all the weight stacked on one side of the scales, this was hardly an easy decision for Gaston to make. And who knows but that he would have chosen to stick with the company and fight to make it profitable if outside events hadn't contrived to make the decision for him. A robbery at the plant, in which thieves made off with the company safe, pushed Brown Belle to a point of crisis. It was not the loss of the little money that was kept in the safe that was the problem; it was the loss of the company records that were housed there that pushed the interest to the brink. The company was already in the middle of a lawsuit brought against it for the use of the Brown Belle name, and the loss of the records would be a total disaster for the court case. Faced with yet another calamity under the Brown Belle imprint, Gaston finally decided he had had enough.

On March 15, 1950, A. G. Gaston penned a response to Emmer Lancaster's latest request to attend the upcoming Negro in Business Conference, and speak once again—this time on the success of his bottling company. "I'm afraid we will not be in a position to give you anything encouraging on this. . . ." Gaston wrote. "It seems as if we will be forced to dissolve the company entirely." All the time and energy being poured into the Brown Belle affair was time and energy diverted from his other businesses, Gaston concluded—businesses that were helping people in tangible ways. It was time to close the door on the bottling company.

In the end the "easy moneymaker" Brown Belle Bottling Company had racked up more than sixty thousand dollars in debt. Shutting the venture down required a settling up of these obligations to creditors and vendors, and it was the responsibility of the stockholders to make up all balances due. Gaston had convinced many of his friends and business acquaintances to back him financially on this endeavor, and the closure of the company in an indebted state would require them to lay out yet more of their own money. Such a move would, necessarily, tarnish Gaston's name and reputation. So once again, Gaston was faced with a choice: let the stockholders bear the brunt of the failure (and thereby risk his standing in the business community) or take the full force of the liability upon himself. As he had done in his battle with Mom Smith, and as he would do for the remainder of his life, Gaston chose to protect his name and reputation. He absorbed the entire loss himself and let his investors walk away unencumbered. For the few faithful employees left jobless by the closing of the company, he found jobs in his other business interests.

The failure of Brown Belle was a public humiliation, and the dissolution of the company produced in Gaston a measure of anguish and plain old embarrassment that he had not yet had cause to deal with in his business career. Down came the posters and banners declaring Brown Belle the product of champions. No more Miss Brown Belle contests would be held. For a man who staked his whole self-worth on his financial success and reputation, this was no small defeat. Though he glosses over his dismay in his own account of his life, it is clear that the Brown Belle fiasco took its toll. He was "exhausted, embarrassed and no little ashamed" of what he had accomplished in trying to get (more) rich quickly—so much so that for only the second time in his life (the first being when he joined the army, looking for "a way out") he felt compelled to leave Alabama—if only temporarily. Gaston had broken his own rules with Brown Belle; he had been propelled by greed and had paid the price for it. Now he needed an opportunity to collect himself and, in some sense, start anew.

In Haiti

Not long after the collapse of Brown Belle, an invitation for travel was floated Gaston's way. The trip that would follow initiated a new era in his life, one of extensive travel that began after the Second World War had been won and America had once again established primacy as a world leader. Beginning with the invitation from President Estimé of Haiti, requesting that the Gastons tour his nation, A. G. and Minnie launched themselves on a series of trips that took them to parts of the world neither had ever dreamed they might see.

That this new period of exploration began in Haiti—a nation of primarily black and deeply impoverished people—was eerily appropriate. The levels of poverty Arthur and Minnie encountered on the island exceeded anything either had seen in their native Alabama, and it was impossible for the Gastons to ignore the nation's profound class differences. The Haitian government was black-run, and an elaborate caste system had been set in place to separate those with power from those without. In truth, this was no different from the situation both Minnie and Arthur had grown up with in the United States. But what made it feel peculiar was the fact that here, unlike at home, blacks were in control—and yet other blacks were still oppressed. As guests of the president they received the best of everything that was available, and it moved both of them to see blacks in positions of power in government. But there was no way to overlook the horrifying living conditions of those who resided beyond the palace gates.

If the trip to Haiti served to reawaken in Arthur the spirit of giving he had temporarily misplaced in his rush to make money, it was also a useful tool in helping him experience his "blackness" in a larger context—an opportunity granted to few blacks in those days (and today, as well). His time in Paris during the First World War had done much to apprise him of the different incarnations of blackness vis-à-vis the world, and more than twenty years later his time in Haiti would help reinforce the notion that life could in fact be different for blacks than it was in America. Haiti had its problems, to be sure, but it also afforded the opportunity to witness a people who had not been completely divorced from their African culture, and to observe a community in which blacks were involved in every level of state and government office. Such a sight served as a powerful indictment of American racism, even for a man like Gaston who believed so forcefully in the American way of life.

On a more practical level, the trip to Haiti was also a boon because it reaffirmed Gaston's belief in his own power as a businessman. Not long after his arrival, it was revealed that the invitation of the president had come because Estimé was, to put it bluntly, looking for a loan. The country was interested in securing ten million dollars in American financing, and the bank it had approached had agreed to lend the sum—but only at a high rate of interest. The president, therefore, decided to approach a few leading black businessmen to see if he could convince them to invest their own capital in the Haiti project.

Gaston was, he admitted, tickled pink to find himself called abroad by the president of a nation based on his business reputation. The hit he had taken with Brown Belle had burned him badly, and this firm pat on the shoulder from a source of authority went a long way toward healing that wound. He assured the president that he would do his best to make contact with banking interests back home, and before the day was out he found his picture splashed across the front page of a number of local newspapers. He was asked to make speeches before large crowds of eager Haitians. By the end of the trip, Gaston had become a genuine star.

Word of Gaston's success overseas accompanied him back to the United States, and he soon found that the Brown Belle disaster was, if not forgotten, certainly behind him. People were still taken by the sound of A. G. Gaston's name and still wanted his backing in matters of business and finance. Gaston was revitalized by the support he had found, both in Haiti and at home, and soon began dedicating himself once again to the maintenance and expansion of his empire. He returned to working his "usual" sixteen-hour day, even though the businesses were so finely tuned by this point that they were truly capable of operating without him. Still, he turned up every single day to oversee operations, to sign checks, to talk with his employees. And, importantly, to plot his next move.

BRITAIN, THE BAPTIST CONVENTION, AND THE BANK

Though Brown Belle had scared him off product manufacture, Gaston had no plan to rest idle. He had, by this point, amassed a large enough fortune to enable him to retire happily—but there was more he wished to accomplish. Through the latter years of the 1940s and into the early 1950s, Gaston focused his attentions on purchasing land throughout the Birmingham area. He bought lots scattered throughout the city, and also—importantly—acquired "the largest Negro cemetery in the area." Real estate was, in Gaston's opinion, one of the safest bets a man could make. It was the means he had used to build his own foundation as a young man (the lot he had paid for with his soldier's stipend was still, all these many years later, in his possession), and after the scare with the bottling company, safety was something he had come to appreciate even more.

In acquiring the extensive New Grace Hill Cemetery (purchased in 1951), along with the Mason City Cemetery, Gaston hammered the final nail into place in his vertically integrated business model. With the purchase of these sites, Gaston could now control every level of the business of dying, from preparation to interment. He owned the company that insured the burials, the mortuaries that prepared the bodies, and now, finally, the place where those bodies were interred. The significance of the purchase of the cemeteries was immense: It turned Gaston's business interests into a true empire, and transformed him into the giant of industry he had always dreamed of being. It was getting hard to live or die in Alabama without coming into contact with A. G. Gaston. As Carnegie was to steel and Rockefeller was to oil, so Gaston was becoming to dying.

In addition to his newly revived passion for real estate interests, in the late 1940s and early 1950s Gaston worked hard to strengthen his ties to community organizations. Though quickly approaching his sixties, he made perfectly certain that free time was not something he had a lot of. Any time not spent working at one business interest or another was dedicated to one of the many charitable or business organizations with which he had become involved over the years. Though Gaston's business affiliations ran the gamut from the Birmingham Business League to the Knights of Pythias, a special place of honor was reserved in his heart for the local African Methodist Episcopal church that he attended. The Birmingham A.M.E. was the same denomination as the church Idella Gaston, A. G.'s grandmother, had worked so assiduously to support, and Arthur had never forgotten her dedication to service. Even in his younger, struggling years in Fairfield, he had relied on the church both as a beacon of hope and as a social outlet. Now, these many years later, he knew it was time to begin giving back in earnest to a source that had given him and his family so much.

Gaston's involvement with the church—in matters both financial (he was a frequent and generous donor) and practical (he became a regular attendee and active participant in church governance)—

Your Decision

For your careful consideration we have presented a factual and pictorial review of our advantages as an institution in which to secure the essential training in the field of business. You will probably attend only one college or business school. Your choice, therefore, is of vital importance.

We have presented the facts. The decision rests with you—a job, a livelihood—a position with satisfying opportunities for going up and up.

This is the point at which many young people hesitate, postpone, and just never do get to making up their minds. They are the ones, who ten years later, are still marking time in mediocre positions, wondering how certain classmates of their school days got all the breaks.

They put off deciding until it is too late. The logical school years of their youth slip by. They take on added responsibilities. Some marry on the strength of jobs that seem adequate at the time and later they cannot go back to school.

We stated in the outset that great vistas of opportunities are gradually being opened to the Negro, that he is being integrated into practically every field and every level of employment, and that we are doing our part to help prepare him to accept these opportunities along with their rewards. In this connection we invite you to visit our modern school, see for yourself our facilities, the fine type of students, and the friendly, able instructors. Come when classes are in session so that you may observe the practical methods of teaching. We shall look forward with sincere pleasure to welcoming you soon and to helping you reap the lucrative rewards gained from taking THE FORWARD LOOK.

From the beginning, A. G. Gaston employed sophisticated advertising campaigns to promote his businesses. Pictured here, an early business school brochure.

quickly ratcheted him up the ladder of parish officials selected from the lay membership. Before long Gaston was a nationally acknowledged figure in the church association. In 1951 he was selected as the "official African Methodist Episcopal Church delegate to the World Ecumenical Conference in Oxford, England." Renamed the World Methodist Council at that conference, the meeting (which occurred every five years) brought together leading members of the worldwide Methodist community for the purpose of debating "theological and moral standards," as well as establishing the direction of church policy. The conference drew delegates from every corner of the world, and Gaston's selection as the U.S. delegate was as big an honor as any he had received to date. Attending the conference required sailing across the Atlantic—a trip Gaston had made once before in his life-

time, with a helmet strapped to his head. This time, however, he determined he would not make the trip alone—and he would make it in
style: He would take Minnie with him and they would explore the
continent of Europe together.

Their departure was scheduled for August 1951, on the grand
ship the *Queen Elizabeth*. The vessel sailed from New York, which
offered the Gastons their first opportunity since their nuptials to tour
the city in a leisurely manner. They had family there now: Minnie's
younger sister Elizabeth (whom she and A. G. had helped raise in
their Birmingham home) had married a man named Edwin Jenkins,
and in the early 1950s the couple had left Alabama and headed for
New York.

Ed Jenkins had spent the first years of his working life looking
out at the action on Birmingham's famous Fourth Avenue from the
windows of the Wheatley Printing Company. A typesetter in the days
when type was set by hand, Jenkins had big dreams that would carry
him beyond Fourth Avenue. He loved the business world (he would
eventually open a bowling alley and start a potato chip factory), and
by the time World War II arrived he had expanded his typesetting
skills into the magazine publishing business. Jenkins created *Newspic,*
the nation's first black pictorial magazine, which preceded *Ebony*
magazine and was distributed to black soldiers. It was a venture,
however, that could not survive the end of the war.

With the folding of this business, as well as of his first marriage,
Jenkins met and married the newly divorced Elizabeth Gardner, and
the two moved to New York, leaving Elizabeth's young daughter
Carol to live with her grandmother on the farm in Alabama. In New
York, Jenkins found employment in the printing industry as a lino-
type operator. Few blacks were allowed to apprentice in the printing
trades (which was generally the only way for printers to gain the requisite skills for the job), so Elizabeth and Ed Jenkins decided to take
matters into their own hands to ensure that blacks in the industry
could secure the proper training. For the next forty-five years, on
Park Avenue South in Manhattan, Mr. and Mrs. J. (as they were
called by their students) trained thousands of the country's black and
white printers at their school: The Printing Trades School. Elizabeth,

like her sister Minnie, not only served as her husband's partner, but also came to be known as a formidable businesswoman in her own right: She, too, served on educational committees, and at one point headed the National Association of Trade and Technical Schools.

Minnie and Arthur Gaston would see much of Ed and Liz Jenkins over the years, and this first trip on the *Queen Elizabeth* was no exception. One of Gaston's diaries from that time reports a meeting he and Jenkins had on that trip. That same diary also mentions what Gaston perceived as the exorbitant prices at the Waldorf Astoria—the Gastons' hotel of choice when visiting New York. The only thing in New York that irritated him, Gaston mentioned elsewhere, were "the Waldorf prices."

In his recounting of the 1951 European escapade, for the first time since becoming a rich man, Gaston vents about his anxiety regarding money—or at least regarding the spending of it. Throughout the chapter of his autobiography entitled "A Long Way from Demopolis," Gaston peppers his tales with constant reminders of the cost of this or that, and the—sometimes wonderful, sometimes awe-inspiring—extravagance of one thing or another. Their stateroom cabin filled with overflowing fruit baskets and flower arrangements; champagne and telegrams; the opulence of the boat itself, with its multiple swimming pools, decks, bars, and shops—not a single detail escaped Gaston's appraisal and comment.

What becomes evident in Gaston's repetition of this theme of luxury is not only his wonder at the excess surrounding him (and his desire to impress us with his ability to be a part of such a display), but the terror the scene induced in him. The boy from Demopolis that Gaston had been might not have worn a hair shirt like Booker T. Washington, but he had just as certainly never been exposed to anything like what he and Minnie were experiencing now. It was what he had worked for all of his days, this opportunity to have the best, but it clearly shook him to find himself in the middle of a reality woven from his dreams. Every corner of the ship housed a new extravagance, and though each was stored in his memory for recounting later, few were to actually be indulged in. The Gastons looked but did not touch much on their voyage across the Atlantic—a rare exception being the seven dollars Gaston allowed himself to lose at a bingo table on board. He always swore he never regretted it, but neither did he ever forget it.

Once in Oxford, Gaston immersed himself in the business of the conference while trying to absorb as much as possible about the town of Oxford itself. Though he was taken by the academic underpinnings of Oxford and its people, by his own account he spent much of his free time exploring the archives of Lincoln College for primary documents relating to early Methodist history. When not sequestered in the college's John Wesley reading room or touring the old town, Gaston attended conference lectures and seminars, listening attentively to and participating in the development of ideas and priorities for Methodist parishes around the world.

Of particular interest to Gaston was a plan, revealed at the conference, to bring a branch of the National Baptist Convention to his hometown of Birmingham in 1954. It was a revelation that would not only have a profound effect on Gaston and his growing fortune, but also ultimately come to play a pivotal role in the unfurling of history in the United States as it struggled to come to terms with the civil rights of its millions of black citizens.

The National Sunday School and Baptist Training Union Congress—the arm of the National Baptist Convention set to consider turning up in Birmingham in three short years—had a membership, Gaston knew, that numbered in the thousands. The influx of so many visitors would be an economic boon for the city—one that it would be foolish to let slip away. But Gaston could think of at least one good, and extremely troubling, reason that such a thing could easily come to pass. The National Baptist Convention's membership was diverse by any standards: Blacks as well as whites would be traveling to Birmingham if the convention were indeed to take place in the Magic City. The central problem, as Gaston immediately saw it, was this: There was simply no place for visiting blacks to stay.

> I began to consider the accommodations available for such a
> gathering in Birmingham. I was proud of the city and had many
> friends in the Convention. . . . It disturbed me that facilities for

Negroes were so limited. White hotels did not accept all races
and, with one or two exceptions, the Negro-operated hotels
were little more than shelter for transients.

The situation in Birmingham regarding travelers' accommodations was hardly inconsistent with the circumstances across the
South. Jim Crow had long since spread its shadow everywhere in the
region; segregation was a fact of daily life, announced without shame
on every storefront, water fountain, and restroom south of the
Mason-Dixon line, and hotel establishments were no exception to
that rule. Though a 1943 survey by the U.S. Travel Bureau reported
529 black hotels in existence across the nation, just under half of
these establishments were located in seven states (only two of
which—Virginia and Texas—were southern). In cities across the
South, black travelers were forced to lodge with friends or relatives
(if they happened to have any in the town they were visiting) or take
a chance on the often meager accommodations that were available to
them. In many cases, when neither option was viable, black would-be
travelers (and their money) simply stayed home.

If, for a time, this scenario suited the white establishment, it
would not continue to do so for much longer. And it certainly didn't
suit A. G. Gaston. What Gaston saw in the body of the National Baptist Convention was a set of consumers—black consumers, at that—
who would be willing to put money in his hand for the service of
providing them with adequate accommodations while in town. These
were blacks who, in service to God, would release their hold on their
discretionary income—who, importantly, *had* discretionary income—and who wanted, and were willing to pay for, the pleasure of
putting more than a tin roof over their heads when away from home.
What Gaston saw (and what many other businessmen, black and
white, were quickly coming to see themselves) was the emergence of
a defined black middle class whose tastes and needs could be catered
to at a profit. It was what Gaston had been doing all along, but here
before him, thousands of miles from home, arose the specter of a new
market segment. It was a simple enough equation: Birmingham
needed a fine black hotel if it was going to keep up with other cities

of its size, and Gaston, with his extensive resources (both financial and community-based) was in a perfect position to make the project happen.

It was an idea that pleased him greatly, one that he determined he "must look into when [he] got home." But for now, there was more work to be done in England—and then a much-deserved vacation.

The necessity of traveling to Oxford for the World Ecumenical Conference had allowed A. G. and Minnie the latitude to make a true adventure out of the voyage. After the conference had concluded they made plans to spend time in London as well as Germany, Luxembourg, Belgium, Monaco, Holland, Italy, and, of course, a return to France. Each destination seemed to impress them more than the last—in no small part, perhaps, because they were treated to the best of everything at every destination. Though associates with corporate interests provided some of these luxuries (the chauffeur and Rolls-Royce at their disposal were provided by friends at IBM), many were paid for by Gaston himself (all of which, again, he felt compelled to describe in detail).

Still, there is a joyfulness and spiritedness present in Gaston's description of his adventures in Europe that are unmatched elsewhere in his autobiography. Perhaps it was the joy of seeing Minnie so happy; perhaps it was the freedom of living for a time outside the boundaries of the United States and its racial segregation; perhaps it was simply that after more than thirty years of constant, grueling work, A. G. Gaston needed a break. Whatever it was, he was clearly happy. At some point during his time in Oxford, A. G. had decided to loosen his chokehold on his own purse strings and have a good time. When Minnie fretted over buying an expensive silver service, he sincerely tried to dissuade her from worrying over it. In Monaco he sidled up to the roulette table clad in his finest tuxedo and played long enough to lose badly and then win handily, at the side of the king of Belgium.

So relaxed was he, in fact, that it was not until Gaston had settled into his seat for his flight back to the United States that business returned to his mind—that is, new business. His first task on arriving back in Birmingham would be to take a closer look at just what stood between him and hotel development in the city. What he would find is that the answer was fairly simple: money. While there would be much agreement among local businessmen that there was a need to fill, few to none wanted to risk their own capital to fill it. So for the second time in his life, A. G. Gaston would step up and fill the need himself.

As a result of his long-standing belief in the solidity of the real estate market, Gaston had rarely passed up an opportunity to acquire pieces of commercial property in and around the larger Birmingham area. One of these lots, adjacent to the funeral home in downtown Birmingham, featured a building that caught Gaston's eye as a suitable site for a first-rate hotel. It would require extensive renovations and an influx of financing to the tune of approximately three hundred thousand dollars, but Gaston was on board. He hired architects to design the place, and arranged financing for the project in his own name. And in the early months of 1954—in time, of course, for the Baptist convention—the doors of the sixty-five-unit, fully air-conditioned A. G. Gaston Motel swung open.

As one Birmingham resident put it in a newspaper interview in *B'ham News,* "It was with pride after the opening that we could journey into other cities and boast of our first-class motel owned and operated by one of our people. It gave us a sense of belonging. . . . Here was the first motel in Birmingham in which Negroes could live. When groups didn't have the means to cover all of the expenses of their out-of-town guests, we just had to say to Dr. Gaston '. . . will you look out for them at your place?' The answer was always, 'Send them on.' "

Because blacks were not allowed to patronize Birmingham's downtown restaurants, Gaston added a restaurant and lounge to the motel as well. Top entertainment acts such as "Little" Stevie Wonder, The Temptations, and Little Richard performed there regularly. Among the famous early guests of the motel were current secretary of state Colin Powell and his brand-new wife, Alma Johnson. The new Mrs. Powell was the daughter of R. C. Johnson, the principal of Birmingham's black Parker High. After their August 25, 1962, marriage in Birmingham, the Powells ". . . spent our honeymoon night at the A. G. Gaston Motel, the only decent place in town for a black couple."

With the motel doing great business, Gaston looked ever further afield for means of expanding his interests. "It must have been divine guidance," Gaston wrote in his autobiography, "which caused me to invest my money in a lot instead of saving the cash, for the Penny Savings Bank failed, and many people in the Birmingham area lost their entire life savings. I only lost $15.00, the last payment on my lot." The lot that A. G. was referring to was the one he had purchased in 1914 for two hundred dollars and paid off over time with his army stipend (a piece of land that, in 1968, he would still claim to own). That lot, and Gaston's renewed consideration of it, would serve as the catalyst for two major businesses added to the Gaston realm in the 1950s: a real estate investment company and a bank.

By 1954 Gaston was renting out that prized original lot and the house on it, as well as a number of other properties, and grew to feel that an independent company was required to manage the increasingly demanding aspects of these real estate investments. Accordingly, Gaston formed the Vulcan Realty and Investment Corporation to manage not only his own properties but those of other landowners as well. Corporate profits from his other businesses were now funneled into land development, and Gaston began offering low-cost homes to those black citizens of Birmingham ". . . with income enough to buy, but without a conventional way to finance." If you happened to already own a lot of land, Gaston Homes would use that as collateral, and build you a house on it with "three bedrooms, one bath, living room, kitchen and dining area . . . for as little as $25 a month." Hundreds of would-be homeowners took Gaston up on his offer, and by 1972 the company was generating $1.5 million in revenues a year—more than half of what the insurance company earned during the same period.

After the incorporation of his real estate holdings, in 1957 Gaston opened the doors on the financial institution that would become the fiscal heart of black Birmingham. There had not been a black bank in the city since 1915, when the Penny Savings Bank folded. A rumor of management problems had triggered a run on the bank, leaving depositors stranded—and blacks in Birmingham with a limited ability to borrow for the next forty years.

Despite this critical gap in Birmingham's banking history, the American black banking tradition was a long one: In the fertile period from 1888 to 1934 some 134 black banks were founded across the country. The infamous Freedmen's Savings Bank, established at the end of the Civil War, was actually a white bank set up to handle black soldiers' pay, and ultimately held deposits of nearly three million dollars. Blacks, though allowed to make deposits, could not borrow from the bank. Famously, robber baron financier Jay Cooke borrowed half a million dollars from Freedmen's Savings, and when his business collapsed so did the bank, leaving thousands of (black) depositors bereft of their life savings.

The legitimately black banks that did exist were generally extensions of fraternal orders. The first, the True Reformers' bank, was established in 1881, and the Independent Order of St. Luke's in 1903—both in Richmond, Virginia. St. Luke's founder Maggie Lena Walker was the country's first woman bank president, and under her leadership the bank evolved into the most powerful banking institution in Richmond. It eventually became known as the Consolidated Bank and Trust Company and survives today. Despite the flourishing of these interests, however, the Depression and World War II took their toll on black banks: Of the 134 in existence as of 1934, only 6 remained in business after the war.

With the collapse of Birmingham's Penny Savings Bank in 1915, blacks were largely unable to secure mortgages and thus unable to invest in housing; as of 1956 the most any white bank would lend a black person to purchase a home was five thousand dollars—and even then the interest rate was inevitably higher than that offered to white borrowers (as banks believed blacks were a higher default risk). Many black businessmen, unable to secure capital investments in their interests, were unable to expand their companies as they would have liked.

Gaston thought it was time to change this dynamic, and with friend and lawyer Arthur Shores began the process of creating a savings and loan association in Birmingham. In 1956 Gaston and Shores submitted their application to the Alabama branch of the Federal Home Loan Bank Board; one major condition of approval was that the existing banks in the community had to agree that another lending institution was a necessary addition to the economic landscape.

The Birmingham banks replied in the negative to Gaston and

Shores's request to open their new bank, either because they feared
competition or were resistant to the idea of blacks having control of
any significant amount of money. The case was appealed to the National Federal Home Loan Bank Board in Washington, DC, and Gaston eventually won. All that was now required was for him to raise
$350,000 in deposits within a six-month period—a means of demon-
strating that investors were in fact interested in utilizing his bank.

As it turned out, many individual black investors, still trauma-
tized by the Penny Savings failure many years before, were frightened
by the prospect of another black bank and were hesitant to invest
their money in such a venture. In this instance, Gaston's saving grace,
as it had been before in his life, was the black church. Just as the Reverend Ravizee had supported his burial business in 1921, the black
ministers of Birmingham now stepped forward to fill the coffers of
his bank. Gaston promised the local churches that he would make
loans available to them for their building and refurbishment projects
if they turned over to him the savings they had collected from their
laity. The church leaders agreed, and within three months Gaston had
raised the requisite amount of money—and then some. By the time
the bank was chartered in 1957, he had raised nearly half a million
dollars.

The Citizens Federal Savings and Loan Association would go on
to become one of the major black banking institutions in the country.
With its help the black middle class was able to finance better homes,
and middle-class neighborhoods took on an increasingly luxurious
air. And true to his word, Gaston extended moneys to the churches,
and a wave of new construction began around the city.

Citizens Federal became known as A. G. Gaston's bank (and indeed it was his invention), but by law any single stockholder could own
only a 10 percent share in a savings and loan. Gaston assumed the pres-
idency of the bank and was offered a salary by its board in appreciation
for the contribution he'd made to Birmingham's black community.
Gaston turned it down. "Why should I be greedy," he said, "and take
money from an institution founded to fill a social need?"

Kirkwood Balton, who joined the Gaston enterprises in 1950 as
an auditor of company records (and would eventually rise to head the
bank), describes Gaston during this period as an incredibly gifted

businessman who kept track of every detail in his domain. Arriving at work early in the morning, he would sit behind his large desk and summon each business and department head to his office, individually. Apparently not a believer in the more egalitarian "conference table" concept of governing, Gaston preferred to have the information flow straight from the manager to the boss, in a one-on-one environment. He wanted to know what was going right, and what was going wrong. No details were meant to be spared.

Gaston made it his business to keep himself well informed—he read the *Wall Street Journal* every single day. He became an expert with the financials. In his dealings, he could be abrupt (with employees and family alike): If he felt his time was being wasted, he had no compunction about cutting a person short. Some people interpreted his style as "ruthless." But one man's ruthlessness is another man's ambition. Regardless, Gaston had evidently mastered the art of employee retention: There were many people, including Balton, who would work for the companies for forty or fifty years or more before retiring.

On the home front, things were similarly copacetic. A. G. and Minnie did a great deal of entertaining in these days—especially of

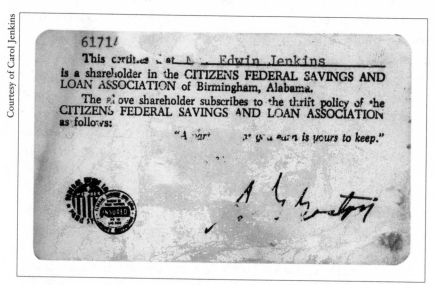

Citizens Federal shareholders card belonging to
Mr. Edwin G. Jenkins (father and grandfather of the authors)

their huge extended family. Every summer the Gastons would take on ten or twelve of the next generation (there were upwards of forty Gardner first cousins and five Gaston grandchildren), for instruction in an evenly divided curriculum: half Booker T. Washington, half W. E. B. DuBois. The expectation was that they would become "The Talented Tenth"—who typed. Attendance at the Booker T. Washington Business School was mandatory, and typing, shorthand note dictation, and business accounting were their summer break fare. Every Sunday they donned their hats and gloves and attended church en masse—*real* church, the kind that lasted for hours and where people sometimes fainted. Responsibility, honesty, and neatness counted above all.

On one infamous summer night, one visiting cousin made the mistake of leaving his or her washcloth in the tub after bathing. When Minnie discovered the lapse in the middle of the night, she roused the children one by one. Each person was marched to the tub individually to wring out the washcloth and hang it precisely on the rack where it belonged, while Minnie delivered a strongly worded lecture on responsibility. Once one child was back in bed, Minnie would throw the washcloth back in the tub and wake another—ready to impart her lesson to her next victim.

Minnie was also a strict believer in hard work and used peach canning time as yet another lesson in dedication to task. The Gaston's country house in Tarrant City sat in the middle of a large peach or-chard, and the visiting cousins were often put to work picking, peel-ing, and cutting peaches for hours on end. Minnie never failed to remind her nieces and nephews how fortunate they were in their lives, and used as an example her own days at Tuskegee, where she had been forced to change the straw stuffing in her mattress—every week. She reminded the young members of her family to "speak to everybody you see; it don't cost you a dime," in the attempt to ensure that this privileged generation of Gardners and Gastons wouldn't think themselves better than anybody they happened to meet. Minnie was the activist when it came to the children, A. G. a more benign presence; handling the children was her domain, not his.

In 1957 the Gastons sold both their city and country houses and bought a small farm in the Birmingham suburbs: a white southern colonial with soaring "plantation" columns. It sat on twenty acres of land and featured a swimming pool (both A. G. and Minnie loved to swim), a pond A. G. stocked with game fish, and gardens to satisfy Minnie's green thumb. It would be the house they would live in until the day they died.

All was ticking along well at Gaston enterprises and at home— even if there seemed to be trouble brewing elsewhere in the South. Though busy with his businesses, Gaston kept abreast of the news, and of particular interest to him was a little girl named Linda Brown who, in 1954, won her case before the Supreme Court of the United States. That case—*Brown v. Board of Education*—effectively destroyed the legality of the separate but equal dogma that had been authorized by the *Plessy v. Ferguson* decision of 1896. The new rule of law, as established in the *Brown* case, made it illegal for the separation, by race, of public education facilities on the grounds that policies of segregation are inherently unequal. Though *Brown* spoke specifically to the question of public education, the decision would usher in the period of civil rights activism that would ultimately define not only an era and a nation, but also a city—Birmingham—and, for better or worse, its people.

Not far from the center of that maelstrom sat A. G. Gaston. And soon, his motel.

THE CIVIL RIGHTS YEARS

*Money is no good unless it contributes
something to the community, unless it builds
a bridge to a better life.*

BIRMINGHAM, 1963

Since the fire hoses had been calibrated to a power strong enough to shear bark off a tree, it shouldn't have surprised him when the water blast lifted the girl high in the air and spiraled her small body down the street. It shouldn't have surprised him, but it did.

No one had a better view of the pitched battle between the dogs, children, and fire hoses that spring of 1963 than A. G. Gaston. From his office window on the third floor of the newly constructed million-and-a-half-dollar building bearing his name, he had an unimpeded vista of the scene unfolding below—one that included Kelly Ingram Park and, just beyond it, the Fourth Avenue black business district, much of which he owned. The Sixteenth Street Baptist Church, where demonstrators had taken to amassing by the thousands, was only one block away.

The phone Gaston had picked up moments before was still cupped to his ear. On the other end was his good friend, a local white attorney named David Vann. The melee ensuing outside his window shocked Gaston, but nothing more so than the sight of the young girl sent airborne by that brutal stream of water. "Lawyer Vann," Gaston remarked in horror to his friend, "they just rolled that little girl down the street." Whatever hesitations Gaston harbored about how this war should be waged were quickly dissolving.

Images captured by reporters on the ground and broadcast across the country would ignite a storm of controversy over Birmingham chief of police Bull Connor's treatment of protestors. Eventually, the national attention would bring down the ever-present WHITES ONLY signs and all they stood for—not only in Birmingham but throughout the South. The unrelentingly racist chief had stepped over a line that day, in more ways than one. What Gaston had seen floating down Fifth Avenue on sheets of rushing water was the dignity and safety of the black residents of Birmingham. As for many others around the nation, these images would transform Gaston, turning him from a reluctant participant in the rush toward desegregation into a powerful, visible broker of peace in his city.

RAGING ALABAMA

The years that had passed between Gaston's opening of the motel in downtown Birmingham and the groundbreaking demonstrations of 1963 had not been quiet ones, for either the Gaston empire or those battling in the arena of civil rights. Throughout the latter half of the 1950s, as Gaston sought to expand his holdings by establishing first the investment management corporation and then the bank, Alabama would be rocked again and again by the turmoil erupting from black demands for equal treatment under the law. To some, the fire began to burn in earnest in 1954—just after the Supreme Court handed down its decision in *Brown v. Board of Education.*

Reaction to the landmark decision had brought swift retaliation across the South, the most vehement of which always seemed to emanate from Alabama. In response to the Supreme Court's ruling, which declared the "separate but equal" doctrine unequal by its very nature, Alabama governor Gordon Persons wasted no time pronouncing integration "unthinkable." And to a large degree, it *was* unthinkable: After all, in Alabama, most service elevators still bore signs reading NIGGERS AND FREIGHT.

In Birmingham proper, city officials had a simple way of circum-

venting unwelcome edicts from above: When the law demanded that
the city integrate schools, the legislature chose to enact another law
that would allow schools to close their doors rather than desegregate.
Thus, in 1956, Birmingham's formerly all-white public schools were
shuttered for over a year to avoid admitting black students. Meanwhile, the state continued its hard work to delegitimize civil rights by
demanding from the NAACP a list of its membership (which had
grown to fifty-six branches with fourteen thousand members by
1956); when the group refused to hand such a list over, the state shut
its operations down wholesale. It would be eight years before the
NAACP would be a presence in Alabama again.

Of course, it wasn't just the politicians who were outraged by the
call to end segregation; white Alabamians of every ilk expressed their
displeasure in the streets. In one incident, a group of Klan thugs cas-
trated a black man and poured gasoline on his wounds, before setting
ten crosses ablaze at local public schools. The homes and churches of
black Birmingham were bombed with such frequency that the town
acquired the name "Bombingham"; the middle-class neighborhood
where many civil rights participants lived, "Dynamite Hill." Those
whites searching for a more "mainstream" way of organizing their
outrage (for some, the white sheets of the Klan seemed a little obvious) formed the notorious White Citizens Council. The group's
spokesmen concentrated on publicizing the perceived sexual threats
to white society that dismantling segregation would entail, and swore
to keep black men "out of the bedrooms of our white women." At its
peak the group claimed more than eighty thousand members in Alabama.

More than anything else, it was the extremity of Alabama's com-
bustible brutality that seemed to set it apart from its neighboring
states. Alabama didn't simply try to brush the concept of civil rights
out the door with a broom; it tried to beat the ideal (and any person
shouldering it) bloody before drowning it in a bucket out back. When
activists decided to test new interstate laws (which forbade segregation on buses and in bus stations) by mounting Freedom Rides
through the South in the summer of 1961, it was crossing the border
into Alabama that marked the beginning of real trouble for partici-

pants. In Anniston one of their buses was set on fire; angry whites attempted to hold the bus doors shut as passengers tried to escape the flames. Elsewhere in the state, things were not better. Student Nonviolent Coordinating Committee (SNCC) leader John Lewis described his experience in the Birmingham bus station as a wild mob of whites rushed the bus's interracial group of activists:

> They carried every makeshift weapon imaginable. Baseball bats, wooden boards, bricks, chains, tire irons, pipes, even garden tools—hoes, rakes. One group had women in front, their faces twisted in anger, screaming, "Git them niggers, GIT them niggers!" . . . I could see Jim Zwerg now, being horribly beaten. Someone had picked up his suitcase, which he had dropped, and swung it full force against his head. Another man then lifted Jim's head and held it between his knees while others, including women and children, hit and scratched at Jim's face. His eyes were shut. He was unconscious.

Alabama was, simply put, a horror when it came to either asking or answering questions of equality. This was of no surprise to anyone black who lived in the state. Nor had the black citizens of Alabama determined to take their treatment lying down. For years before the full-scale explosion of the civil rights movement would be sparked by the events of 1963, leaders of the black Birmingham community had been quietly (and, some may argue, effectively) agitating for changes within Birmingham's (white) power structure. A. G. Gaston was first among them.

AUTHERINE LUCY AND THE UNIVERSITY OF ALABAMA

Despite his critics' claims to the contrary, Gaston had waged a lifetime long effort to forward the cause of equality—if not in the most popular or predictable ways. Dating to as far back as 1920, when he established a "civic association" while still working in the mines, he had been involved in the Birmingham struggle for civil rights. In 1947 the local black newspaper *Birmingham World* reported that

Gaston was the author of "a [written] protest of the racially inspired revocation of a city permit for the construction of a Negro theatre." Aside from his deep involvement with the National Negro Business League in this period, Gaston was also among the group of white and black city leaders that founded the Birmingham branch of the Urban League. A more conservative organization than the NAACP, the association was invested in the creation of an interracial group that would focus its energies on the issue of black employment in the corporate world. In 1948 twenty-five blacks and fifteen whites met in Birmingham under the league's auspices for the first time, and twelve whites and twelve blacks were nominated to the board. Gaston was one of them.

Gaston had also played a unique role in the early-1950s integration attempts at the University of Alabama in Tuscaloosa. Birmingham lawyer and old friend Arthur Shores, along with NAACP Legal Defense Fund head (and future Supreme Court justice) Thurgood Marshall, had taken up the case of Autherine Lucy and Polly Myers. These two young women had been granted admission to the all-white university in 1952, but their offers of admission were rescinded when it was determined that they were black.

As Carl Rowan writes in his biography of Marshall, whatever his successes had been in other cases, Marshall "would soon learn that the universities and statehouses of the South were full of dream breakers, and that no state would put up more resistance to desegregation in higher education than Alabama." It would require four years of legal maneuvering to finally succeed in getting Autherine Lucy back into the University of Alabama (Polly Myers would fail in her attempt)—a blink in the eye of the justice system, but a sizable chunk of time in the life of a human being. Autherine Lucy was not a woman of means; she was a student in search of an education and, more immediately, a young woman in need of job. *Birmingham World* editor Emory Jackson, who was at the time assisting Marshall and Shores in the case, told Gaston about Ms. Lucy's need for work. Gaston instructed Jackson to send Lucy down to see Mrs. Gaston at the business college. There she was given a job doing secretarial work at a rate of pay that was more, in Jackson's estimation, than what she would have earned teaching school.

Once the case had been decided in her favor, Autherine Lucy headed back to Tuscaloosa to meet her fate, with Gaston also inadvertently figuring in her first, traumatic day at UAB. Arriving on campus in February 1956 to register for classes, she drove up to the school doors in one of Gaston's cars—described variously as a Cadillac and a Pontiac, but in either case too expensive a car for a black girl to be riding in by white Tuscaloosan tastes. They did not like that she arrived in that fancy car, was well dressed, and had paid for her registration with a crisp hundred-dollar bill. All of these elements added fuel to the building rage of the white students and agitators, who had begun to mount increasingly violent campus protests. At one point twelve hundred people gathered around a burning cross on the UAB campus, singing "Dixie" and shouting, "Keep 'Bama White!" In another instance, a mob chased after a dean's car that was transporting Lucy, throwing stones and eggs, bashing in a rear window, and shouting "Lynch the nigger!"

Lucy lasted only three days on the UAB campus before university trustees expelled her (ostensibly for her own safety), and legal action to reinstate her at the school failed. Following her departure, the University of Alabama would remain segregated until 1963, when self-acknowledged racist and then governor George Wallace would make a grand show of his momentary "stand in the schoolhouse door" before stepping aside to allow black students Vivian Malone and James Hood to enter.

Gaston's usefulness in the Lucy case had hinged on his ability to provide financial backing in an instance of need. And this wasn't the only instance. Gaston also took the opportunity to use his financial clout as a wedge for civil rights in Tuskegee, Alabama, throughout the 1950s. Though the city had four times as many black residents as whites, whites controlled the local government. This was a direct result of the fact that in Alabama, as in most southern states, literacy tests were required to register to vote. These tests were designed and administered by local government structures, often operating with the direct purpose of denying blacks the vote (in order to maintain white control of government). The (black run) Tuskegee Civic Association attempted to ameliorate registration conditions by launching a voter registration drive, but met with little success. "Many from the staff of the Tuskegee Institute, holders of advanced degrees including Ph.D.'s, failed to pass the voter registration test," Gaston reported in his autobiography.

Opting for another, more efficient, tactic, black residents of Tuskegee initiated a "business boycott in the late 1950s," which succeeded in closing a number of white businesses. White business owners retaliated by way of a twofold maneuver. First, a massive gerrymandering plan was instituted to cut the "cancer" of black influence out of the heart of Tuskegee. In 1957, "the Alabama legislature unanimously altered the city boundaries . . . putting all but four or five Negro voters outside the city, and changing the city map from a 4-sided to a 28-sided figure resembling a paralytic sea horse." Next, blacks in possession of home mortgages and business loans were targeted: Immediate repayment of all outstanding loans was demanded, as a means of breaking the wills (and the banks) of those who had had the temerity to ask for full inclusion in the American system.

Gaston once again stepped in to offer what few other blacks could: a financial alternative to certain ruin. Speaking before the angry and "frustrated" membership of the Tuskegee Civic Association, Gaston "assured [them] that our company was willing to take up any mortgages where undue pressure was being applied, and to advance mortgage money for Negro businesses and homes." As a part of this commitment, Gaston provided "over $100,000" to guarantee the opening of the black-owned ABC Super Market in Tuskegee.

A City on the Edge

Gaston was also willing, in certain instances, to take on the power structure in his hometown of Birmingham. In October 1961 Judge H. H. Grooms had ordered that all city pools and parks comply with local desegregation ordinances by January 15 of the following year. But the city's mayor, Art Hanes, opposed this action and hoped to use Gaston's influence (and perceived conservatism) to keep blacks away from white pools and parks. Rather than capitulate, Gaston took the reins of a group known as the Committee of 14 (a biracial subcommittee of the larger Committee of 100) to seek resolution of the issue. It was in this role that Gaston seemed to take his first steps into the public forum, calling for mass meetings to determine "what the Negro community wanted them to do in the future." Despite the committee's efforts, however, attempts at mediation failed and "sixty-seven parks, thirty-eight playgrounds, eight swimming pools, four golf courses, [the] zoo, art museum, state fair, municipal auditorium, and Legion Field stadium" were shut down as a result.

It was Sidney Smyer, president of the Birmingham Chamber of Commerce, who first invited Gaston to join the political fray in Birmingham. Smyer, who would himself become a major participant in 1963's events, believed it was important to keep the parks open and functioning; toward that end he had formed the Committee of 100— representing every significant white leader in the city—to begin meetings with black leaders to negotiate some kind of agreement. The white group filed a petition asking the city to reconsider the closings. Few blacks believed the businessmen were acting out of anything but self-interest, but if that self-interest happened to mesh with black aspirations, many blacks were willing to come on board.

What spurred Smyer to action? Simply put, money. Aside from serving as president of the chamber of commerce, Smyer was a successful businessman in his own right. Through his real estate company, he owned several downtown buildings and therefore had a very personal interest in keeping the Birmingham economy thriving. On a recent trip to Tokyo Smyer had found himself embarrassed in business meetings by news accounts of Bull Connor's legalized lawlessness back home, pictures of the battered Freedom Riders having traveled that far abroad.

Eugene "Bull" Connor had been terrorizing Birmingham since 1937. He had served four consecutive terms as public safety commissioner, skipped one, and was in office again in 1957 and 1961—for a combined total of twenty-six years in the commissioner's post. A former radio sportscaster and state legislator, Connor was a rabid and unabashed segregationist, even refusing to allow blacks and whites to even convene in the same place within the city limits. He was, effectively, the "boss" of Birmingham (despite the fact that he served with two other "co-commissioners") and quickly became known not only for his virulent politics but also his penchant for cruelty when it came to dealing with anyone who had dared cross him.

What Smyer began to understand on his trip to Japan (making him perhaps the first white leader of the city to do so) was that segregation and Bull Connor were bad for Birmingham's business. Connor's violence in dealing with protestors had raised the stakes; this was no longer a "family matter." The world did not like what it saw in Birmingham.

Motivated by the "dollar and cents thing," Smyer began to cultivate black leaders, and A. G. Gaston was at the top of his list. Smyer's advance would signal of the opening of a years-long and serious dialogue between the two men. When the city's commissioners finally rejected Judge Groom's order to desegregate—with Bull Connor publicly lecturing the "Big Mules" (as the white businessmen had come to be known) on the evils of integration—a movement to replace Connor, along with the entire system of Birmingham government, was born.

The Ambassador and His Wife

According to historian Barbara Ransby, during the civil rights movement black involvement fell into one of two distinct categories: "There were the deal-makers, who bargained for incremental change, and then there were troublemakers, who raised a ruckus." Placing Gaston in his proper place along this continuum is not a challenge. Gaston believed in incremental change; he was, unabashedly, a deal maker. But if accommodationist he was, he was at least an equal opportunity accommodationist. He believed in negotiations, not demands, no matter whom they were coming from.

In the period just before the street protests of 1963 bore down on the city, Gaston was an intrinsic part of Birmingham life: certainly the most successful, connected black businessman in the city, and astute enough to have honed his negotiating (some would say *compromising*) skills to a fine art. That art would turn out to be a crucial component to the resolution of the Birmingham problem.

As it happened, there were few in Birmingham who were fluent in the languages of all the combatants: poor blacks, middle-class blacks, and the white power structure often went head to head with little to no understanding of where exactly their opponents were coming from. Gaston had the advantage (and, in some cases, disadvantage) of having lived on both sides of the fence, as a person with power, and also as a person without it. He certainly understood the language of poverty and discrimination; he knew what black Birmingham meant when it called for "equality," even if he didn't always agree with the methods used to secure it.

Gaston was just as assured when he spoke the language of the rich businessmen, the corporate leaders he'd dealt with in running his own business interests for more than thirty years. Though he never forgot that his race made him different from the white business owners with whom he had dealings, he was unafraid of standing his ground on the issues he felt were important. In one instance, he threatened to close his account at the (white-owned and -run) First National Bank unless it removed the WHITES ONLY signs from its drinking fountain. The signs came down.

While it was A. G. Gaston who would go on to get most of the credit (and criticism) for his role in the movement, Minnie Gaston, too, played a formidable and important role in Birmingham city life. Ossie Ware was Minnie Gaston's right hand woman for some forty years, serving as her assistant at BTW Business College. Today she speaks of Minnie Gaston's compassion, above all. According to Ware, Mrs. Gaston was the kind of person who tried to help every single person she came in contact with—and succeeded in most cases. No matter what the request, or apparent need, she looked for a way to oblige. When others would caution Mrs. Gaston about her generosity, she would simply say "If they ask for something they don't need—that's on their conscience. But if they needed it, and I didn't give it, that's on my conscience. I'd rather give."

It was a philosophy she made sure to instill in her family, by way of example. She systematically set aside her own earnings over a forty-year period—in savings bonds for sisters and brothers and nieces and nephews—leaving a financial legacy of wealth sharing, and putting her own twist on one of her husband's rules: For Minnie, "pay yourself first," meant providing for the generations to come; it meant taking care of your sisters' children's children.

Minnie's sphere of influence was wide, and the company she kept stellar: Eleanor Roosevelt, Mary McLeod Bethune, and Charlotte Hawkins Brown were all women she counted among her acquaintances. Upon first meeting the young Ossie Ware, Mrs. Gaston set out to secure her a position with the renowned educator Charlotte Hawkins Brown. Brown had founded the Palmer Memorial Institute in Sedalia, North Carolina, in 1902 when she was only nineteen years old. Named for its white benefactor, Alice Freeman Palmer, the Palmer Institute was founded to teach its students improved agricultural methods (the accepted training for African American boys and girls at the time), but quickly evolved into a respected academic institution and an elite finishing school. By 1941 black families across the country were sending their children to the coed boarding school run by the formidable Hawkins Brown. In the small circle of black women educators, Minnie had become familiar with Hawkins Brown and her work, and suggested that young Ossie Ware would make a good assistant at Palmer. Soon enough, however, Minnie was enticing Ossie back to Birmingham—first to work as an assistant to A. G. But "Mrs. G couldn't give me up," Ware remarked, so she began her long career at the business college, watching Minnie Gaston at work.

Much like Charlotte Hawkins Brown, Minnie Gaston knew that there was more to success in life than merely acquiring work skills. She ran her own "finishing" school for students, where polished social skills were taught and practiced. Social events like cotillions, where refined young women were formally introduced to society, became regular events for middle-class blacks.

According to Ware, one of Minnie Gaston's greatest fans was the revered Mary McLeod Bethune. "Dr. Bethune adored Mrs. Gaston," Ware reported. Another great educator who like Minnie Gaston did her early teaching in Georgia, Mary McLeod Bethune founded a school for girls in Daytona Beach, Florida, in 1904. By 1923 her school had merged with an all boys academy to become Bethune-Cookman Institute, later Bethune-Cookman College. Dr. Bethune

From A. G. Gaston Enterprises promotional material

Booker T. Washington Business College Spring Dance
and Miss BTW. Mrs. Gaston insisted that her students
develop social skills along with their more practical education.

exercised enormous power as a friend and advisor of Eleanor Roosevelt. The lead member of black advisors known as the Black Cabinet, Dr. Bethune headed the Negro Affairs Division of the National Youth Administration during the New Deal and was a vocal presence during World War II. In 1935 she founded the National Council of Negro Women (which remains today a forceful organization in African American life). Minnie Gaston would later serve as an officer of the group, traveling to its Washington, D.C., headquarters to participate in formulating educational policy under the leadership of Bethune's successor, Dorothy Height.

Minnie Gaston had much in common with Bethune's good friend, Eleanor Roosevelt. Both were the wives of powerful men whose own works were overshadowed by their husbands'; both were nevertheless dedicated to building and maintaining their husbands' legacies. Eleanor Roosevelt's support of black Americans was well-known—most famous was her resignation from the Daughters of the American Revolution when the group refused to let African American

opera singer Marion Anderson sing in Constitution Hall. Roosevelt
helped arrange and attended Anderson's recital on the steps of the
Lincoln Memorial. But her concern was exhibited in her stand for the
rights of many less celebrated African Americans, as well: Letters,
now in the National Archives, were written by Mrs. Roosevelt on behalf of black elevator operators who had been fired from their jobs
and replaced by whites during the Great Depression. She spoke before the Urban League, A. Philip Randolph's Sleeping Car Porters'
Union, and the NAACP in the 1930s and 1940s.

In November of 1938 Eleanor Roosevelt appeared in Birmingham
as the keynote speaker for a biracial group, the Southern Conference
for Human Welfare. Objecting to the segregation of blacks on one side
of the room, and whites on the other, Roosevelt sat on a stool in the
center aisle. While we don't have evidence that Minnie Gaston was at
that early meeting, we do know, through Ossie Ware, that the two
women would eventually meet and manage to talk—despite the local
segregation laws that expressly forbade blacks and whites convening
together. Their courage in meeting at all cannot be understated—particularly given Bull Connor's penchant for prosecution.

Minnie, in the early years, was not afraid of much, and she made
a point of lending her support to the young activists and protestors
who made their way to Birmingham. Wyatt T. Walker remembers her
showing up at meetings and at the press where they were printing flyers to give them encouragement. While her plate of civic activities
was full—she worked with both the YWCA and the Girl Scouts
(where she spearheaded efforts to secure funds to renovate the old
wooden houses that served as their headquarters and worked to
make sure new buildings were erected), and with social organizations
like the Links and Alpha Kappa Alpha Sorority—she always, it
seemed, made time to give the activists her attention.

Soon enough, everyone else would be forced to give them their
attention, as well.

THE BUSINESS OF BOYCOTTS

When protests did finally erupt in Birmingham in 1962, activists' initial target was industry—not government. The protestors out on the

streets arrived with the goal of exacting concessions from white merchants, specifically the owners of the large department stores in
downtown Birmingham. Blacks spent a great deal of their money (an
estimated forty million dollars a year) in these stores without benefit
of either significant employment or access to basic amenities such as
dressing rooms or bathrooms. Shopping was therefore a compro-
mised experience for black patrons: With no alternative, many a
black mother had been forced to scurry her child into an alleyway to
urinate.

The indignities suffered at the hands of the department stores became a symbol of the breadth of discrimination blacks experienced
throughout Birmingham. And evidence trickling out of the Montgomery and Tuskegee boycotts served as proof that threatening to
cripple the establishment economically could be an effective bargaining tool. In Birmingham, discontent was turning quickly to rage.
Black citizens of the city had had enough.

Students from Miles College (located in nearby Fairfield) had
been staging sporadic protests at the downtown stores since 1960.
Spurred to action by the example of the four North Carolina A&T
students who on February 1, 1960, had taken their places at the
whites-only lunch counter in a Greensboro Woolworth's, black students across the South initiated a wave of direct actions in segregated
campus towns. Within a two-week period eleven southern cities
would become targets of the student sit-ins.

Black leaders in Birmingham, however, were aware that Bull
Connor's fuse was much shorter than that of most law enforcement
officers, and that he would have no compunction about resorting to
violence to maintain order in "his" city. As a result, the leaders did
what they could to blunt the students' enthusiasm for bringing direct
actions to Birmingham. A. G. Gaston sat on the board of directors of
Miles College, and in February 1962 he became directly involved in
the students' activist interests. His goal was to try to save the young
protestors from the brutality that was sure to be suffered at Connor's
hands. The students had planned to launch a black boycott of the
downtown stores, but Gaston and Miles College president Lucius
Pitts urged them to call it off (city laws forbade "boycotts," which
gave Connor a legitimate reason to arrest and thus harass them). To-

gether with Pitts, Gaston employed his adroitness in the business world to try to barter an agreement. He worked with the students to draw up and present their list of demands to the white merchants in a civil fashion, arranging for the students to meet with Smyer and other businessmen to discuss their concerns. The meetings took place in Smyer's downtown office. Since Smyer couldn't be seen meeting with blacks (for fear of Connor's response), Gaston and the students entered his office by way of the back alley.

An Activist of a Certain Ilk

The results of these meetings with Smyer were initially disappointing. Smyer himself seemed unaware that in one of his own buildings (the Frank Nelson Building), if the freight elevator happened to be unavailable or out of order, blacks were forced to climb as many as seven flights of stairs to conduct business. According to author Diane McWhorter, he asked Gaston and Pitts, "You mean those niggers can't even get an elevator?" (How such a shrewd and sympathetic businessman could be so totally unaware of the discriminatory policies of his own companies is something to be pondered.) However, upon learning of the situation, Smyer made the gigantic leap of desegregating the elevators in his buildings, and began working on getting the COLORED and WHITES ONLY signs removed from water fountains on his property.

That said, there was little else to make the nascent protesters feel hopeful. But for Gaston, the Miles College meetings were monumental. Working with the students seemed to ignite a spark in him, and had what has sometimes been described as a "militarizing effect." Perhaps his dismay at Smyer's ignorance played a part as well. Whatever the impetus, on February 12, 1962, Gaston made his first formal appearance at the movement meetings that had been taking place at various churches around the city. Since 1956, under the Reverend Fred Shuttlesworth's guidance, a network of fifty-five working-class churches had been rotating the hosting of these Monday-night "mass meetings," often drawing three hundred to four hundred people each week, and eventually thousands.

In response to the shutdown of the NAACP in 1956, Shuttlesworth (then pastor of the local Bethel Baptist Church) had formed the Alabama Movement for Human Rights (ACMHR). Its very first meetings were held in the Smith & Gaston Funeral Home. A fiery activist and organizer, Shuttlesworth had managed to coalesce the working-class "masses" of Birmingham into countless actions and protests over the years. Eventually ACMHR became an affiliate of Martin Luther King's Southern Christian Leadership Conference— organized after the successes in Montgomery in the 1950s. King, who sometimes opposed Shuttlesworth's style, nevertheless had to give the man his due: "Bull Connor doubtless regarded [ACMHR] as just another bunch of troublesome 'niggers,' " King wrote. "It soon became obvious even to Connor, however, that Shuttlesworth was in dead earnest." He was not a man to be messed with. Shuttlesworth was the most litigious of the civil rights activists, filing a record-breaking eleven lawsuits that reached the Supreme Court (including the Birmingham parks suit). Over the years, however, Shuttlesworth would pay a price for his outspokenness: His house was bombed and destroyed, his church dynamited, he and his wife "mobbed, beaten, and stabbed," and he himself jailed eight times.

Gaston, it is true, viewed Shuttlesworth with some "distrust." It had become clear very early on that the two men had directly opposite approaches to solving the problem of Birmingham's racism. Gaston had always wanted a peaceful denouement; Shuttlesworth hurled himself flagrantly against the obvious injustice. What they would come to realize, however, is that these differences didn't mean they couldn't work together as an inadvertent "good cop–bad cop" team, with Shuttlesworth threatening, and Gaston approaching the negotiating table with open arms.

On the night in February when Gaston first spoke to the crowd, things were not as usual. That night, it was not Shuttlesworth running the meeting, but the young preacher Martin Luther King, come to visit from Atlanta (Shuttlesworth spent the months of January and February 1962 in jail, at Bull Connor's specific request). Gaston addressed the crowd first. He used the platform to praise black efforts on behalf of desegregation, before adding his trademark appeal to "the good white people in Birmingham." It was a stance that would define his civil rights involvement, as well as one that would generate his most vehement opposition. Perhaps reading the thoughts of the crowd that evening, in his own speech King wisely cautioned against the widening distrust among Negro leaders.

Beginning with his speech that night, Gaston—along with Lucius Pitts, attorney Arthur Shores, and insurance executive John Drew (who was also vice chairman of Gaston's Citizens Federal Bank)—stepped forward to represent the moderate wing of black leadership in Birmingham. Where before he had publicly held his tongue on matters of integration, working behind the scenes by lending his money but not his mouth, now Gaston felt ready to speak out when called upon. He might have felt that without him, the situation would explode beyond repair. He may very well have been right.

———

By March 1962 Shuttlesworth (who had also been serving as adviser to the Birmingham students from prison) was released from jail. It was clear by this point that the white retailers had no plans to respond to the students' entreaty. No reply had been received to letters that Frank Dukes, the Miles student body president, sent to the merchants requesting desegregation of restrooms, water fountains, lunch counters, and hiring practices. Backing away from the threat of boycotting was not an option (it would only weaken the movement's bargaining power), and so, with the Miles students in the lead, the Easter "selective buying" protest began. On March 29 Lucius Pitts issued a statement to the press proclaiming widespread endorsement of the boycott, "from Shuttlesworth on the left to A. G. Gaston on the right."

With near-total support from the black middle class (including a car pool established by black society women to "[transport] students from campus to assignments patrolling downtown"), in its early days the protest was estimated to have operated with 85 to 90 percent effectiveness. Over the two-week Easter period, sales in Birmingham dropped 15 percent. The boycott was effective enough to raise the ire of Bull Connor, who quickly denounced the action and declared, "I don't intend to sit here and take it for a minute." And he didn't. In response, the city canceled its surplus food program for the poor, most of whose recipients were black. At least in part as a result of this pressure, over time, black resolve to "Wear Your Old Clothes for Freedom"—the boycott's motto, meant to remind blacks to resist the urge to patronize the department stores—diminished significantly.

THE NEGOTIATIONS

As enthusiasm for the boycotts began to flag Fred Shuttlesworth believed he had the key to igniting the next phase of Birmingham's civil rights movement: Martin Luther King Jr. and the Southern Christian Leadership Council. King was the head of the SCLC, a church-based civil rights group founded after the success of the Montgomery bus boycott in 1955. Then a minister at Montgomery's Dexter Avenue Baptist Church, King was just twenty-six years old when Rosa Parks famously refused to give up her seat on a bus. The Montgomery Improvement Association chose him as leader despite his youth. Blacks in Montgomery refused to ride local buses for a year under the MIA's (and thus, King's) orders and eventually forced the integration of bus services in the city. King, a follower of Gandhi's nonviolent philosophy of resistance, had become a national hero after the success in Montgomery. In 1959 he relocated to Atlanta to join his father as pastor at Ebenezer Baptist Church.

Shuttlesworth had long been trying to convince King that a demonstration in Birmingham would be central to desegregating the entire South. "I assure you," Shuttlesworth famously wrote to King, "if you come to Birmingham, we will not only gain prestige but really shake the country. If you win in Birmingham, as Birmingham goes, so goes the nation." King, however, was hesitant—the SCLC had just backed away from an unsuccessful protest in Albany, Georgia, where the local police chief's refusal to contest their action had caused it to fizzle. With Bull Connor, King knew, there would be no such lack of response; the question in this case was precisely the opposite: Just how brutal would Connor be?

After much resistance, at an SCLC board meeting in Chattanooga, Tennessee, in May 1962, King finally made a concession. He announced that the organization would indeed be going to Birmingham that September—but only with the purpose of holding its annual convention there. Still, Shuttlesworth knew the impact of the decision. He knew that most of Birmingham, black and white, believed that if King was as much as in the same city as Bull Connor, there would be trouble. And Shuttlesworth did nothing to dissuade anyone of that supposition.

Sid Smyer heard the rumor that King was coming to town and promptly called A. G. Gaston. The chamber of commerce had recently formed a "Senior Citizens Committee" made up of the leading white men of Birmingham, commissioned to solve the city's racial problems before King did it for them. Smyer, as head of the committee, wanted to know what he had to do to prevent demonstrations in the city. Gaston and the other moderate black leaders (Pitts, Shores, and John Drew) told Smyer that he would have to deal directly with Shuttlesworth, as he was the one who had extended the invitation to King in the first place. Moreover, they informed him, Shuttlesworth was the man who led the people; he was the one who'd be doing the marching, not them.

The "Senior Citizens" were resistant to the idea of negotiating with Shuttlesworth, but the U.S. attorney general, Robert Kennedy, wanted to hear what Gaston and other black leaders had to say and encouraged the white businessmen to at least hear them out. Movement leaders initially hoped that Kennedy would use his influence to convince the white retailers to make concessions. This, however, was not to be. Kennedy had other things on his mind—namely, at that point, getting James Meredith enrolled at the University of Mississippi. Negotiations stalled.

With little help coming from Washington (for either side), back in Birmingham A. G. Gaston took another stab at moving things along by reiterating his advice to Smyer. "Fred's the man that's got the folks," he told the Senior Citizens. "I got some money, but that's all. Money don't run this thing now. He's the man with the marbles. You have to talk to the marbles." It seemed that this time, the white establishment was willing to listen. With just a few days left before the

September SCLC gathering in Birmingham, a meeting was called: Smyer, Roper Dial of Sears, Roebuck & Company, and Isadore Pizitz of Pizitz Department Store were among its white participants; Gaston, Shuttlesworth, and Pitts sat across the table from them, there to speak on behalf of black interests. Smyer was not vague about what he had to say: He told Shuttlesworth that his group just couldn't make promises for all the merchants. Rising swiftly from his seat, Shuttlesworth offered his simple reply: "Well, I'm talking to the wrong crowd then. Let's go, gentlemen. Y'all wasting my time. I'm busy. I'm fighting segregation." He exited the room directly.

Cooler heads prevailed when talks resumed the next day. Gaston, realizing that he had the best perspective on the problem, turned first to Isadore Pizitz and appealed to his family history. Pizitz's father had started in the retail business much as A. B. Loveman had, carrying fabrics door-to-door on his back, and both of his parents had been supporters of the Tuggle Institute. The Pizitz store was a favorite of black shoppers, including Minnie Gaston, who shopped for her nieces and nephews there. "Your father and I," Gaston remarked to Pizitz, "started in the business at the same time. Both of us got our fortunes off poor folk and black folk." Drawing the link between the elder Pizitz and himself, Gaston—ever the statesman—calmly encouraged Pizitz toward reason.

Shuttlesworth, true to his "bad cop" role, then threw everything he had at the waffling merchant. He promised Pizitz that both he and Martin Luther King would have to be dragged from his store by Bull Connor himself if he didn't acquiesce, that the two men would go to jail and not eat or shave if Pizitz didn't make the required concessions. Shuttlesworth warned, "Folks will see how bad we're treated, and I'm sure there won't be nobody shopping with you."

Roper Dial, manager of the local Sears, perhaps envisioning the scene and recognizing that an impasse could lead to disaster, quickly offered that *perhaps* his janitor *could* paint over the WHITES ONLY signs in his store. Before anyone could object or demand, he excused himself to make a call. Upon returning, he announced, "My janitor accidentally painted over a sign." Shuttlesworth, flush with satisfaction, commented, "Now you're a white man with some sense."

Reluctantly, the other merchants followed Dial's lead. The offensive signage came down all over town. Water fountains and restrooms lost their labels of WHITE and COLORED and a feeling of joy settled over black Birmingham—at least temporarily.

Connor's Revenge

On September 25, 1962, three hundred attendees of the annual SCLC convention arrived in Birmingham. Baseball pioneer Jackie Robinson and outspoken New York congressman Adam Clayton Powell were featured speakers at the event. Sammy Davis Jr. performed as part of an SCLC fund-raiser. Many if not most of the convention participants were staying at the A. G. Gaston Motel, dining in the restaurant, or holding meetings in the A. G. Gaston Building.

Late on the morning of Friday, September 28, as King addressed the convention's final session in the L. R. Hall Auditorium of the Gaston Building, a young white man seated in the sixth row rose from his seat and rushed the stage. He attacked King, striking him about the face and body a number of times. King never retaliated. He "made no move to strike back or turn away. Instead he looked at his assailant and spoke calmly to him." The Birmingham police detained the attacker, Roy James, a twenty-four-year-old member of the Nazi Party from Arlington, Virginia, but King refused to press charges.

It was a scene Gaston would always remember—in part because it brought to light one of his major differences with King. In a 1975 interview Gaston was known to have remarked that the one thing he never understood about King was his dedication to nonviolence. Martin, Gaston commented, was always talking about "love," and that was one thing Gaston, in his own words, couldn't quite get along with. Gaston, for all of his skill as a mediator and his deference to the white community in many situations, was not the biggest believer in turning the other cheek. "I always felt," he told one *Ebony* reporter, "that if somebody hit me, I would have to hit them back."

The incident was the violent end to what had been an essentially peaceful gathering. What black residents of Birmingham could not know at the time was that Roy James's actions had set the tone for life in the city for months to come.

As soon as the conference ended, the WHITES ONLY signs that had come down from Birmingham's fountains and restrooms went right back up where they had been for decades. White businessmen claimed that Bull Connor had threatened them with fines if they refused to comply with the signage ordinance. Connor had apparently forced one merchant to spend nine thousand dollars on unnecessary repairs on a newly desegregated elevator in retaliation for those missing signs. The police chief, it was said, had the town in the palm of his hand. The whole city, blacks as well as whites, rich as well as poor, obeyed him out of plain old fear.

If things seemed bad in Birmingham with Connor in power, matters only got worse when the state governorship changed hands in January 1963. The new head of state, George Wallace, wasted no time proclaiming his position on the subject of race from the mountaintops. Speaking in bold, grandiose terms, he declared, "In the name of the greatest people that have ever trod this earth, I draw the line in the dust and toss the gauntlet before the feet of tyranny. And I say, Segregation now! Segregation tomorrow! Segregation forever!"

However lyrical their declarations, the combination of Wallace and Connor proved too much for even some white Alabamians to bear. Despite the political current that had brought Wallace to power, many white citizens of Birmingham were beginning to grasp that segregation's days in the city were numbered. Specifically, Gaston's friend Sid Smyer had begun to work to remove Bull Connor from the Birmingham equation. In the end, the issue for Smyer and others in business wasn't race baiting; what galled them into action was Connor's superior attitude in relation to the white business elite. It was one thing to treat blacks as if they didn't matter, a whole other to treat privileged whites the same way. In refusing to allow Smyer and his compatriots to honor their pledge to black leadership, Connor signed the deed on his own political demise.

Back in February 1961 Smyer had contacted the Birmingham Bar Association about a change in the form of the city's government. As it stood then, the city was set up to be run by three commissioners and a mayor. Bull Connor was one of these city commissioners and, by way of his consistent bullying tactics, effectively ran the city, overriding his fellow administrators as well as Mayor Art Hanes. Smyer wanted to replace this system with an arrangement that called for a mayor and a nine-member city council. He felt that this kind of structure would be more representative of the desires of Birmingham citizens—and would also help in cooling the city's racially charged environment. The Birmingham Bar Association agreed, and in February 1962 recommended the change. A young white lawyer, David Vann (who would become a close friend of Gaston's and, some years later, mayor himself), was enlisted to head up a petition drive. He managed to get eleven thousand white voters to sign in favor of implementing the measure. A referendum was set for November 1962.

Remembering his father-in-law's passion for voting rights, A. G. Gaston led the effort to get blacks into the booths that November. With John Drew, he headed up the Jefferson County Voters League Progressive Democratic Conference. When the election was held it was clear that the black vote had carried the reform to victory: The referendum passed, 19,317 votes for, and 16,916 against.

Gaston's old employer, Tennessee Coal and Iron, inserted itself into the electoral discussion at this point, siding with Connor, who was fighting to keep the old system (and his power) firmly in place. The steel interests wanted to maintain their control over labor in the mines and mills, and any change to the status quo would jeopardize their standing. They forced the referendum into court, challenging the legality of attempting to change the city's government system. While the court eventually upheld the new form of government, the question that remained was *when* the measure would take effect: immediately, or not until after Connor and his associates' terms were completed in 1965. The Alabama Supreme Court would supply the answer—but only after the upcoming mayoral elections had been held.

The elections were set for March 1963. Though Bull Connor deplored the new configuration of government, he decided he would run for mayor, anyway, alongside his fellow commissioner Jabo Waggoner, and Tom King, a liberal who had lost to Art Hanes in the 1961 mayoral race. Sid Smyer and the white businessmen chose as their candidate a man named Albert Boutwell. Hardly pro-integrationist, Boutwell had been the architect of the law that had allowed Birmingham whites to avoid implementing the *Brown* decision by shutting down the city's schools. As a result, Boutwell had the support of white supremacists as well as that of the moderates pushing his candidacy.

Voters cast a historic 44,736 ballots in the March election: 17,434 for Boutwell, and 13,780 for Connor. Liberal Tom King won most of the black vote, despite Gaston's efforts to turn the tide in Boutwell's favor. Apparently even Gaston—who had worked in cooperation with David Vann to try to get Boutwell elected—had not been able to persuade black voters that it was in their interest to vote for the man who kept Birmingham's schools segregated when given a more liberal option. While Boutwell's strong showing was an indication that Connor was losing ground with the citizens of Birmingham, it did not garner him enough votes to forestall a runoff, scheduled to take place one month later, in April.

The rematch, on April 2, set yet another new polling record: This time around, 51,278 citizens turned up to cast votes. And this time, black voters had few doubts. Given the choice between a continuation of Bull Connor's terror tactics, with which they were all too familiar, and the uncertainty of life under Albert Boutwell, they chose Boutwell en masse. Boutwell's margin of victory was eight thousand votes. Virtually all ten thousand black voters had cast their ballots in his favor. Though only a small percentage of Birmingham's blacks were actually able to vote, their votes had made the difference in creating a new government—and electing a new mayor. For Gaston, who had worked tirelessly to "get out the vote," it was a triumph of leadership in the public domain.

But Bull Connor wasn't gone yet. The state supreme court still hadn't issued its ruling on *when* exactly the referendum on the new system of government would go into effect. The steel interests advised Connor to stay in office until a ruling was handed down. Newly elected Mayor Boutwell moved into an office next door to Connor's in city hall, and for six weeks both administrations attempted to run the municipality according to their own logic.

As Birmingham edged its way closer and closer to outright confrontation, it began to gain renown as the only city in the world with two mayors, a King, and a parade every day.

The Call to Demonstrate

By April 1963 King and Shuttlesworth had postponed the opening of their planned protests three times to avoid interfering with electoral politics. They had no interest in energizing the pro-racist, pro-Connor electorate, but there was also little expectation that a change in mayor would bring down segregation. King felt that while Boutwell was obviously a gentler man than Connor was, they were both, in the end, segregationists. Protests were inevitable if things in Birmingham were going to change, King was certain. It was a question of when, not if.

Replicating the tactics of the Miles College students, King and Shuttlesworth finally chose the Easter shopping period to stage their strike at the downtown stores. The Birmingham Manifesto, issued by the movement the day after the runoff, declared to the public that the protests represented "Birmingham's moment of truth in which every citizen can play his part in her larger destiny." As the manifesto's imposing language suggested, the stakes on this one were exceedingly high.

A. G. Gaston's part in this particular drama would be prominent, and conflicted. Gaston adamantly believed that demonstrations would be destructive to the delicate political process that he had been involved in on a day-to-day basis for years. He was not in support of them. Having helped put Boutwell in office, Gaston now lobbied to give him the chance to negotiate an end to segregation. Yet at the very time that Gaston, the man, was arguing against the "invasion" of King and his troops, the Gaston Motel was being retrofitted for what would turn out to be one of the most important battles of the civil rights era. There was no more likely place for King's group to set up its official Birmingham headquarters than the A. G. Gaston Motel.

King and his colleagues Ralph Abernathy and Wyatt Walker had descended upon the motel as of February to plot what would come to be known as "Project C." The C ominously stood for "confrontation," and Gaston wanted none of it.

Nevertheless, Room Number 30, the motel's best suite, was taken over by King and Abernathy for use as the "war room" where strategy sessions and debriefings would take place. Their staff occupied other rooms throughout the motel. Shuttlesworth (who had accepted a job in Ohio years before but returned to Birmingham frequently) stayed here, too. Abernathy described the accommodations in this manner:

> The Gaston Motel was Birmingham's only acceptable black inn,
> the place where black business and professional people stayed
> when they visited the city. It was not luxurious, but it was as
> well furnished and well decorated as most of the white motels
> and hotels. We were given the best suite in the motel—two
> rooms located right above the lobby—one bedroom with two
> double beds and a sitting room with chairs, a table, and a desk.

It was a motel, courtyard, and restaurant that would become as well known to America in 1963 as any other Birmingham landmark. King's daily news conferences announcing plans and successes were held there. In his autobiography, Andy Young, King's young aide (who would go on the become the mayor of Atlanta and a UN ambassador), reminisced about the time spent at the Gaston Motel in the Birmingham years. As interest in the movement grew,

> . . . the gatherings in the courtyard and restaurant of the
> L-shaped, two storied motel increased. Gaston's was beginning
> to resemble Grand Central Station at rush hour. The motel
> bubbled with activity and discussions on a twenty-four hour
> basis. It had become the site of a national meeting and greeting
> convention, an ongoing debating society on the pertinent
> questions of the movement, a place where supporters
> might meet or see or talk with Martin if he was available, a

continuing educational seminar on the movement conducted
by Wyatt for visiting reporters and supporters, and a magnet
for the curious and for celebrity hounds.

The movement paid for its rooms, even though there were those
who thought Gaston should have given them to the leadership rent-
free. Ever the businessman, Gaston did give them what he considered
a discount. Furthermore, the vacant Smith & Gaston Building, formerly the funeral home (which had moved to a new location), was
annexed for office space; the A. L. Smith Auditorium was provided
for large meetings. And according to Wyatt Walker, office supplies
and printing presses (whose operation was overseen by A. G. Gaston
Jr. and which were used to create the movement's endless flyers)
were supplied to the movement free of charge by Gaston.

It wasn't just Gaston's possessions that were important to the
movement. Abernathy spoke openly of the group's realization that in
any fight in Birmingham, it was better to have Gaston on your side
than opposing you. "Gaston was one of several important community leaders we wanted to enlist in addition to the clergy," Abernathy
wrote. "He was very sympathetic to our cause and very generous
with his financial support. We knew that more than any other man in
black business circles, he could help us establish our credibility in
Birmingham."

But Gaston, like most of middle-class black Birmingham, was in
no mood to abandon the results of what had been the most effective
voter registration effort for blacks in the history of the city. With a
string of successes—first effecting a referendum, and then tossing
Connor out of office—Gaston saw evidence of increasing possibilities for participation *within* the system. It was unlikely that he could
turn his back on the biracial committees that had produced the
change in order to now support widespread sit-ins and street
protests. The whites on these committees expected him to exert his
influence to prevent these actions, not encourage them and Gaston
was, as ever, loathe to burn any bridges. Therefore, the opening
salvos of the campaign came and went without Gaston's participation.

On April 3 the protests began in earnest. Demonstrators targeted lunch counters at Loveman's, Britling's, Newberry's, Woolworth's, and Pizitz's department stores. The first arrests were made at Britling's. No one knew then that ultimately there would be thousands.

The next day, April 4, a news release was issued stating the protest's aims. The leaders called for:

1. Desegregation of all lunch counters and all public facilities in all downtown stores.

2. Immediate establishment of fair hiring practices in those stores.

3. The dropping of all charges against those who had been arrested during sit-ins.

4. The establishment of fair hiring practices in all city departments.

5. Reopening of city parks and playgrounds, all of which were closed to avoid desegregation.

6. The establishment of a biracial group to work out a timetable for desegregation of all Birmingham schools.

The list was broad, and ambitious. Over the next few days, protests continued, without much incident. Then, on April 7, Palm Sunday, the movement got the spur it needed: During a peaceful parade, a nonmovement spectator got into a fight with a couple of Bull Connor's dogs. According to eyewitnesses, "a knife flashed" when the young man rose to defend himself, and then, in an instant, "a German shepherd tore his arm and police knocked him to the ground and kicked him. Suddenly onlookers, officers, and other dogs rushed over the fallen man." The project had its first "confrontation." Extensive news coverage would follow. Back at the A. G. Gaston Motel,

Wyatt Walker was said to have started jumping around Room 30, yelling, "We've got a movement. They brought out the dogs. We've got a movement."

The incident may have energized the campaign, but A. G. Gaston still wasn't fully on board—and that angered some movement leaders deeply. Abernathy, at one late-night mass meeting, preached about the danger of "Uncle Toms" and how to get rid of them. No one had to guess too hard about which Uncle Tom in particular he had in mind. Gaston remained steadfastly opposed to what King and his people were doing on the streets of his city—and he wasn't alone: In the early days of the campaign few middle-class blacks volunteered to participate in movement activities.

On Monday, April 8, Gaston called a meeting at the Gaston Building with King and one hundred local black leaders to allow the preacher to make his appeal for their support. Before he could get it, though, King would be forced to answer a few hard questions. There was much reluctance, even resentment, on the part of some in the crowd that day, but King faced it down. He would not be moved. He told his audience bluntly, "This is the most segregated city in America. . . ." and informed them in no uncertain terms that they would have to "stick together" if they ever hoped to have a better life in Birmingham.

If King was trying to teach Gaston and Birmingham's black middle class a lesson in radicalism, Gaston, at least, was in no mood to listen. The young man's presumptiveness was beginning to get under his skin. Rather than helping matters, the meeting on April 8 only seemed to further polarize Gaston and his contingent from where King and the SCLC were headed. Gaston, however, was not going to simply go away; neither were the protests. So the next day Gaston released a statement to the press:

> I regret the absence of continued communication between the
> white and Negro leadership in our city and the inability of
> the white merchants and power structure of our community
> to influence the City Fathers to establish an official line of
> communication between the races in our city.

... There is no doubt in my mind, or in the minds of any of
us, concerning the aspirations of the Negro citizens in this community and throughout the country. We want freedom and justice; and we want to be able to live and work with dignity. ...
Today, Birmingham stands on the threshold of transition, and I
feel it will be a transition to greatness. ... I, therefore, call upon
all the citizens of Birmingham to work harmoniously and together
in a spirit of brotherly love to solve the problems of our city, giving due recognition to the local colored leadership among us.

That last line, singling out "local" leadership (which King, who
had come in from Atlanta, was not), infuriated both King and his followers. Some suggested that Gaston's businesses be added to the list
of those that were being picketed by activists. That idea met a quick
end: Ed Gardner—an aide to Fred Shuttlesworth and Birmingham
citizen who had grown up under the Gaston aura—wasted no time
informing the group that "If you picket Gaston, we'll send every last
one of you back to Atlanta." Civil rights were one thing; loyalty, it
seemed, was another.

Though it was his own aide who had saved Gaston from picketing by the movement, Fred Shuttlesworth was as furious about Gaston's statement as anybody. It was a slap in the face to movement
leaders, and Shuttlesworth, who had been putting his life on the line
in service to the cause for years now, resented it. The minister publicly accused Gaston of charging too much for rooms at the motel,
and called him a "*super* Uncle Tom" to the press. Soon enough,
though, Shuttlesworth realized the error of his move and offered an
apology to the businessman. Despite Gaston's age (seventy) and size
(quite small), it was rumored that these two men had had to be pulled
apart physically once before. Gaston was tough, and had garnered a
reputation (deserved or not) for being vindictive when crossed.

Shuttlesworth apologized because the movement needed Gaston,
but also because it was absolutely necessary to project at least the appearance of solidarity to the world at large. Wyatt Walker and Shuttlesworth took pains to defend Gaston from New York reporters who
had picked up on Gaston's critique and lambasted him for it. Instead

of acknowledging the "local" slap, black movement leaders spun Gaston's statement into an endorsement. Walker and Shuttlesworth issued separate statements highlighting how Gaston had been advising on the effort for more than a year, serving as a negotiator. For those who knew about Gaston's indefatigable mediating efforts before the SCLC conference, it was the truth.

In a further attempt to bring Gaston into the fold (and to appease the "local" black businessmen and clergy), King set up an advisory committee of twenty-five men and women who would meet every morning at the Gaston Motel to "approve the day's strategy." At least for the time being, it gave Gaston (and others like him) some say in how things would be done. It wouldn't take long for it to become clear that Gaston disagreed in a fundamental way with the SCLC's methods—but by then there would be no way he could hold shut the floodgates opening on the streets of Birmingham.

"Damn the Torpedoes:" Demonstrations at Last

On April 10, 1963, Bull Connor got a temporary injunction from state circuit court judge W. A. Jenkins prohibiting the movement from any more direct actions: no marching, no picketing, no sit-ins or parades. The court order was served to Martin Luther King, Ralph Abernathy, and Fred Shuttlesworth as they held forth in the Gaston restaurant at one o'clock in the morning on April 11. King read the injunction to the ever-present reporters gathered around him, noting ever so calmly that the injunction appeared to be a violation of their constitutional rights.

At a formal news conference later that day, there was more clarity about whether or not the injunction was to be obeyed. "Damn the torpedoes. Full speed ahead," Shuttlesworth announced. On April 12, Good Friday, there would be a demonstration, and the leaders would submit to arrest. King's statement gave the reasoning: "We believe in a system of law based on justice and morality. Out of our great love for the Constitution of the U.S. and our desire to purify the judicial system of the state of Alabama, we risk this critical move with an awareness of the possible consequences involved."

The morning newspaper on that Good Friday put a damper on the planned action. The *Birmingham News* contained a letter, signed by eleven of Birmingham's leading white ministers, labeling the planned march as "unwise and untimely." Ralph Abernathy said King "brooded" over how to respond. Shortly, there was a knock on the door of Room 30. A. G. Gaston and other members of the recently appointed "advisory board" were there to talk King out of defying the injunction. As Abernathy wrote:

> We recognized the line they were taking. It came from the white Birmingham merchants, who did a brisk business during Holy Week and were terrified that they would lose money . . . they had been influenced by these white men they regarded as their friends . . . it was precisely the greed of the white merchants on which we were counting. In the end, we were betting they would care more about dollars than they would about Jim Crow.

Abernathy remembered Gaston lecturing King about the sanctity of the Easter season and the need to obey the law, as well on the dangers of the violence that seemed to be more and more certain. The scolding went on for a while. At some point, according to Abernathy, King said, "Ralph, I'm going to march regardless of what they say." Though the visitors to Room 30 had managed to "convince themselves all over again" that ceasing and desisting on the protests was the way to go, King, in Abernathy's recollection, remained firm. Addressing the pillars of black Birmingham society seated about the room, he ended the meeting politely. "Thank you for your words of advice," King said, "but we're going to have to march. Now."

Gaston and the group were left behind in the motel as King, Abernathy, and Shuttlesworth made their way to a rally at the Zion Hill Church. Then, with hundreds of supporters following them, they marched straight up Seventeenth Street. Bull Connor was waiting for them. King and Abernathy were unceremoniously picked up by the seats of their pants and thrown into the back of a paddy wagon. They were carted off to the Jefferson County jail and placed in solitary confinement. Fifty other protestors were arrested right along with them. Shuttlesworth was arrested at his home later in the day.

Direct actions continued through the weekend, with blacks attempting to attend white churches across the city on Easter Sunday. Two churches admitted them.

On Monday, April 15, Albert Boutwell was inaugurated as mayor. An estimated one hundred blacks, including A. G. and Minnie Gaston, attended the ceremonies. Boutwell declared that "the city government of Birmingham would not submit to intimidation or interference" of protesters. By this point, 260 people had been jailed for taking part in the weekend's actions. Arthur Shores and NAACP Legal Defense lawyer Norman Amaker spent that Monday in court, filing an application to dissolve Connor's injunction.

It was during this time, while still "brooding" about the white ministers' newspaper criticism, that King composed his famous "Letter from a Birmingham Jail." Begun on the margin of a newspaper that someone had smuggled into his cell and on tiny slips of paper, King's letter was released to the press on April 16. "You may well ask," he wrote, " 'Why direct action? Why sit-ins, marches, and so forth. Isn't negotiation a better path?' " It was a direct challenge to Gaston's proposed methods. But King would answer his own question in his own manner, writing: "You are quite right in calling for negotiation. Indeed, this is the very purpose of direct action . . . to create a situation so crisis-packed that it will inevitably open the door to negotiation." Erudite in the extreme, King had turned his black opponents' arguments into a mere extension of his own. Some bought it; others, notably Gaston, did not.

On April 20, eight days after being arrested, King and Abernathy were suddenly freed from jail. According to Andy Young, the news that someone had posted bail came as a surprise to movement leaders. King and his supporters had felt it was a better move politically for Martin to stay in prison; the "Letter from a Birmingham Jail" was creating interest around the world, and the extended jail time made King look good as a leader, willing to endure great deprivation for his cause.

It is Young's theory that it was Gaston who put up the bond, in order to "persuade [King] to stop the demonstrations and leave Birmingham." Young believes Gaston acted, in this case, out of self-interest, fearing retaliation against his businesses if King persisted with his direct actions. But even Young was forced to admit that, "notwithstanding his possible role in Martin's untimely release from jail, A. J. [*sic*] Gaston played an important part in supporting the Birmingham movement." Gaston himself refused to comment on the matter of King's bail one way or another.

D-Day and the Children of War

If Gaston did in fact provide the money for the leaders' release in this case, had he known what was coming he might have kept his cash in his pocket. Once King and Abernathy were out of jail, they almost immediately created the "crisis-packed situation" King had been searching for. It was determined that schoolchildren would, from that point forward, become an integral part of the Birmingham protests. David Garrow has suggested that the turn to the use of students may have been prompted by the fact that the news media was tiring of the Birmingham story. King is said to have told a confidante, "You know, we've got to get something going. The press is leaving. . . ." And without the press in their corner, King knew, the mountain would be that much harder to climb.

In truth, the movement had still failed to generate active participation in much of the black population—middle class, working class, or poor. As Taylor Branch put it, by this point the "grand Birmingham campaign showed signs of terminal weakness. . . ." King and his crew may have made for a good story, but by and large the black citizens of Birmingham just weren't showing up to put their lives on the line for the cause. The lack of turnout was a serious problem for the leadership, and members of King's staff had become desperate for solutions.

The scheme to incorporate children into the movement's actions was devised by one of King's aides. James Bevel, who developed the plan, believed that children would be more willing to fill the streets than their parents; their activism and idealism was more rabid (and thus more useful) than the elder generation's. Putting the children in the streets—and watching Connor's response to them—had the makings of great drama, and the movement sorely needed something to jolt it out of the doldrums. King, however, was concerned. Although he would later hold that using the children was the right thing to do, during its planning stages, he was not immediately convinced of the sagacity of the move. He was, after all, a father himself.

On Thursday, April 25, Sid Smyer and David Vann indicated to Gaston that renewed negotiations between white merchants and the black leadership might be able to take place "soon." Gaston was glad to hear it, but it was obvious even to him that the merchants were moving much too slowly for the SCLC's satisfaction. By the next Tuesday, leaflets encouraging students to join demonstrations in the streets had made their way into the local high schools. School principals, attempting to keep students away from the protests, padlocked the school doors. At Parker High, students climbed out of windows to escape. A disc jockey at WENN (the black radio station that Gaston would later buy) broadcast coded messages over the air detailing where and when students should meet.

Thursday, May 2, was known as "D-Day" to organizers. As preparation for the noon march took place, King reportedly wrestled with his conscience regarding using the children. Nevertheless, things went ahead as scheduled. While King remained inside the motel, wave after wave of students—some as young as six years old—set out from the Sixteenth Street Baptist Church and walked straight into the arms of Bull Connor's police. Six hundred children were arrested that day—so many that the jails were literally filled to overflowing. So many that more than a few had to be penned in the open stockyards at the state fair. It rained that day, and Edna Gardner (Mrs. Gaston's sister-in-law) remembers taking newspapers to the children in the stockyards so they would have something to cover their heads. Condoleeza Rice, who would become national security adviser under President George W. Bush, was a young child in Birmingham at the time. Her parents had not let her participate in the demonstrations, but her father, a minister, did take her to see her friends who had been detained. She never forgot riding on his shoulders through the crowd that day, watching as he consoled his parishioners.

Watching, too, was A. G. Gaston. And he was livid. He was not alone in his outrage. Local blacks, the national press, and even the ruling clan in Washington all registered their disapproval. Robert Kennedy made an official statement condemning the action, stating that "school children participating in street demonstrations is a dangerous business. An injured, maimed or dead child is a price that none of us can afford to pay."

Gaston pulled no punches in vocalizing his objections to what King and others had done. When asked about the protests Gaston replied, "As a responsible citizen of Birmingham, I deplore the invasion of our schools to enlist students for demonstrations during school hours. I do not condone violence or violation of the law on the part of anyone and I am sure all responsible Negro citizens share this thought." At the motel the next day, Gaston told King face to face, "Let those kids stay in school. They don't know nothing." King, by now accustomed to going head to head with Gaston, replied, "Brother Gaston, let those people go into the streets where they'll learn something."

That day—D-Day + 1, May 3, 1963—things finally turned not just ugly, but brutal. On the first day of the children's march, Bull Connor had shown some restraint in the use of dogs and fire hoses. But by day two, the sight of an endless supply of willing prisoners made Connor snap. "Bring the dogs," he commanded. And the dogs came, snarling and lunging ferociously, straining against their leather leashes, ready to attack.

As Andy Young remembered it, "The police ran through the park, swinging their billy-clubs at marchers, onlookers, and newsmen—anyone in the way. Kelly Ingram Park was exploding with insanity and terror."

The fire hose attachments had been ratcheted up. The monitor guns were now fed by two hoses, making them twice as powerful as what the city had determined was necessary to put out any major fire. The fabric of shirts and dresses peeled away under that level of pressure, the people wearing them knocked straight off their feet. Or, if you were a small girl, you might have taken flight, hoisted as you were in the air and pinwheeling down the street, head over heels.

Gaston, surveying the scene from his office window, had finally been converted. If the image of that little girl spinning through the air proved anything to him, it proved how truly debased Bull Connor was—and how morally negligent any person who allowed his actions to continue unabated. That meant white businessmen, the U.S. government, and A. G. Gaston himself.

David Vann was still on the line. "Lawyer Vann," Gaston said, "I can't talk with you now or ever. My people are out there fighting for their lives and my freedom. I have to go help them." With that, he hung up the phone.

BROKERING THE PEACE

*Never spit in a lion's face when you've
got your hand in his mouth.*

BIRMINGHAM, 1963

Featured in newspapers across the country, the page-one pho-
tographs of police dogs ripping the clothing and flesh of Birmingham's children meant many things to many people. It spoke of the
end of an era, the depravity of one particular man, and the desperation of a class of people willing to face any threat in order to escape
their oppression. But perhaps most importantly of all, the dissemina-
tion of those pictures of bruised and beaten children meant, finally,
that Washington would have to help Birmingham, too. Watching the
melee had made him "sick," Robert Kennedy said, and he put Assistant Attorney General Burke Marshall on a plane to Birmingham to
try to negotiate a peace. Marshall was not new to the Birmingham
saga; he had long been trading daily phone calls with Gaston, King,
and David Vann. He already knew how tense the situation had become. The question now was, what could actually be "negotiated."
What did King want?

Upon arriving in Birmingham, Marshall began meeting separately
with the black and white factions. At his urging, on Sunday, May 5,
white businessmen "reluctantly agreed" that their only option was to
meet with their black counterparts if they intended to end the de-

structive events. Even though the idea of granting concessions was "offensive to all present," they instructed Smyer and Vann to contact A. G. Gaston and request a meeting "that night."

The two groups met together at John Drew's home that same evening, and, in a discussion led by Gaston and Arthur Shores, the blacks presented their four "Points for Progress." They were:

1. The immediate desegregation of all store facilities, including lunch counters, restrooms, and fitting rooms.

2. The immediate upgrading of store employees and nondiscriminatory hiring.

3. Merchant pressure on the city government to drop charges against the jailed protestors.

4. Merchant pressure on city government to establish a biracial committee to deal with future problems.

The white businessmen's response to the presentation didn't give much cause for optimism. No one present at the meeting seemed willing to give. Shuttlesworth warned the merchants that the protests could be kept up indefinitely, causing continuing damage to local businesses. The white merchants were unmoved. Perhaps they didn't believe the protesters had the fortitude to carry out their threats.

On Tuesday, May 7, as King, Gaston, and 125 white businessmen met downtown to continue negotiations, four thousand young people gathered at the Sixteenth Street Baptist Church to deliver the message that would finally make the businessmen understand what lay ahead if they refused to concede. According to King, the two groups had reached a point in discussions where he felt no progress would be made. They broke for lunch. Emerging from the building, negotiators realized that "Negroes had marched on the town. . . . There were Negroes on the sidewalks, in the streets, standing, sitting in the aisles of downtown stores. There were square blocks of Negroes, a veritable sea of black faces." The jails had been filled to capacity, so only a few arrests could be made. It was, by all accounts, an astonishing sight.

Three hours later, the white merchants acquiesced to some of the movement's demands. King, feeling flush with victory and believing that the merchants were negotiating in good faith, called a twenty-four-hour truce.

The victory was to be short lived. Upon learning of the merchants' capitulation, Bull Connor (in an attempt to derail the settlement) ordered King and Abernathy to be hauled back to court to face the Good Friday charges of parading without a permit. Judge Charles Brown found them guilty of the charges, and set bail not at the expected three hundred dollars per man but at the exorbitant twenty-five hundred dollars apiece. Stunned, King and Abernathy protested the excessive bond and, rather than paying it, opted to return to jail.

In response to Connor's interference and the court's obvious pandering, Shuttlesworth and others threatened to start up the protests again. The president and attorney general became alarmed that the settlement was falling apart. Marshall, under pressure from his bosses, decided (along with black leaders) that the best way to neutralize Connor (and save the peace) was to post the bail. Gaston—the richest black man in Birmingham—was asked to front the money for the bonds. He wrote the checks without hesitation.

If the events of the preceding months had proved that no single black man held the power to influence white Birmingham, Gaston nevertheless wielded enormous power within the parallel construct of black Birmingham: By 1963 he employed some five hundred people, with a payroll of a million and a half dollars. The bank he had founded in 1957 continued on its trajectory of expansion, growing its holdings "from an initial $350,000 in 1957 to 1.7 million in June 1958, $3 million in July 1959, and $4 million in June 1960." Though he had often been accused of taking a soft line on desegregation for his own business benefit, what is true is that Gaston left behind a legacy of passionate involvement in the civil rights cause—not least of all by providing crucial financial backing when the movement was in need.

While the struggle for equality rocking Birmingham had been

nominally aimed at ameliorating life for the "masses," there was no better example of the absurdity of segregation than Gaston himself—a fact of which he was patently aware. In his memoir of the era, Andrew Young tells of an interview in the early 1960s with a black citizen of Birmingham. The man had witnessed A. G. Gaston entering a Chinese restaurant in town. Gaston pulled up to the establishment in his luxury sedan, and then, like every other black person in the South, went around to the back "colored" entrance for takeout. "The stinking kitchen door!" the man exclaimed. "And he's the richest black man I ever heard of." The man named Gaston who owned a bank, an insurance company, a motel, funeral homes, a business school, and office buildings—a man who employed hundreds of people and contributed tens of thousands of dollars to the city's coffers—had no more authority than the next black person to walk through the front door of any given restaurant, take a seat, and have lunch.

Nevertheless, Gaston had a perspective on the events of the 1960s that few active in the movement could claim to share. Viewing the city though the lens of nearly sixty years of living and working there, Gaston knew that things had truly gotten better for blacks in Birmingham. His moderation stemmed precisely from this knowledge. As he pointed out in his autobiography,

> A 1957 survey revealed that Negro family income in Birmingham was the highest in the Southeast. The number of families earning over $4000 had increased more than 300% between 1950 and 1957, when almost half the Negroes in the city owned their own homes. New apartments had been constructed and subdivisions built. Negroes were building fast . . . homes, churches, hospitals, businesses.

For Gaston, the measure of success was to be calculated, at least in part, on appreciating assets. And along those lines, blacks in Birmingham were making slow, if meaningful advances.

Gaston was outspoken in his belief that for blacks "economic potential should equal our civil rights advancement. A first class broke man will find it very difficult to use his civil rights to the fullest. . . . We cannot fight and beg from those we fight at the same time." His age and experience had taught him this much, though it would be years before most participants and observers of the movement understood what he meant by this economic imperative. In the meanwhile, Gaston determined to use his own financial advantage to keep the movement afloat—and to maintain his own influence over events as they played out.

The Banker and the Preacher

Gaston may not have been a huge fan of King's over the years, but in 1963 he had a strong rationale for keeping the preacher out of prison: "While Martin Luther was confined, more militant splinter groups of the Movement were whipping the Negroes into an ugly mood. I put up $2,500 bail and got King out. He was needed to calm and control the colored community. I felt his continued imprisonment would further agitate my people."

King, however, had had other ideas. As in his original Good Friday arrest, King had hoped to use this incarceration as a bargaining chip in the larger battles being fought. He did not want to be released from jail. Despite repeated requests, the white businessmen had refused to use their influence (or money) to free the more than two thousand movement protestors—many of them children—still languishing in jail. King was looking for a way to force the point, and felt that his imprisonment, with its attendant risk of further protests, would make the retailers relent.

Gaston, believing he knew the businessmen better, was convinced that King was wrong—and that this time around someone was going to get killed. With the "active encouragement" of Robert Kennedy (who believed that Connor was counting on a riot to bring federal troops into the city), Gaston bailed King and Abernathy out of jail—once again against their wills.

There was, however, still the matter of the jailed protestors. With King out of jail, there was little reason for the merchants to cave. Having effectively destroyed King's perceived "bargaining chip,"

Gaston agreed to step in to help secure the protestors' liberation. As Gaston remembered it, "Bond for their release was $237,000. I was asked to guarantee $160,000 of the bail money, which I gladly did." The remainder of the bond was financed by four local guilds of the United Auto Workers, each of which agreed to post forty thousand dollars, matching Gaston.

On May 10 King, Abernathy, and Shuttlesworth held a news conference in the courtyard of the Gaston Motel, officially announcing the truce that had been negotiated on the 7th. They represented the black movement only; there would be no "joint" statement with their white counterparts. Shuttlesworth, it must be said, objected to what he felt was King's caving in to the white businessmen. He had been out of the loop when the terms were agreed to, hospitalized by a blast from one of Connor's fire hoses. Shuttlesworth was shocked when he learned of the final terms of agreement; they fell significantly short of what black leaders had originally asked for. So enraged was he that he threatened to take his people back to the streets to fight for more. Only a direct order from Robert Kennedy dissuaded him. Therefore, it was a reluctant Shuttlesworth who read that day, "The city of Birmingham has reached an accord with its conscience. . . ."

The terms were, unquestionably, short of what had been originally demanded. There would be no "immediate" moves in any direction. Instead,

1. Lunch counters, restrooms, and drinking fountains would be desegregated in planned stages within ninety days of signing.

2. The upgrading in hiring would take place within sixty days.

3. The merchants would cooperate with movement lawyers in getting jailed protestors out on bond (not eliminating bond, as had been hoped).

4. Communications would be established between black and white factions to prevent the necessity of further demonstrations (another biracial committee).

In addition to the loss of immediacy, any expectation that the merchants would exert pressure on the city disappeared from the agreement. The businessmen had always maintained that they spoke only for themselves—and what could be accomplished in the downtown shopping district of Birmingham—and they held to that idea in their agreement.

King, at least publicly, was satisfied with the settlement, offering this optimistic statement to a waiting public: "I am happy to report to you this afternoon that we have commitments that the walls of segregation will crumble in Birmingham, and they will crumble soon."

THE MOTHER'S DAY RIOT

What crumbled in downtown Birmingham on May 12, 1963, was not segregation, however. It was the facade of the A. G. Gaston Motel, blown to bits by a bomb strategically placed to kill anyone who happened to be in Room 30: King and Abernathy's headquarters. As it turned out, its occupants had vacated the room only a short while before the bomb went off. There had been a victory celebration after the announcement of the settlement on May 10; the next day King and Abernathy returned to their churches in Atlanta to preach. In the early-morning hours of that Sunday, just as nightlife was ending in the black section of town, the bomb at the Gaston Motel exploded, obliterating Room 30 and destroying adjacent rooms and offices below. To leave no doubt about whom the bombers were after, another explosion was detonated that same night at the home of A. D. King, Martin's brother. Fortunately, no one was home there, either.

At the scene of both incidents, blacks became enraged. In Kelly Ingram Park, across the street from the motel, some two thousand spectators gathered. Rocks and bricks were thrown, a car overturned. Police quickly labeled it a riot, and came in swinging billy clubs. Blacks yelled for Bull Connor. "We'll kill him," they chanted. An ambulance carried away the four people who'd been injured in the motel blast—none of them seriously.

As movement workers spread through the crowd, urging people to go home, Colonel Al Lingo of the Alabama state troopers appeared on the scene. Lingo, sent into the fray at the direct request of Governor George Wallace, led a merciless charge of his men, clubbing any blacks who still happened to be left on the street. The troopers entered the Gaston Motel compound, searching for more "rioters." Claude Sitton of the *Times* wrote that, "the 'thunk' of clubs striking heads could be heard across the street." Wyatt Walker's wife was assaulted as she tried to get into their room at the motel. Walker found her on the floor, victim of a rifle butt to her head, and carried her to the hospital. On his way back to the motel, he was beaten by police himself.

The degenerate behavior of the state troopers further inflamed black onlookers, who, infuriated, now began their own rampage through town. By dawn six businesses, a two-story apartment complex, and several cars were destroyed—and seventy people had been taken to the hospital. A twenty-eight-block area of the city had been sealed off, including the motel, which was now without water, telephone, or electricity. It was Mother's Day in Birmingham, 1963. The incident would come to be known as the Mother's Day Riot.

In the aftermath of the insurgence, the question on everyone's mind was whether the settlement had been destroyed. Burke Marshall was called into President Kennedy's office to answer just that question. Kennedy believed that the segregationists' intent (Connor's first among them) was to obliterate the agreement. He had Marshall call King. King assured the assistant attorney general that he was encouraging blacks to remain peaceful. He warned him, however, that if the white businessmen backed away from the agreement, all bets were off. Sid Smyer made his own phone call to Washington to assure Marshall that for their part, the white businessmen planned to live up to their end of the bargain.

The settlement seemed safe, at least for the moment. In a live broadcast to the public that night, President Kennedy announced to the nation, "The Birmingham agreement was and is a fair and just accord. The federal government will not permit it to be sabotaged by a few extremists on either side." Just in case the extremists weren't paying attention, Kennedy moved federal troops to the outskirts of the city.

The presence of these troops would prove persuasive in another ongoing conflict a few miles from Birmingham in the town of Tuscaloosa. George Wallace had been brought into office on his "segregation forever" pledge, and it came to a test at the University of Alabama at Tuscaloosa on June 11. Wallace had vowed to "stand in the schoolhouse door" to prevent black students from entering the university. But pressure from the Kennedy administration made it seem as if that promise would be difficult to keep. Instead, Wallace negotiated a face-saving compromise with the administration: They would give him the opportunity to stand in the schoolhouse door, living up to his political promises, but he would then step aside and the students would enter another part of the campus. While federal troops stood guard, this is exactly what played out.

That night, President Kennedy went on television to announce his new civil rights legislation, forbidding discrimination in education, employment, public accommodations, and transportation. "The events in Birmingham and elsewhere have so increased the cries for equality that no city or state or legislative body can prudently choose to ignore them," he declared. The legislation was sweeping in scope, as were Kennedy's words. If any doubt remained about whether Jim Crow was on the run, Kennedy's address sought to squash it, once and for all.

As always, however, the segregationists had their own answer. Hours later, just after midnight on June 12, civil rights activist Medgar Evers was shot dead in Jackson, Mississippi. Kennedy himself would never live to see his legislation enacted.

Three Bombings, Four Deaths

In comparison with the spring events, the summer of 1963 was a relatively quiet one in Birmingham. But there were presentiments of trouble ahead. Arthur Shores's home was bombed; at Loveman's Department Store, as it began to comply with the desegregation settlement, a tear gas explosion sent twenty shoppers to the hospital.

The March on Washington on August 28 unequivocally captured the world's attention, as nearly three hundred thousand people gathered peacefully at the Lincoln Memorial to hear Martin Luther King deliver his "I Have a Dream" speech. King himself later observed that the major benefit of the event may have been that for the first time, national news coverage showed blacks in serious discussion about important events—as opposed to the by now familiar images of them fleeing dogs and being beaten by police.

As September 1963 rolled around, A. G. Gaston was busy running his businesses and watching warily as the city began to boil again. The home of Gaston's friend and attorney Arthur Shores was bombed once again. Blacks took to the streets yet again, staging an all-out battle with police that ended with one black dead and another twenty-one hospitalized. Integration of the public schools had long since been ordered, but the new mayor, whom Gaston had fought so hard to get elected, was using delay tactics. At Governor Wallace's demand, Boutwell had closed the targeted schools, asking the court to consider the "inherent differences in the races" in making its decision—not moves bound to reassure the black voters who, following Gaston's lead, had put him in office.

In the midst of this new erosion of civility in Birmingham, there was, however, one "cheerful" episode for Gaston: an invitation from President and Mrs. Kennedy for Dr. and Mrs. Gaston to visit the White House. The occasion was a state dinner for the king and queen of Afghanistan.

The invitation was the most cherished sign of recognition A. G. Gaston had yet received. He recalls reading and rereading the invitation, showing it to his friends, convinced by the very fact that he was holding it in his hands that "America was the greatest country in the world. . . . If I, as a Negro with little education and no influence, could progress from a Black Belt farm of Alabama to a seat at a White House dinner, then anybody could." The invitation reinforced Gaston's philosophy that a person's success was an individual, not a group endeavor, and that any American who did not build "a purposeful, satisfying life for himself just didn't have it on the inside." (He did concede that by this time he'd been a longtime contributor to the Democratic Party, which may have helped him garner the request for his company; however, he never considered his acquiescence to the Kennedy administration's request to bail King out of jail as having played a major role.)

Gaston described the dinner as a "grand affair," involving various international and national officials. After Kennedy had introduced everyone in the room, he singled out the couple from Birmingham. "I am so sorry, Mr. Gaston," the president offered, turning to face A. G., "to hear of the racial disturbances in your Birmingham." Gaston thanked the president for his concern. He then sat down beside his wife to enjoy his meal, more elated, by his own estimation, than he had ever been in his life.

Gaston's euphoric mood would quickly fade. Back at home the following evening, A. G. and Minnie had just retired for the night, their live-out staff all having departed, when a firebomb sailed through a first-floor window of their house. The bomb exploded and began to burn through the living room, filling the house with smoke. A. G. awoke to Minnie's cries: "I started running for her . . . she was in the living room, standing beside a burned lamp shade, and tears rolled down her terrified face."

Minnie placed the call to the sheriff. She thought she had heard someone come up the drive earlier, but hadn't thought it was cause for alarm. Though an intercom had been installed at the entrance gate to the property (through which it was necessary to call to gain entrance), it was possible that the gate had been left open by a departing employee. Upon arrival, sheriff's deputies sealed off the grounds to the estate, which included (as the front-page newspaper accounts made ample note) the main house, a guest cottage, and a swimming pool.

Investigations revealed that two bombs had actually been thrown. One made its way inside the house while the other scorched an exterior wall and fell back outside. They were amateur bombs (gasoline-filled milk bottles wrapped in rags), but Gaston attributed the minimized damage to the flame-retardant materials in the drapes and rugs. Otherwise, he was convinced, flames would have consumed the entire house—including its two occupants.

Round-the-clock guards were hired by the Gastons, who had reached the chilling conclusion that somebody wanted them out of the way. What they couldn't tell then was whether it was the racist white members of the Klan who had thrown the bombs, or the more militant blacks who considered Gaston a hindrance to the civil rights effort. They would in fact never know.

Many more bombings continued to take place in what was becoming an increasingly violent era. Unlike some of those who watched Molotov cocktails fly through their windows, both A. G. and Minnie had escaped unharmed. But no such blessing would befall four black schoolgirls attending Sunday school in the basement of the Sixteenth Street Baptist Church one warm fall day. Instead, Addie Mae Collins, Denise McNair, Carole Robertson, and Cynthia Wesley were all killed instantly when a bomb detonated on the bright Sunday morning of September 15, 1963.

The Smith & Gaston Funeral Home sat only a block away from the church. It was the first funeral home on the scene after the blast, and Smith & Gaston hearses transported what was left of each girl to the city morgue. But Smith & Gaston was not chosen to handle any of the funerals. Carole Robertson, whose parents chose a "personal" funeral, was buried by Poole; Denise McNair, Addie Mae Collins, and Cynthia Wesley's funerals were conducted by Davenport Harris. Edna Gardner, whose husband, Thomas, ran the funeral home, said the family was surprised not to be asked—they were friends of the victims' families. One of the mothers even worked at the business college.

Nevertheless, A. G. and Minnie were VIP attendees at the funeral—a place of honor reserved for them right behind the girls' families. Eight thousand people turned up to hear King deliver his eulogy and mourn the loss of the young lives. He used the occasion to remind the crowd that ". . . we must be concerned not merely about who murdered [the girls], but about the system, the way of life, and the philosophy which produced the murderers."

The church bombing had realized Gaston's worst fears of what would come of openly defying the white establishment. The warnings Gaston had for years leveled at King and his followers had finally come to fruition in the deaths of these four little girls, and as miserable as he was made by their deaths, he was also irate. King's response to the *We-told-you-so* anger of the moderates was just as heated. "What murdered these four girls?" he asked his critics. "The apathy and the complacency of many Negroes who will sit down on their stools and do nothing and not engage in creative protest to get rid of this evil."

If each faction blamed the other for the loss of the girls, each was nevertheless heartsick. King had been forced to return from Atlanta and Shuttlesworth from Cincinnati to face, with all the other adults, the consequences that had befallen the children. The streets were once again full of rioting.

A meeting was arranged to take place at the White House between movement leaders and President Kennedy. Gaston wrote that he was invited to join. He and King traveled together to Washington in what must have been an uneasy trip. Both men had been devastated by the bombing—Gaston feeling that his attempt to forestall violence had failed, King shouldering the burden of having pushed matters to their breaking point. Neither was in a good mood.

Before the meeting with Kennedy, the Birmingham contingent gathered at a hotel to discuss their plan. According to Gaston, the question of asking for federal troops was put on the table. Gaston opposed it; there had been enough violence already. Instead he urged his cohorts to "try to settle this without federal troops." King, however, wanted the troops, and was determined to ask for them.

As the session began, the president greeted A. G. "Mr. Gaston, I was certainly distressed to read that your house was bombed. I give you my sympathy. It must have been a bad shock to you and your wife." As in their first meeting, Gaston thanked Kennedy for his concern, and then the men got down to business. When the issue of federal troops came up, King made it clear that he was in favor of using them. Gaston offered up his opposing view. The president agreed with Gaston—for the time being. "I don't want to invade Alabama," he remarked, before adding, "but troops must be sent if the danger grows more acute."

As to the larger issue of peace in the city of Birmingham, Kennedy's solution was to send two representatives—both white men, both army men, one of them a former football coach—down

south to sort things out. On the president's order, former army secretary Kenneth Royall and former West Point football coach Earl
"Red" Blaik traveled to Birmingham and began holding separate
meetings with white and black citizens. No one attempted to disabuse
the president of the idea that his solution would work.

King, the public face of what was supposed to be the more radical wing of civil rights agitation in America, was soon made to regret
having been so accommodating to the president's suggestion. Activists such as the writer James Baldwin were furious he'd let
Kennedy get away with it. And in the meantime, the merchants had
yet to comply with their agreement as part of the settlement to begin
hiring blacks.

While King was taking the heat for the perceived capitulation,
Gaston was openly advocating that everyone involved give the emissaries a chance. But on September 27—apparently fed up with his
critics' attacks—King announced that he would be returning to Birmingham and the streets. Gaston and Shores denounced the plan immediately and (in a statement that was all too willingly splashed
across the front pages of the white papers) once again labeled King an
"outsider," urging him to keep away from the city.

Ignoring Gaston and Shores's provocation, King issued an ultimatum to the city: Hire Negro police officers by October or face
more protests. The deadline came and went without any action—
from the city or from the movement. Shuttlesworth complained that
the middle-class leaders of black Birmingham (Gaston, Shores, Drew,
and the like) were undermining progress by talking to Boutwell behind their backs. Indeed, Gaston *had* written a letter to Boutwell,
suggesting that hiring police would be "a great shot in the arm for
those of us in the Negro community who want to avoid outsiders
coming . . . and taking the leadership of our people for more direct
action." It was another direct (if private) slap at King.

King was reportedly demoralized by the lack of support from
black Birmingham in the matter, and despite Shuttlesworth's urging refused to lead another demonstration in the city. Not long
after, Kennedy's emissaries would return to Washington and report
what everyone who'd spent any time in Birmingham already knew:

Progress would only be coming to the Magic City slowly and grudgingly.

Marching for Selma

Exhausted from the bombings and the intense negotiations that had followed, A. G. and Minnie Gaston left Birmingham at the end of October for a vacation in Hawaii. When their return flight landed in San Francisco on November 22, 1963, a hotel clerk informed them that President John Kennedy had been shot and killed. Like most blacks, in Kennedy the Gastons had felt that for the first time a president was willing to address the conditions of black America. Gaston had dealt with John Kennedy on a personal level and had found him both charming and attentive. Kennedy had given Gaston his most meaningful tribute by inviting him to the White House. In the absence of this man's influence, the Gastons wondered, what would become of black America?

They didn't have to wonder for long. The next president did not waste any time making himself clear on the subject of blacks. In Lyndon Johnson's first address to the country, he stated his intention to go forward with Kennedy's civil rights legislation: "We have talked long enough in this country about civil rights . . . a hundred years or more. . . . So let us here highly resolve that John Fitzgerald Kennedy did not live—and die—in vain."

Exactly a year from the date that President Kennedy proposed the civil rights legislation, his successor Lyndon Johnson succeeded in getting it passed. The Civil Rights Act of 1964 gave blacks free access to hotels, restaurants, and all other public places; it gave the Justice Department the right to enforce desegregation in schools and made it unlawful to discriminate against blacks in employment, union membership, or any state program receiving federal aid. Johnson signed the legislation into law on July 2 of 1964—just two days before Independence Day.

Even as Johnson and blacks across America celebrated the historic legislation, it was clear that more than paperwork would be required to transform the South. Three young civil rights workers—Michael

Schwerner and Andrew Goodman (white students from the North) and James Chaney (a black activist)—had gone missing while canvassing in Neshoba County, Mississippi. Their bodies would be found on August 4, buried in an earthen dam near Philadelphia, Mississippi. The murders were a blow to the morale of all those who believed in and had been fighting for equality. The battles, it seemed, were far from over.

On December 10, 1964, Martin Luther King was awarded the Nobel Peace Prize in Oslo, Norway. In his acceptance speech, King declared, "I conclude that this award, which I received on behalf of the movement, is profound recognition that nonviolence is the answer to the crucial political and moral questions of our time—the need for man to overcome oppression and violence without resorting to violence and oppression." It was a reminder many in the movement, after years of casualties, needed desperately to hear.

Energized, perhaps, by his own performance in Oslo, King returned to America with a new objective in mind: to secure the voting rights of the black citizens of Selma, Alabama. Practically speaking, 77 percent of blacks still did not have the right to vote in Alabama in 1965. In Selma, only 335 of the town's 15,000 black residents were actually registered to vote, despite the determination of the many black citizens who had dutifully shown up to register. Birthplace of Bull Connor and site of the first White Citizens Council meeting, by the 1960s Selma had its own Connor look-alike presiding in office: Sheriff Jim Clark. And like his temperamental doppelganger Connor, Clark would prove a vicious opponent.

King first addressed the people of Selma in the Brown Chapel A.M.E. Church in January 1965. His tone was stern: "We are not asking," he told them, "we are demanding the ballot." Following up on the work done by local residents and SNCC, King led progressively larger groups of blacks to the registrar's office, attempting to get their names on the voter rolls. They were consistently turned away. On February 1 Sheriff Clark arrested the newly minted Nobel laureate, along with Abernathy and several hundred marchers. Five hundred schoolchildren, protesting at the county courthouse, were taken off to jail, too. It was beginning to look like Birmingham all over again.

Before long, the formerly inconspicuous town of Selma was swamped by reporters, there to detail Clark's brutality as much as report the full story. Clark was not afraid to let his officers beat women and prod at children; he took a page right out of Connor's book and made it his own. After a marcher was finally shot and killed by Clark's troops, King made a proposal from his jail cell: The protesters would march from Selma to the state capital of Montgomery (some fifty miles away), and place their demands at the feet of Governor George Wallace. The plan was quickly brought to fruition.

The marchers' first attempt to cross the Edmund Pettis Bridge that leads out of Selma became known as "Bloody Sunday." In King's absence, John Lewis of SNCC had taken leadership of the group. Having gained advance warning of the group's intentions, Governor Wallace had instructed Clark to stop the protestors from crossing the bridge, whatever it took. In the fifteen minutes of film broadcast that night on television, the country watched as Clark's "posse" rode on horseback through the crowd of peaceful marchers, swinging bullwhips and clubs, setting off tear gas, driving the marchers back.

A. G. and Minnie Gaston watched the attack and its replays on television from their home in Birmingham. They worried, prayed, and waited for more news.

President Johnson took to the airwaves himself the next week, announcing federal legislation to ensure voting rights for blacks. "Their cause must be our cause too," he warned the nation. "Because it is not just Negroes, but really it is all of us who must overcome the crippling legacy of bigotry and injustice. And we *shall* overcome." Johnson then detailed his proposal for a voting rights act that would attempt to make pleading for that right, and being beaten for trying to secure that right, unnecessary.

Regardless of Johnson's measures, King planned to go forward with the march. It would take five days to traverse the fifty-plus miles that separated Selma from Montgomery, and marchers needed secure places to sleep along the way. Gaston came forward to offer aid. He suggested that marchers use the Gardner family's farm in Lowndes County as a stopover site. The offer was accepted by movement leaders; it was agreed that the marchers would spend night three on the Gardner property.

On Sunday, March 21, thirty-two hundred people started out on the historic march from Selma to Montgomery. Led by (a newly released) King and other black icons such as Rosa Parks, Ralph Bunche, and Roy Wilkins, the marchers were joined by a host of celebrities: James Baldwin, Harry Belafonte, Sammy Davis Jr., Joan Baez, Dick Gregory, Johnny Mathis, Elaine May, and Peter, Paul & Mary all turned out to show their support. Those who didn't walk lined the sides of the highway, cheering the marchers on.

Just as the celebratory mood was overtaking the marchers in Selma, back in Birmingham, the U.S. Army was frantically trying to disarm five bombs that had been discovered around the city—one of them at the Smith & Gaston Funeral Home. Two demolition experts had been rushed in from Fort McClellan, sixty miles away, to handle the situation. A parishioner on his way to early-morning Sunday services at a local Catholic church had spied a green box lying against the side of the building. He picked it up, heard it ticking, and alerted the parish priest. It was the beginning of an all-day race as bomb after bomb was discovered by passersby, each attached to an alarm clock, transistor batteries, and enough dynamite (forty to fifty sticks) to blow ten-foot holes in concrete—more than enough to kill.

All the devices had been set to go off at noon. The team of experts raced around the city clipping wires, reaching the funeral home only *after* the time set on the clock for detonation. (They managed to clip the wires anyway, and became instant heroes in the city.) The other targets? Once again, A. D. King's former house (he had moved out of the city by then); once again, attorney Arthur Shores's frequently bombed home (he commented that by this point his home had been bombed so much, "it never excites me"); the mayor's manse; and a black high school, Western High. Mayor Boutwell called the attempted bombings "a particularly vicious and calculated crime against the whole community."

Had the bombs gone off, the chaos and bloodshed would surely have distracted from the victorious march in Selma. Luckily, no such thing occurred, and the focus was kept on the marchers. The long line of protestors stretched down Route 80 as they made their way to the state capital. At the end of day three of their five-day journey, the protesters camped, as planned, on the Gardner family farm—where Minnie Gaston and all of her brothers and sisters had grown up. In 1965 Minnie's brother Robert, his wife, Mary, and their children were still living on the farm, and they greeted the arriving protesters personally. What Mary remembered about that night was the rain, and how excited people were despite it. Two large tents were erected on the property: one for the men and one for the women. The decision to allow the protestors on their property had been a complicated one for the Gardners—the threat of violence was everywhere. But the attorney general had given them his personal promise that their family would be kept safe. "We just went on our faith," Mary said. In the end they knew that what they were doing would benefit everyone.

Marchers arrived in the capital on March 25 and held a rally that swelled to fifty thousand strong. The Confederate flag flew above the capitol as the protesters gathered to hear King proclaim, "No lie can live forever . . . the arm of the moral universe is long, but it bends towards justice." And it would not be long, he promised them, until justice was served in the state of Alabama. Governor George Wallace was nowhere to be seen.

That same night, however, the segregationists would level their punishment: As she transported marchers back to Selma from Montgomery in her car, white Detroit housewife Viola Liuzzo was murdered by a group of Klansmen. The four white men who committed the crime (one of whom was an FBI informant) had seen Liuzzo traveling up and down the stretch of road that led from Selma to Montgomery with her black passengers aboard; when her car pulled up to a stoplight, the men drove up beside her, their guns pointed directly at Liuzzo's green Oldsmobile. When Mrs. Liuzzo turned to face the car, Collie Leroy Wilkins, sitting in the passenger's seat, extended his arm out of his window and fired two shots through the glass of Mrs. Liuzzo's driver's-side door and directly into her head. After riddling the car with the rest of their bullets, the Klansmen drove away, only to be captured later.

According to Mary Gardner, the shooting took place just five or six miles down the road from the Gardner farm on Route 80. Secu-

rity presence was visible around the farm and its surroundings for a
year following the march; agents in a car patrolled the Route 80 strip,
while helicopters kept continual watch from above.

Mrs. Gaston Goes to Washington

While her relatives in Lowndes County were busy hosting the Selma
protesters, Minnie Gaston was occupied with a project of her own.
Over those final days of March, Minnie spent day and night at her
desk at the Booker T. Washington Business College, collating documents and organizing her files. She combed over the speech she had
written countless times, looking for errors or inconsistencies, or even
just a bad turn of phrase. When she wasn't working on the project at
the college, she was at home doing the same. It didn't matter how
many times A. G. told her the presentation was perfect—to Minnie,
there was always some way it could be better. Minnie Gaston was
going to speak before the U.S. Congress, and she had no intention of
being taken less than seriously.

Hearings for the National Vocational Student Loan Insurance Act
of 1965 (also known as HR 6468) were scheduled to take place in
Washington, DC, on April 5–7. As described by the House subcommittee that held the hearings, the bill was intended to "establish a system of insurance on reduced interest loans to assist students to attend
postsecondary business, trade, technical and other vocational schools."
In plain English, that meant the Congress was holding hearings on
whether to establish a federal student loan program. From the fifth
through the seventh of April the committee would be considering the
specific case of vocational schools.

The Congress's Committee on Education and Labor, chaired by
Congressman Adam Clayton Powell of New York, sent out requests
to experts across the country in the field of vocational education—
professors of education as well as institute directors—to come to
Washington and testify before the subcommittee on the need for a
federal student loan program for vocational institutes. The issue in
question was whether students in vocational programs required separate consideration in federal lending than students attending four-

year academic colleges. Student loans, and the paucity of them for vocational students (in particular, *black* vocational students), were a matter Minnie had struggled with for years at the business college. When the request to testify on the subject before Congress landed on her desk, she was happy to oblige.

After weeks of preparation, Minnie traveled to Washington to submit her case. At ten o'clock on the morning of April 5, 1965 (the first day of hearings), Mrs. Gaston took her seat in Room 429 of the Cannon House Office Building. At the subcommittee chair's request, she began her presentation. Her argument in favor of the bill was formulated on two central points: the nation's growing need for skilled workers, and the general inability of many students to pay for their education. "The vast need for unskilled labor is past," Mrs. Gaston announced to the committee. "What we need now is more skilled workers, which student loans would make available."

At the time of Mrs. Gaston's testimony, the Booker T. Washington Business College had an enrollment of 360 students. It had by that time graduated more than eight thousand students into the business world. Over the course of the school's twenty-five-year history, Mrs. Gaston had observed that the major impediment to securing education for those who were seeking it was a simple lack of money. During the academic year preceding her testimony, Mrs. Gaston claimed, the college had received "over 700 applications for admittance." But two-thirds of those who applied were unable to enroll because "they were unable to pay just the first month's tuition." Though the Gastons themselves had granted hundreds of scholarships personally, as well as through A. G.'s businesses, the demand for education was more than they could supply out of their own checkbooks. Offering evidence of the myriad ways in which the work of the Booker T. Washington Business College and its graduates had bettered their community over the years, Mrs. Gaston made an unimpeachable case for the need for federal support. When she had finished her presentation, the congressmen not only thanked her for her time, but also praised her as being "highly professional in every sense."

Aside from the eloquence and astuteness of Minnie's appearance before the subcommittee, what is striking about the speech is its total lack of racial specificity: the word *Negro* appears exactly twice in the entire address. Still, if Mrs. Gaston was aiming to keep the issue of race off the table to temper the discussion, it was impossible for the issue to not sublimate itself in the margins of the debate. The vast majority of the students whom Mrs. Gaston worked with, and was speaking on behalf of, happened to be black (Booker T. Washington Business College operated, as noted previously, with an open-door policy in regard to race; there were, over the years, some white students who attended). Mrs. Gaston herself was a black woman from Birmingham, Alabama, scene in the recent past of some of the nation's biggest battles for civil rights. The hearings were taking place less than two weeks after the Selma marches; the protesters had stayed on Mrs. Gaston's family farm on their way to the capital. All of this was known, if not spoken. *Nobody* in that room could have been unaware of the latent racial implications of all that Mrs. Gaston was arguing.

Though not often listed among the major triumphs of civil rights legislation, the passage of HR 6468 was indeed a significant gain in the arena of equal access to education. Getting an education was often not just about being able to get through the schoolhouse door. It was also about being able to afford to stay there. The new legislation to fund vocational colleges would have a profound effect on the ability of vocational students—many, many of whom were black—to get into and remain in school, and Minnie Gaston had played a crucial role in making it happen. In return for her hard work on the bill, Mrs. Gaston was later invited back to Washington by President Johnson to witness its signing. She "was also elected Businesswoman of the Year by the United Business Schools Association for her efforts in its passage." For her husband, Minnie's success was yet another example of how working within the system could, with patience, bring about real change.

———

Later that same year another legislative victory would come to fruition—this one much more grandly celebrated. On August 6,

1965, Lyndon Johnson signed the Voting Rights Act into law. Symbolically, the ceremony took place in the President's Room of the Capitol Rotunda, where President Lincoln had signed the Emancipation Proclamation 104 years before. The act, as promised, guaranteed blacks the right to vote, authorized federal examiners to travel to certain states to conduct the registration process, and banned the so-called literacy tests. As a direct result of the act's passage, more than a quarter of a million blacks registered to vote before the close of 1965. A. G. Gaston came out publicly to support the legislation, advising blacks to get on the voter lists and reminding them that "your vote is a sacred privilege, and it is not for sale."

The cooling winds of the fall brought with them a relative calm to Birmingham. King, true to his word, had not staged any other actions in the city; he and the leaders of the movement were focusing their attentions elsewhere. For those who remained behind in the city of Birmingham, it was time to try to put life back together after so many years of turmoil. For A. G. Gaston, that meant getting back to business.

The King Is Dead

On April 4, 1968, Martin Luther King was assassinated in Memphis, Tennessee. Gaston responded to the news with disbelief and a deep sense of grief. The period of King's campaigns in Birmingham had been trying ones for Gaston in very personal ways. Before King's arrival, he had spent years working behind the scenes with white businessmen and moderate black leaders to improve the conditions of the black citizens of Birmingham, and he had always considered King's involvement disruptive at best and at worst dangerous. But it was also true that the seventy-one-year-old businessman admired the young preacher, having observed and even supported some of his more masterful acts of leadership—in particular the year-long bus boycott in Montgomery in 1956 that had brought the state capital to its knees.

Gaston and King had disagreed on fundamental principles, but as part of the governing black middle class, they knew each other well and had developed a grudging affection for one another. They had even conducted business together. According to historian Glenn Eskew, the year after Gaston launched his Citizens Federal Savings Bank, King sent him a thousand dollars to open an account, along with a note: "This is just a little expression of the interest I have in the great work that you and your associates are doing in the area of economics." King also promised that a considerable deposit would be forthcoming from the Montgomery Improvement Association, the organization that had transformed Rosa Parks's one-woman stand against segregated seating on buses into a massive political action— with donations pouring in from around the country to support the cause. Gaston had responded to King's advance by inviting him to serve on the bank's advisory board, an invitation that King accepted. According to Eskew, King's name went on the bank's official letter-head.

The esteem had clearly traveled both ways. King respected the ac-complishments of a man from humble beginnings who had succeeded in the world. Birmingham newspaperman Jesse Lewis remembers that the future Nobel laureate waited for an appointment with Gas-ton just like everybody else: patiently, leafing through a magazine until his turn came for an audience.

Now, after more than a decade of turmoil in which they were rarely to be found on the same side of the fence, King was dead and Gaston was profoundly sorry to have lost him. In his autobiography Gaston wrote, "I had long supported [King's] philosophy of non-violent protest and knew he was sincere and dedicated. . . . He did not try to throw his weight around. His voice was quiet and his man-ner unassuming." Without King, Gaston wondered, what would come next? It was a dilemma a whole new generation of young, angry blacks would have to ponder as well.

INVESTING IN LIFE

I am looking forward to a day when
all our people have learned the secret
of organizing their money and making it work
for the future of our race.

THE REMAINS OF THE DAYS

If the assassination of our nation's president in 1963 had sounded the initial rumblings of the loss of America's fabled innocence, then the events of 1968 represented the true death knell of the era. Martin Luther King was dead. Bobby Kennedy, too. Images of great men lying on their backs, drenched in their own blood, became metaphors for all that had been hoped for and all that had been lost in the decade. Ours was a nation forever changed by the events of the 1960s, but also undeniably battered by the transformation.

There is a tendency in the American national consciousness to perceive the violence and emotionality of the civil rights era as having ended at approximately the same time that Dr. King lost his life. This appreciation of the historical record would lead us to believe that with the passing of the Civil Rights Act, the chief concerns of black people in America had been redressed. For black people, however, parity was nowhere in sight. For while the gains of the decade of the 1960s answered many of the "big picture" issues pertaining to the black community, the real conditions of daily life remained bleak.

What had not changed amid the social gains of the 1960s was poverty, and its discontents raised themselves with a vengeance in the

years after King's death. As a result, the end of the decade, violence
was on the rise.

The numbers on black poverty in the middle years of the movement were staggering: While one-fifth of whites lived at or below
poverty levels in the United States, *one-half* of blacks in the U.S.
were living in poverty. And things did not change in a hurry after
the passing of the civil rights legislation. As of 1977, it was reported
that the median black family income "was only about 60 percent
that of whites," indicating the persistence of the problem for black
Americans.

Though many poor blacks had supported the movement despite
its relative lack of focus on economic issues, the silence invoked by
the formal passing of the hard-won legislation and the death of Dr.
King provided many blacks with the first opportunity to sit back and
reflect on the actual, physical quality of their lives. What many of
them saw was nothing that they liked, and much of the agitation that
followed stemmed from the economically based inequalities ignored
by the mainstream civil rights movement until it was, in the eyes of
many, far too late.

The Economics of "Equality"

It is no secret that the movement was, from its earliest incarnations, divided on matters relating to the black poor. Though just before his
death Dr. King had turned his attention to the needs of the underclass,
during the heyday of the movement, the great issues under debate were
arguably middle-class concerns. As historian Robin Kelley explains,
"Very few civil rights leaders were . . . necessarily knowledgeable
about or sensitive to the specific problems, needs, and desires of the
poor. And, with few exceptions, mainstream civil rights spokespersons
did not encourage poor blacks to participate in decision-making or
leadership capacities within their organizations."

One extreme example of this issue of class division can be seen in
the creation of the Birmingham Interracial Committee (BIC) in the
early 1950s. Formed, it would seem, primarily to help ameliorate relations between the ruling elite of black and white Birminghamians,

the BIC took as its earliest tasks "the construction of a nine hole Negro golf course" and "development of a real estate subdivision for high class Negro homes." This, during a period in which the *average* black citizen of Birmingham made less than half of what his white counterpart could hope to make.

Though it is true that organizations such as the BIC were not agitating for "civil rights" as we know them, its interests are nevertheless indicative of the schism between middle-class interests and the bulk of the black population. The argument here is not that the broader movement was simply agitating for country club facilities; it is, however, to say that in some cases, the privilege of middle-class perspectives allowed bourgeois concerns (rather than, for example, providing critical care for those lowest on the economic ladder) to take precedence.

King, as the movement's unequivocal leader, kept his focus on what had been termed "social ills" affecting blacks—and, in particular, southern blacks. This meant, in many instances, confronting policies of segregation in schools and in public accommodation; it meant challenging the social mores of the region when it came to broadstrokes questions of what was "fair" and what was "right"—and all this in a specifically southern context. Pointedly, the movement never truly addressed the differences in life circumstances experienced by northern blacks versus their southern compatriots. Yet, as Jay R. Mandle reveals in his book *The Roots of Black Poverty*, the disparity between the southern and northern economies was such that the gains of the southern-based movement would necessarily have little effect on the lives of the 50 percent of the black population living in the northern United States.

Blacks now had the right to sit at lunch counters in towns and cities across the nation, the guaranteed right to vote—and much more. But on the issues of employment and, critically, money, few answers seemed to be forthcoming. In neglecting to ask and answer the question of what, economically, the black community would require to raise itself out of its chronic un- and underemployment, movement leaders had set the stage for a revolution that refused to ignore the importance of class in the name of racial solidarity.

This question of economic stability was one that held particular relevance in a place such as Birmingham, Alabama, which had its own very distinct black employment and poverty problem. The deindustrialization of Birmingham proper had had a devastating impact on the employability of the black community. The mines, which had provided thousands of jobs for Birmingham's black residents, began to cut jobs in the latter years of the 1940s, and by the middle of the 1950s, seven out of ten black miners in the metropolitan area were out of work. Racism in union activities further curtailed blacks' ability to secure jobs in other industries; the housing projects of Birmingham's inner city were filled beyond capacity. Levels of homelessness exploded, and the city was quickly unable to meet the needs of its growing indigent population.

These were the circumstances, it is important to recall, that *preceded* the movement for civil rights in Birmingham. What the movement left behind was hardly much better from an economic standpoint. In fact, between 1960 and 1970 the percentage of families living below the poverty line in Birmingham *increased significantly,* with more than a third of black families living in poverty by 1970. Moreover, the programs devised by the federal and local branches of government to aid the poor more often than not failed to reach those most in need. What became obvious in Birmingham, as in many other cities around the country during the 1970s, was that "civil rights" had had little to do with the ability to make a living. Poverty, it seemed, was going nowhere.

If the critical nature of economic independence was a revelation to many, it was no such surprise to A. G. Gaston. Gaston was not a man who would or could have ignored the importance of economics when considering the welfare of the larger black community—least of all because economics was his personal obsession. His doctrine of self-improvement had never varied from the lessons he learned early on in Booker T. Washington's *Up from Slavery;* Gaston had never believed that there was any other way "up" than through economic success. And he had been unafraid to say so in the midst of the demonstrations taking place throughout Birmingham in the mid-1960s. There was no question in Gaston's mind that as important as government recognition of equality under the law might be, there were some other equally important issues for blacks to consider— first among them financial solvency. If true parity were going to be achieved, blacks would first be required to reconfigure their monetary relationship to white culture.

For as obvious as this argument may seem by today's standards, the sentiment Gaston was advancing was not one echoing from many other corners in the mid-1960s. His focus on economics appeared callous (at best) or opportunistic (at worst) to those around him in Birmingham fighting a war for equality. What Gaston knew then (and what the black community and leadership have come to accept increasingly over the years) is that without economic power, *equality* becomes merely a catchphrase for rights guaranteed but never fully accessible. This, however, was a position few people wanted to give credence to at the time. Furthermore, it was a position that had, along with his refusal to relinquish his business, political, or personal ties to the white community, earned Gaston the hard-to-shake label of *Uncle Tom*.

Though wealth had shielded Gaston from many of the daily indignities and dangers that the average black citizen faced, it could not protect him from the impact that these confrontations had on Birmingham as a community. The social revolution in his hometown had put Gaston in a bad position from a business perspective. He knew that the trust of the white community was crucial to his survival as a businessman; he was similarly aware that he needed the respect of the black community if his businesses were to thrive. The divide was one that was difficult to reconcile by any means, and well nigh impossible if you were (as Gaston was) unwilling to abandon one side, whole cloth, in favor of the other.

It is difficult to find an account of Gaston's life in the aftermath of the movement that doesn't take him solidly to task for what have been described, in polite terms, as his accommodationist attitude. Civil rights supporters both black and white hated Gaston for what they perceived as his capitulation to white interests, not only in the business realm but in the social and political worlds as well. From Gaston's perspective, however, the economic viability of the black community should always have been central to the civil rights equation—the issues of social, civic, and economic welfare being inseparable in his mind. The refusal of movement leaders to address this question directly seemed to Gaston exceedingly shortsighted, if not just plain dangerous. It infuriated him to watch the economics of inclusion given short shrift when it came to the well-being of the black community. Though requests had been made on the part of leadership for increased employment opportunities for blacks, these were often the points that fell to the wayside first in multiparty discussions. While Gaston was a negotiator nonpareil, and well aware that some gains would have to take a backseat to others, it seemed to him that King and his followers failed to appreciate just how important it would be for blacks to have control of their economic futures—which meant not merely *asking* for jobs, but, critically, having the power to *create* them.

By the end of the decade, the name *A. G. Gaston* was no longer the shining symbol of success and admiration that it once had been. Though he wouldn't have admitted it to anyone but Minnie, the public relations beating he had taken during the 1960s as a result of his leanings had hurt him deeply. The derisive tone with which author Diane McWhorter refers to Gaston is typical of the shadow that clung to him by the end of the decade. McWhorter's repetition of the characterization of Gaston as a "Responsible Negro," the kind of man who could "shuffle his feet and keep his eyes on the ground when he's talking to white people and at the same time stand up before colored people and demand immediate racial equality," echoes a common complaint about the man: It was a more detailed iteration of the same old "Uncle Tom" charge. It was an indictment frequently voiced in the late 1960s, and, importantly, one that Gaston was aware was being bandied about in connection with his name.

Green Power

As a longtime public figure in Birmingham, Gaston was accustomed to hearing people talk about him; the Brown Belle debacle alone had taught him a lesson about riding the storms of public opinion. No

one who strove to stand out as Gaston did could hope to get away
with a lifetime in the public eye without accumulating some ill will—
this much he knew. But he also knew that something more serious
was going on in the minds of black Birminghamians in the years after
the police dogs had been kenneled and the fire hoses re-coiled. When
his house had been bombed a few years earlier he had spoken from
his heart when he said that he couldn't be certain if it was blacks or
whites who had perpetrated the crime. It honestly could have been
either. And now that things were relatively quiet, now that the children were out of the streets, when people—black or white—saw his
name, what, he wondered, did they think? Did they remember him as
the man who had built a bank, funeral homes, an insurance company,
an empire, out of nothing and against every odd in the books? Or did
they simply think of him as the man who had tried to keep King—
their hero—out of Birmingham? Did anyone understand what he had
meant by his actions? Or was he doomed to remain an "Uncle Tom"
for eternity?

Gaston realized that the only way to set the record as he would
like it was to write a version of that record himself. Having watched
President Kennedy, Malcolm X, King, and then another Kennedy die
well before their time (and all much younger than he), Gaston was
conscious that counting on tomorrow was a risky bet—and he was not
by his nature a betting man. Whether he constructed the tale alone or
with the help of an aide we do not know, but in short order Gaston sat
down at his desk and began to write a story he knew well: the story of
a boy who started with nothing and came to greatness, and not without challenges. It was the story of his life—just as Booker T. Washington would have written it.

In 1968 *Green Power*—Gaston's account of his own life and
times—was published. Publication was funded by Gaston himself,
and all proceeds were directed to benefit Gaston's newly formed
Boys Club in Birmingham. Gaston's rationale for self-publishing is
not documented, but given his penchant for control, it is certainly
possible that he preferred to handle the business of writing his life
without interference from higher-ups. The allure of an advance from
a publishing company, if one had been forthcoming, would likely not

have been impressive to Gaston. He had the clout in Birmingham to entice a local publishing house to print the book for him—that is, he could essentially contract their presses without having to be under contract to their editorial division himself—and with his publicity machine already well oiled, and a staff in the hundreds at his beck and call, it would require little effort on his part (beyond an initial layout of money and the time it took to actually write the text) to get the book out the door.

Though this is precisely how the book got published in the end, it is also quite possible that Gaston chose to release the memoir on his own for one other very simple reason: lack of interest in his story from any major publishing house (and given that *Green Power* has remained out of print since its third reprint by Troy State University in 1978, it is not an implausible notion). This was, after all, still the 1960s, and the perceived hunger of the reading public to see black lives in print was largely underestimated by mainstream publishers. Moreover, Gaston had taken a real hit in popularity as a result of his conservatism. His was not a voice people were necessarily clamoring to hear. Gaston's importance to the struggle would truly reveal itself only with time.

In its final version, the book spanned the years from Gaston's earliest memories in Demopolis to the highly fraught battles of the 1960s. This was Gaston's chance to clear his name—or, at the very least, to tell his side of the story. And he chose to tell this story through the filter of Washington's own autobiography—the first book Gaston had ever read from cover to cover. Like Washington's account, Gaston's is one that most contemporary readers find troubling. As Washington related licking a drop of molasses from a tin plate with overwhelming gratitude, pointing out how *lucky* he had been to even receive such a treat, so Gaston chose to relate not what was absent in his life but what was present and good. "Negroes' time spent in seeing all the things that were wrong with us and all the reasons we couldn't get out of a rut," Gaston believed, "could be far better spent in finding ways to lick problems." So he was *lucky*, he recalled, not to have had to wear a hair shirt like young Booker Washington; he was *lucky* that his mother had a job with the Lovemans, even if it meant she was away from him for months at a time.

Truth be told, relative to most blacks of his generation (and many after) he *was* lucky—for all of this and more. But if escape from the stigma of Uncle Tomism was what Gaston was looking for in publishing this account, it is unlikely that stories like these were going to engender it.

Nevertheless, publishing *Green Power* finally gave Gaston a chance to respond to the criticisms of movement leaders and people on the street alike. And he was not afraid to mention that he knew he had been called an Uncle Tom. Rather, he took the term in his own hands and, in explaining how and why he had behaved as he had, remarked, "If wanting to spare children, save lives, bring peace was Uncle Tomism, then I wanted to be a Super Uncle Tom." Though he was, he admitted, "disturbed" that blacks had failed to appreciate his intentions in resisting certain movement initiatives, he stood his ground, refusing to apologize for what to his mind remained a solid position. He hoped that through his explication he might make an impression that could revive his popularity and respect in the black community.

The black community's response to the book was overwhelmingly positive. Edna Gardner remembers that there was a signing scheduled at the bank, which was well attended. Copies of the book were given away free to every new customer at both the bank and insurance company. *Ebony* and *Jet* magazines, which kept constant track of Gaston's doings as a figure of national importance, featured the publication in their magazines as well. But the coup de grace came when Gaston was invited to New York to appear on *The Today Show* to discuss his life as detailed in *Green Power.* One of the show's producers had gotten hold of a copy of the book and, entranced by Gaston's tale, invited him to appear on national television. The businessman was flown in from his home in Birmingham; his niece Carol Ann (one of the authors of this book) accompanied him to the interview.

THE A. G. GASTON BOYS CLUB

The publication of *Green Power* did have some small effect in turning the tide back in Gaston's favor, and it allowed Gaston the satisfaction of feeling as if his voice had been heard on the issues at hand, once and for all.

Furthermore, in publishing the story of his life, Gaston hoped to leave behind a record of encouragement and possibility for the future generations of blacks. If the preceding decades had to some degree been focused on securing Gaston's own success, these later years of his life would be just as much about ensuring the success of other blacks, first and foremost by providing them with a model of success who looked like they did.

Primarily, however, the publication of the book allowed Gaston to promote and fund what had become his new passion: The A. G. Gaston Boys Club. In the early months of 1966 Gaston, fresh from his dispute over the use of children in demonstrations, had been taken with the notion that black boys in Birmingham could use a better outlet for their energies than the city was currently providing. Though there was already one Boys Club in existence in Birmingham, it was underfunded, understaffed, and incapable of meeting the needs of the city's entire young black male population.

Gathering together a group of "civic leaders" both white and black, Gaston pitched the idea of constructing a new facility. The project met with enthusiasm, but as in times before, Gaston was the first to step forward with a generous financial gift. He donated an aging two-story brick building on Fourteenth Street and Seventh Avenue North (in the heart of Birmingham's blighted inner city) to the cause, and then began a heated campaign of fund-raising to cover the costs of renovation. By the time the doors of the club were set to open in the fall of 1967, Gaston and his cohorts had raised $350,000 to fund the enterprise, in addition to Gaston's donation of the $50,000 building and the plot of land on which it sat.

There was nothing lacking at the A. G. Gaston Boys Club. It boasted a brand-new fully stocked library, gym facilities, arts and crafts, and music and game rooms. Athletic fields were constructed on the land that adjoined the building. Not only could boys receive scholastic tutoring and mentoring through the club, but Gaston and his board of directors made certain that medical attention was also available to clients (in many cases, this was the only avenue to medical care a member would have received in his life). In Gaston's eyes, beyond the physical and literal opportunities the club offered, its fundamental purpose was to make it clear to each of these boys that *somebody* cared about him. As he wrote in *Green Power*, "Nothing destroys an individual like the feeling that he is nobody and of no good to anybody." The building on Fourteenth Street stood as a testament to the fact that he and other members of the community believed that young black boys deserved to be cared for, in a measurable manner.

By May 1968 the center was serving 150 boys, and that number was on the rise. Though initially there had been a certain reluctance to join this kind of "do good" organization, soon enough kids were lured by tales of what awaited them inside. Boys from age six on up eventually found their way to the club, having been pointed there by their families or engaged through the outreach efforts of the club's director, Frank Clayton, a former Birmingham schoolteacher who had come on board to administer the club's programs. Most of the boys, Gaston surmised, came from "broken homes": They were poor, without fathers, and often without much purpose in their lives. Gaston knew a little something about what growing up in those circumstances was like. His purpose in founding the club was to give these boys direction. He was only too happy to offer himself and Clayton up as the father figures the boys were lacking.

Donating money, if you have it to give, is an easily accomplished feat. What is harder is living out the tenet of putting others before you by actually taking their needs into account before your own. Like every other initiative he had undertaken in his life, Gaston took the boys club project not only seriously, but personally. Caring, he knew, could be demonstrated by dollars. But what the members of the A. G. Gaston Boys Club needed (at least as much as they needed money and a route to securing it) was to feel that they mattered. And in Birmingham, being guests in the home of Mr. and Mrs. A. G. Gaston certainly meant you mattered—a whole lot.

Gaston not only took it upon himself to attend to the boys in a personal manner while at the club (all the boys knew him by name and rushed about straightening the building and themselves in preparation for his daily visits), but—with Minnie's encouragement—he took his involvement a step farther. In the same suburban mansion that had been bombed by vigilantes in the mid-1960s, A. G. and Minnie now hosted scores of their young pledges for barbecues and swimming parties. Business school students and boys club members alike crowded the grassy backyard of the Gastons' home throughout the year, mixing in the summertime with Minnie's many nieces and nephews come to visit from their various homes around the state and country, along with the Gaston grand- and great-grandchildren. There was more food than anyone could ever eat (hot dogs, hamburgers, fried chicken, potato salad, and, always, a special steak for Mr. Gaston), and nobody was ever made to feel ashamed for asking for more of anything, whether it was another morsel of food or one last cannonball off the diving board.

In addition to his work with the Boys Club, Gaston also offered his services (both financial and influential) to national organizations such as the 4-H clubs, the YMCA, and the Boy Scouts of America. The YMCA, in particular, became a special interest of his. Though the organization had supported the "separate but equal tenet" of the *Plessy v. Ferguson* decision (not unlike nearly every other social organization operating in the South prior to the mid-1960s), it satisfied its more liberal need for inclusiveness in building "less well-equipped" and generally "poorer" Negro branches for its black constituents. Gaston, undaunted by the institutionalized inequality, invested himself in the organization, raising dollars and volunteering his personal service toward increasing black membership. So dedicated was he to the membership drive that he was quickly made a division leader, and by 1972 the organization had rewarded him for his devotion by honoring him five times with distinguished service awards.

Like any good businessman, Gaston was not blind to the fact that his investment on the front end of these boys' lives might enable him to reap great rewards over time. The club's slogan, *Help build boys . . . not mend men,* held not only a bona fide social imperative, but a business-related one as well. By taking an active, charitable role in the lives of young blacks, Gaston established the first loop of a system that encouraged its participants' fidelity to the company—and, most especially, to the man who ran it. Boys who frequented the club knew very well that Gaston was a rich man, and that he stood in a position to help them obtain both jobs and the skills necessary to succeed in them. While it was impossible for Gaston to offer employment in a Gaston enterprise to every boy who walked through the Boys Club doors, what he could submit to them were opportunities to the broader end of securing employment *somewhere.* Many a former Boys Club member found himself led to a classroom at the Booker T. Washington Business College, from whence he might emerge to be employed almost anywhere in the South. The luckiest and most skilled among them were offered positions in Gaston's own interests.

In simplest terms, what Gaston was building among his young clientele was what we now call "brand loyalty": Boys who began as youngsters under Gaston's umbrella of charity became men who recognized not only their indebtedness to this man, but also his power to effect positive change for them, and thus returned to take advantage of his services (whether as consumer or employee) throughout their lives. Gaston was offering them answers to real-life questions—how to earn a respectable living; how to put food on the table; how to survive as a black man in the post-civil-rights-era South—and by and large boys, men, and their families responded to his interest in their well-being. The benefits that Gaston reaped from his efforts were appreciable, as well. For the businesses, the success of the Boys Club created a reservoir of potential employees who had already been schooled in the proper ways and attitudes of successful black folks— elements of comportment that both Mr. and Mrs. Gaston deemed essential to the success of any working person, and nonnegotiable in the demeanor of either a Booker T. Washington graduate or Gaston employee.

If we believe in the dictum that "there is no wiser investment than opportunity, no better way to hold the country together than to make sure everybody has at least a chance to get ahead," then in building his Boys Club, Gaston proved himself not only a shrewd investor, but also a true American in the most capitalistic sense of the term. In an era in which it was becoming increasingly obvious that race would not be the only factor in determining success, in which issues of class would emerge as key features of the basic inequality of American society, Gaston situated himself in the vanguard of ameliorating conditions not by theorizing about the depredations of poverty on blacks but by actively participating in eradicating its ill effects. Whether the fact that these charitable endeavors served Gaston's own business interests negates the advantage conferred upon those who received the benefit of his generosity is a question each person must answer for him- or herself, according to his or her own convictions.

PROFITS AND LOSSES

By the early 1970s Gaston was approaching his eightieth year. In the case of many men it would be safe to assume octogenarianism as an ample excuse for scaling back on business, or a wholesale retirement from the companies that had already provided more than enough financial success for Gaston to live out the remainder of his days in quiet comfort. In Gaston's case, however, no such retirement appeared forthcoming. He continued to play a daily role in administrating his business interests and expanding his companies' reach throughout the state of Alabama.

What did Gaston's empire look like by this point? Bountiful, to say the least. In 1969 Citizens Federal Savings had moved into its grandly planned and executed new office space and settled in as a major institution in the heart of downtown Birmingham. As of 1972, the bank could claim nearly $16,000,000 in assets and had approximately $12,000,000 of loans in force. The bank held the honor of acting as "a depositor for the city of Birmingham, its county government and the state of Alabama" and served as the largest individual financial holding in Gaston's growing domain.

Though the bank had become the focal point of the empire, the Booker T. Washington Insurance Company retained its place as the foundation of Gaston's works. While the insurance company fell just behind the bank in a ranking of individualized hard numbers, because it served as the holding company for all of Gaston's other interests (including the business college, the funeral home, and the motel), the

company's total assets just edged out the bank's. The insurance company had continued to expand its numbers and reach across the state
over the years, growing its assets from approximately $112,000 in
1941, to $728,000 in 1949, to $1.2 million in 1951. As of 1951 it reported insurance holdings of $15,559,277 to the government, and by
1982 it would be able to claim $535 million of insurance in force,
making it the United States' eighth largest black-owned insurance
company.

While the bank and insurance company continued their steady
accumulation of wealth, Gaston utilized his financial leverage to invest in and promote a number of new interests. Among the most successful of these were the Vulcan Realty and Investment Corporation
(formed to keep a handle on Gaston's ever-expanding real estate
properties) and the A. G. Gaston Construction Company. These two
interests worked in cooperation with one another to help revitalize
the downtown Birmingham area in the aftermath of the civil rights
movement: Vulcan managing the purchase and administration of
properties, and Gaston Construction overseeing their production or
refurbishment. (Gaston Construction would eventually become the
largest black-owned construction company in Alabama.) In addition
to his purchase of a nursing home and a drugstore, in the mid-1970s
Gaston also availed himself of the opportunity to invest in the world
of mass communications. In 1975 he bought not one but two local
radio stations in Birmingham: WENN, which became an R&B station, and WAGG (bearing its owner's initials as its call sign), dedicated to playing a steady rotation of gospel favorites.

One version of how Gaston acquired the radio stations indicates
that age certainly hadn't affected either his business acumen or shrewd-
ness of purpose. According to newspaperman Jesse Lewis, an old business associate of Gaston's, the idea to buy the radio stations was
Lewis's own: He had gone to A. G. for advice, describing to him the
terms of the deal he was prepared to negotiate with the seller of the stations. Gaston gave him some counsel regarding the purchase (i.e.,
agreeing that it was a sound investment) and bid Lewis good-bye. The
very next day Gaston called Lewis back to his office to inform him that
he needn't worry about those radio stations anymore—Gaston had

arranged to buy them himself. Lewis was, understandably, upset by Gaston's shenanigans, but Gaston (conscientious as he was shrewd) offered to cut Lewis in on the deal. Though Lewis missed out on reaping the bulk of the profits, Gaston had not forgotten him when the pie was divided.

Though most of Gaston's interests continued their general success throughout the 1970s, some had begun to show signs of trouble. The most notable of these was the place that had played such a large if silent role in Birmingham's struggle for civil rights: the A. G. Gaston Motel. Its downfall was a result of one of the most profound effects of the civil rights movement: With the end of segregation blacks were free to take their business anywhere they chose, and to the detriment of the black business community, many black citizens chose to spend their money where they could get the best deals—which was more often than not in white-owned stores, whose larger financial bases and backing generally allowed them to offer deeper discounts and broader selection than their black competitors.

In the case of the Gaston Motel, being undercut in the price wars was one problem. The other, of course, was the effect of a decade of racial unrest on Birmingham's image as a welcoming vacation destination. Fewer and fewer people were choosing to visit Birmingham for either business or pleasure, and blacks especially were keeping their distance. Those who did visit could usually find better prices and more plush accommodations at the franchise hotels that now had no choice but to accept them. Over time, more and more of the Gaston Motel's rooms were going empty. Gaston was faced with the option of either shutting down operations or coming up with a new strategy for stopping the hemorrhaging of money from the motel's coffers. Rather than shutting the door on so much history (and, of course, in the name of good business), Gaston decided, in 1982, to transform the motel into the A. G. Gaston Gardens: a housing complex for elderly and handicapped citizens that is still in existence today.

Though there were glitches to be dealt with and decisions still to be made on a daily basis, the majority of Gaston's enterprises remained fiscally healthy. Moreover, Gaston believed he had selected a board of directors and administrators upon whom he could rely to keep his companies moving ahead, with or without him. As Gaston put it, "I've got a fine, solid organization. The system is solid." And it was indeed. With millions of dollars of holdings and policies and a history of sixty years of business under his belt, Gaston had been able to produce a network of companies that were mutually sustaining and financially secure. Having made the decision early on to build his empire vertically, Gaston was now reaping the rewards of having established a foundation that could, to some extent, protect his companies from the vagaries of the markets.

As at other crucial junctures in his life, however, just as Gaston's financial fortunes were on the rise, his personal life was taking another hit. In 1971, Gaston's only son, Arthur George Gaston Jr., passed away. He left behind five children—Arthur-Jean, A. G. Gaston III (called Brother), Creola, Rachel, and Patricia—and his wife, Sally. Though the relationship between Gaston and his son had sometimes been troubled, the two had remained close. A. G. Gaston Jr. and his family lived in one of his father's houses in the country, and Gaston's grandchildren grew up visiting their grandparents regularly. Minnie was often credited with cultivating the relationship between the families, but after years of working together, father and son had built a relationship of their very own. Whatever ambivalence remained in their interactions, Gaston was certainly rocked by the loss of his only heir. But as with the losses of all those who meant the most to him (Dad Smith, Creola, Rosie), he had little to say on the matter—at least publicly. Now, as before, Gaston threw himself into his work to dull the pain of his loss.

It was a difficult time—and the heartache was not yet over. For soon Gaston would be dealt another cruel reminder of just how unpredictable life can be.

BOUND AND GAGGED

Friday, January 23, 1976, started off like any other day in the Gaston household. Arthur and Minnie awoke, as always, in the early-morning hours to begin their respective duties in preparing for the day. Each maintained a separate, richly decorated bedroom on the second floor of the house on the hill, Arthur occupying the master suite and Minnie the guest rooms just next door. After rising from his large mahogany bed, but before dressing for the day, Arthur would have donned his bathing suit and ventured down to the pool to swim a few early-morning laps (a practice he would keep up well into his nineties). Once his morning exercise was complete, he headed to his closet to choose from his array of suits, shoes, and hats, pausing first at the desk he kept in his bedroom to look over whatever papers might apply to the coming day. By this point, on the other side of the wall, Minnie would have wrapped herself tightly in a bright robe and made her way downstairs and into the kitchen, to oversee the preparation of the couple's breakfast.

Climbing into his silver 1972 Cadillac El Dorado after finishing his meal, Arthur pulled out of the long, sloping driveway, with a full schedule ahead of him. His newly acquired radio stations were set to go on the air in just a few weeks, and any number of programming and technical issues to had to be dealt with before then; he wouldn't return home until late in the evening. Minnie, too, was gone all day, managing operations at the business college.

That evening, upon returning home, eighty-three-year-old Arthur Gaston turned in on the early side; his hectic day had worn him out. Minnie, on the other hand, wasn't quite ready for sleep. So after kissing her husband good night, she settled herself down to peruse literature from her various charities, turning on her television for company. Sometime just before midnight, Minnie Gaston fell asleep. What she could not know was that as she slept, her life was—once again—in danger.

Downstairs, at the back of the house, someone was drilling a long series of holes in the back door—so many holes, in fact, that police would later estimate that it took the intruder close to two hours to accomplish the feat. The man working steadily outside had already found a way to bypass the first of two alarm systems installed at the Gaston home, and when his work on the door frame was complete he would succeed at breaching the second as well. Upon entering the house, the intruder—later identified as Charles Lewis Clayborn Jr., a mentally disabled local man—made his way silently up the stairs and into the bedrooms of Arthur and Minnie Gaston.

When, precisely, the Gastons became aware that someone had entered their home is unclear. What is certain is that the assailant attacked Arthur Gaston with a hammer, opening a wound in his head that required twenty-three stitches to close. He assaulted Mrs. Gaston as well, dislocating her shoulder and knocking her unconscious before handcuffing her. Though he left Mrs. Gaston behind, before leaving the attacker availed himself of a number of items from the Gastons' home, including Mr. A. G. Gaston himself.

Handcuffed, with a paper bag placed over his head, and covered with the blood that was draining from his wound, Gaston was thrown in the backseat of his own car and covered with a pile of blankets. Not long before sunrise, the car lit out down Gaston's driveway and turned onto Lawson Road, headed to an unknown destination. Unfortunately for the assailant, Mrs. Gaston was not long for the world of the unconscious. She awoke, dazed and bruised, and worked her way over to the telephone in her room, which had been knocked off the hook in the scuffle. After contacting the operator, Mrs. Gaston convinced her to call the funeral home with news of the attack. Whoever was working at the funeral home that day had the good sense to call the police, as well as Thomas and Edna Gardner, Mrs. Gaston's brother and sister-in-law.

The Gardners and the police arrived at the Gaston home at the same time, and an immediate all-points bulletin was put out with a description of Gaston's car and his license plate number. Within hours, the car was spotted by deputies and stopped, and Charles Clayborn was taken into custody. A. G. Gaston, black multimillionaire, was found buried under those blankets in the backseat of the Cadillac and rushed directly to Baptist Medical Center in the Montclair section of Birmingham. Mrs. Gaston had been admitted to the same hospital after a harrowing trip to the fire department to remove her handcuffs so as to release her dislocated shoulder from its distorted position. Both Arthur and Minnie Gaston were treated for their injuries, and spent the months following the attack recuperating in the hospital.

At his trial for the burglary and kidnapping, Charles Clayborn received a lifetime sentence for the crimes of which he was accused, to be served in an Alabama state penitentiary. There was, however, some controversy over the conviction, based on Gaston's own statements to the police. In the aftermath of the attack, while still lying in the emergency unit of Baptist Medical Center, Gaston was interviewed by police officers working the case. During this interview, Gaston claimed that the masked man who had attacked him was white. Clayborn was black. And though Clayborn had indeed been discovered by deputies driving Gaston's car, with Gaston bound and bleeding in the backseat, his defense team claimed that Clayton was simply a pawn in a larger operation, "merely a delivery boy caught in the abortive kidnap attempt which followed the Jan. 24 break in."

The jury didn't buy that argument, though, and with less than forty minutes of deliberation, Charles Clayborn was convicted in May 1976, ostensibly never to set foot in the world as a free man again. In the five months that had passed between the attack and the trial, Arthur and Minnie Gaston had recovered as well as was physically possible, given their advanced age. But the emotional toll of the event was one that was harder for either of them to escape, though each negotiated that burden in very different ways.

Ever since the bombing of the house in 1963, Minnie had been besieged by an unrelenting fear regarding the Gastons' safety—and the events of January 24 only served to increase her anxiety. The double alarm system she had insisted be put in place after the bombing had failed to stop one determined intruder from entering their home and battering them. Who knew what a more calculated effort could produce? So severe were Mrs. Gaston's misgivings about their security that, for a time, guards were positioned around the property in an attempt to provide her with a modicum of peace. Her nephew Paul moved in with the couple, as well, as a means of making her feel more secure. Though the guards and the presence of family members helped ameliorate the present, they could not obliterate her memories of what had occurred. Minnie Gaston was, in a very real sense, haunted by that night for the rest of her life, until her mind was no longer capable of memory at all.

In a 1982 interview with a local newspaper to mark the occasion of his ninetieth birthday, Gaston admitted that the events of the break-in remained, six years later, frighteningly alive for his wife. Moreover, Minnie was not shy about sharing her fear with either family or friends, or, repeatedly, with Arthur. She was truly terrified—and perhaps for his well-being more than her own. The topic of the kidnapping was one that came up often in Minnie's consciousness and she was, it seemed, powerless to stop herself from expressing her fear. Perhaps as a result of this, or perhaps just as a matter of his nature, Gaston himself became increasingly reticent on the topic. In the same 1982 interview in which he revealed his wife's inability to let go of the terror of the night, he claimed that, as for himself, he tried not to think about it. "I forgot about that thing," he told the reporter. "I figure if a guy is going to get you, he's going to get you anyway."

There is something more than a little telling in Gaston making this kind of claim in the wake of the severe traumas he and his wife had suffered. It was neither true nor possible that he had literally forgotten "that thing"—Minnie's articulation of her fear on a daily basis was enough to ensure that much. But his words do reveal the strain of Gaston's personality that tended to become most visible when he was under stress: denial. As when Dad Smith and Creola has been suffering under the weight of their various illnesses, Gaston eschewed the emotional approach here in favor a "grin and bear it" mentality. He meant it when he said, "If a guy is going to get you, he's going to get you anyway"; it was a reaffirmation of his conviction to trouble himself only with the things he could control in his life. Random violence, he determined, was not one of them.

Yet none of this is to say that Gaston was unaffected by the attack. In interviews after the events of January 24, Gaston began rejecting, for the first time ever, the label *millionaire*. He was upfront about precisely why he had begun to shun the term, telling reporters that he blamed media portrayal of his wealth for the kidnapping and burglary that had almost claimed his life and his wife's. "My name is not A. G. Gaston Millionaire," he remarked. "There's a lot of folks in this town with as much or more money than I have, and you never hear them referred to as 'millionaire.' " The publicity surrounding his millionaire status, Gaston felt, put a real, public number to his level of personal wealth, which inspired resentment more often than pride from the black community. As Gaston himself is reported to have said in 1972, "The only thing the black people had against me was I was a success."

Practically speaking, the term *millionaire* amplified Gaston's position as a target for kidnapping and ransom—and even if he had come to terms with the idea of "fate" he described in interviews, it is also true that he lived with and loved a woman who was being driven to her wit's end by worry over their welfare. But there were ideological implications attached to this kind of identification as well, its most obvious effect (as noted above) being that of alienating the Gastons from the larger black community. The repetition of the term *millionaire* in front of or behind his name set Gaston farther and farther apart from the average black citizen of Birmingham, and while he had never felt any real need to be "like" the bulk of the black community in terms of the quality of his life, he also had no desire (nor could he afford) to isolate himself from that population. As the days of segregation had disappeared, so had his captive clientele. So, too, had any sense of security based on wealth and position. Being well liked, it would seem, had become as important to staying alive as it was to maintaining business.

Charles Clayborn's attack on the Gastons had the profound effect of reminding both Minnie and Arthur, simply and inevitably, of the capriciousness of life. While Mrs. Gaston's response was to try to fight uncertainty by attempting to set order to the world around her (guards, gates, ever more intricate alarm systems), Mr. Gaston chose instead to relinquish his grip on trying to control what he knew he could not. And though this had always been the case in terms of his personal life, what came to be true, in the aftermath of the events of January 24, 1976, was that the same model of behavior began to apply to his businesses dealings, as well. Perhaps it was that at eighty-three he was beginning to feel his own frailty (the diabetes that had killed Dad Smith had by now been diagnosed in Gaston as well), or perhaps his run-in with the hammer in Clayborn's hands had put a good scare in him. Whatever its origins, the latter half of the 1970s and early 1980s saw an undeniable change in Gaston's outlook on his life—and his businesses.

Minnée

A person only turns ninety once in his or her lifetime, and that only if the gods are truly smiling. On July 4, 1982, Arthur Gaston crossed over yet another major threshold, entering into the tenth decade of his remarkable life. He chose to mark the occasion not in Birmingham, or anywhere in his home state of Alabama, but hundreds of miles away, in his condominium in Florida.

The decision to commemorate this milestone in a place so far from home certainly wasn't, at face value, a monumental one. However, it did underscore the shift in Gaston's demeanor that began to filter into view in the later years of his life: Florida meant rest and relaxation; it meant time away from the businesses and the spotlight. And more and more, it appeared, this is what Gaston was craving. The resort town of Fort Myers, Florida, had become a home away from home for the Gastons in the late 1970s—a place they could retreat to when either felt it was necessary. The Gastons had become extensive travelers over the years, with their trips tending to take them to ever-new and different locales, including visits to the president of Liberia in the 1950s and a tour of communist Russia in 1972. Over time, however, the toll of these trips began to register on Arthur. At ninety it was becoming increasingly difficult to muster the requisite strength and enthusiasm for these extended voyages (not to mention the media attention they attracted). Florida, however, offered the comfort of home with the exoticism of a beach destination and respite from the public eye. It was time to step back, and Fort Myers provided Gaston with an easy means of doing so.

At the insurance company, a man named Louis Willie had already been picked to steer the corporation into the next stage of growth. Willie had been hired by Gaston himself to fill a midlevel position at the company in the mid-1950s, and had steadily worked his way up the ranks to position himself as heir apparent. At the bank Kirkwood

Balton (another longtime employee) had taken the reins and was, in Gaston's estimation, doing a fine job of moving the company into the future. Though Gaston would continue to visit his companies daily, management had effectively been turned over to the next generation.

Yet as Gaston sought to withdraw from his business interests, Minnie—who for nearly forty years had focused the bulk of her attentions on running the business college—began to churn over her own enterprising notion. The Booker T. Washington Business College would shut its doors in 1988 (a victim of a newly integrated Birmingham and the attendant increase in competition), and in the years before it actually closed down, Minnie found herself with more time on her hands and plenty of energy to spare.

One of the most frequent compliments Mrs. Gaston had received over the years was on the youthfulness of her husband's appearance— for which she, justifiably, took full credit. It had all started in the early years of their romance, after Creola's death and the struggles with Mom Smith. A. G. had begun to suffer physically under the strain of so much emotional upheaval. So Minnie took it upon herself to heal him through natural remedies. She concocted various vitamin-enriched potions for him to drink, and on their travels throughout the world kept a close eye out for any and all herbal remedies native to their destination.

Like most women of a certain age, Minnie eventually began to be concerned about the condition of her skin. She found she was disappointed with the results of most mass-market skin creams and began mixing up her own suspensions at home, which she tested on herself and her family over a period of years. When she had found a formula that suited her, she encouraged Arthur to use it, which he did. Over time, as people began to remark more and more effusively about the condition of the Gastons' skin, Minnie concluded that perhaps she had hit on a business idea of her own, and Minnée Cosmetics was born.

Launched first in Birmingham and then in New York in 1984, the company started small, as had all Gaston ventures since Rosie Gaston gave her son the wise advice in his youth. It offered only two products: a rich face cream called Skin Saver, designed to fight wrinkles, and a lighter body lotion for allover skin hydration. Both products were made with natural ingredients and packaged sleekly in sable-colored containers with silver lettering. A splash of hot pink in the company crest added a suggestion of joie de vivre to the elegant, understated design.

The company's New York launch took place in the Rainbow Room at Rockefeller Center on a warm September day. The event was well attended and drew attention from local media outlets in New York and back in Alabama. Minnie's family in the Northeast helped host the event and feted Mrs. Gaston like the celebrity she had become. The one person conspicuously absent from the proceedings, however, was A. G. Gaston.

Minnie made no secret of the fact that her husband disapproved of her business venture, offering as much to reporters who questioned her about his involvement in the company. "He isn't supporting it," she revealed in one interview, and whether she meant emotionally as well as financially is unclear. Minnie had accumulated wealth of her own over the years, and was a particular fan of savings bonds as a means of growing capital—her own as well as her family's. Because she partnered early on with an already existing cosmetics manufacturer (M & M Products), the level of production costs Minnie herself incurred were relatively low (they were originally estimated to be in the range of thirty thousand dollars). When Gaston refused to help, she covered these costs by dipping into her own savings accounts and seeking investments from members of the extended Gardner family.

In any case, it would not take long for the issue of Gaston's support to be resolved. Though the products received good marks from those who tried them, they failed to ever truly catch on in a large-scale fashion. Eventually, Minnée Cosmetics met the same fate as the Brown Belle Bottling Company: closed for business.

In some ways the story of the collapse of Minnée is no different from the millions of other tales of failed companies that pepper the cultural landscape. The equation for success is as simple to state as it is difficult to achieve: If your income doesn't supersede your expenses, you're out of business. And that is precisely what happened in

the case of Minnée. But in another sense, Minnée wasn't just any
other company—or at least it didn't have to be. Its founder was the
wife of one of the richest black men in America, who possessed, if he
was willing to use them, the tools to protect the fledgling company
from some of the harsher realities of the growing pains all companies
experience in their infancy. It is what Gaston had done to secure the
foundations of his own companies, feeding and sustaining the one
with the fruits of the other until the less secure enterprise could stand
on its own two feet. Yet curiously, in the case of Minnée, no such support was forthcoming from the Gaston empire.

All of which begs a few questions. Why would a man whose personal worth hovered in the range of thirty to forty million dollars—
that is, with the financial capacity to do so—refuse to provide
financial support to his wife of forty years in her pursuit of a dream?
It's certainly a question Minnie's family asked more than once. No
definitive answer was ever forthcoming, but there are any number of
plausible scenarios. In the first place, it is possible that Gaston refused to support the project because he simply did not believe it
could succeed. His own experience with the aforementioned Brown
Belle operation had sincerely burned him on the wisdom of product
manufacture, and there is no indication in any of his dealings that he
ever again became interested in expanding in that direction. The
ratio of potential reward to financial exposure clearly did not yield
the kind of bet Gaston was willing to take.

Secondly (and perhaps most compellingly), it is possible that
what Arthur objected to in Minnie's business venture had less to do
with business than it had to do with personal dynamics. Arthur and
Minnie's marriage was one that had been founded from its start on a
system of inequality: He had always been older than she and wealth-
ier; he was, unmistakably, the Very Important Person in their relationship, the one who was to be deferred to in any given situation.
Quite simply, he was the husband in their very conventional marriage, and in return she was expected to play the wife—which may
have included supporting roles in the drama of business life, but was
never intended for a star turn. Gaston may have balked at the very
notion of Minnie stepping out from under his shadow and establishing herself as a businesswoman in her own right. Though he had al-

ways been supportive of her extensive volunteer work (she had assumed leadership roles in the Alpha Kappa Alpha sorority, the 29th Century Club, the Links, the Girl Scouts of America, the local Women's Business League and Nurses' Association, as well as at the St. John A.M.E. Church), and was proud of her dedication to shaping the business school, Minnée was a project that would place Minnie in the driver's seat. A. G. was not likely to have relished the idea of watching his wife's star ascend just as the sun began to set on his career.

The internal scuffle over the creation of Minnée was not a minor issue between husband and wife, but neither, in the end, was it surprising to people who knew him. Arthur Gaston was who he was, and was still who he had always been: a shrewd businessman who expected total loyalty and devotion in all aspects of his life—perhaps from Minnie above all others. Over the decades Gaston had become accustomed to deference from all around him, and nobody who ever spent any time with the Gastons could mistake the fact that (as close as the couple was, and as much as Gaston respected her input on matters) Minnie was also expected to toe that line. But now, after having been together for nearly fifty years and for the first time, Minnie was striking out on her own. How could Gaston not feel a sense of loss? Maybe even anger?

Things were changing, in the world as well as at home, and it was simply getting harder to keep up. Moreover, Gaston may have begun to wonder just what the *point* of trying to keep up would be. "There's just so much you can do," he remarked late in his life, and by 1987, Gaston felt, he had done it all. In his ninety-fifth year he determined to divest himself of the majority of his companies and live out the rest of his life in a relatively more relaxed manner. Of course just *how* he went about this was, like everything else about the man, totally out of the ordinary.

LOYALTY PAYS

There's a story that A. G. Gaston liked to tell about his early life in Demopolis, something his mother taught him that he never forgot. He had been sitting at the kitchen table in his grandparents' log cabin, his cousin Gaston Stern seated just beside him. Rosie, Art's mother, had placed an apple on the table between the two boys and handed Art a knife to divide the fruit for sharing. Grasping the knife in his small hand, Arthur had proceeded to cut the apple "in such a way that I had about two thirds of the apple for myself." He passed the smaller portion to his cousin and reached for his own, larger slice. Before his hand could close around his piece of fruit, Rosie intervened, silently taking Art's piece and placing it in front of Gaston Stern, and moving the smaller piece in front of her son. As Arthur remembered, she looked him hard in the eyes and offered him this piece of advice: "This is the way good people think. This is the way you're supposed to think . . . always. God first. Others second. Me third."

God first. Others second. Me third. The rules were that simple. They were rules that Gaston had tried to follow over the course of his life, despite the fact that his chosen profession was not one that necessarily lent itself to that kind of code. Over the years he had been accused—repeatedly—of being ruthless in his business practices, of being out to make a dollar above all else. But Gaston simply never believed this to be true of himself, telling a group of students in the 1980s, "I didn't get into business to get rich . . . I kind of made my millions by accident." Which, along a certain line of thinking, is true. Gaston had turned to a career in business out of desperation: first, as a child, to reclaim his lost friends, and later as a young man, to save himself from the life of debt and dependency he saw waiting for him if he continued on in the mines. And with the exception of the Brown Belle bottling plant, he had always kept to the model of "finding a need and filling it"—a different iteration of his mother's dictum regarding first-, second-, and third-order responsibilities.

One testament to how seriously he took his mother's lesson is that there was never a period in Arthur Gaston's life in which he was not engaged in community service in one form or another—and he had the commendations to prove it. Starting in the early days with his work with the Fairfield A.M.E. church and stretching into the final decade of the twentieth century, Gaston had the honor of being recognized hundreds of times over by the many organizations to which he had lent his time through the years, and to which he continued to donate his money. He hung each and every one of these honors in the room that adjoined his corner office at the insurance company.

But there would be another, perhaps bolder, demonstration of just how sincerely Arthur believed in putting others first. In 1987 the insurance company and its holdings were valued at approximately thirty-five million dollars. Gaston's personal wealth hovered in the realm of forty million. He had decided it was time to sell, to let the companies he had built stand without him. If negotiations went well with a qualified buyer, the sale would put him in a position to nearly double his wealth (and given the solid earning projections of the companies, there was little reason to believe they wouldn't have sold for their full valuation).

It was an easy play, a pop fly to left field on a cloudy day, one that any of a thousand good businessmen could have transacted with their eyes closed. But A. G. Gaston had never taken the easy or predictable route. There are precious few among us who, given a near-certain chance to double our money, would walk away from the table jingling mere change in our pockets. But that is almost precisely what A. G. Gaston did.

Rather than selling the conglomerate of nine companies held under the umbrella of the Booker T. Washington Insurance Company to any one of several outside buyers, Gaston chose instead to reward the loyalty of the people who had made the company what it had become over the years. He had his lawyers draw up a deal in which ownership of the company would shift into the hands of 350 long-time employees. His asking price? Three and a half million dollars—*one-tenth* of the company's actual worth.

After what had amounted to more than sixty years in business, Gaston had learned a few crucial lessons about making money, and one of them was that loyalty and dedication should not go unrewarded among employees. There are many stories of the wrath incurred by those whom Gaston felt had failed him in this department—he was not above raising his voice to express his displeasure when his standards were not met (either practically or ethically speaking), or summarily dismissing anyone who couldn't measure up. But he had in his employ hundreds of workers who *had* met his expectations and then some, and who would be left with much less to rely on than the forty million dollars Gaston already had in the bank, if he sold to an outside buyer.

Was it a difficult decision to make, this relinquishing of an extra thirty-five million dollars? If it was, Gaston never admitted it, nor did he ever make public any regrets about his decision. It was a move so radical that strangers and his familiars alike were stunned. The man who appeared to many to have treasured money above all else had walked away from a windfall, for the betterment of 350 black employees. Why? As Gaston explained it, the answer was in that apple he had sliced unevenly almost ninety years before. He had spent a lifetime in business, which had resulted in the creation of great personal wealth, but it was clear to him now that filling that particular cup to overflowing would help only a privileged few. The point, as Rosie might have said, was to spread it around. This was Gaston's chance to live the letter of his mother's law, and he grabbed at it, with both hands.

If Gaston was looking for someone at home to pat him on the back regarding the sale of the company, it wasn't going to be his wife. Though there was no one who was more dedicated to helping those in need and rewarding the hard work of their employees than Mrs. Gaston, she had her own, very grave concerns about her husband's decision. The employees who were set to take over the companies had assured Gaston that he would be allowed to continue to exert some influence once the sale was final. But Mrs. Gaston had her doubts. To be fair, it is also true that by this time, relatives of Mrs. Gaston's had begun to notice changes in her affect—changes that would eventually develop into Alzheimer's disease. Nevertheless, Minnie Gaston was still functioning in the world at the time of the sale, and she did not like what she saw in Gaston's deal with his employees. As the launch (under her own financial steam) of Minnée had made clear, through years of saving and investments, Mrs. Gaston had amassed a nest egg of her very own upon which to rely—so her concerns were not solely financial. What Arthur determined to do with his money was, in the end, his business (though she might have liked to see the family considered more fully, had she been making the decisions). But watching A. G. remove himself from the company he had spent his entire life building, however, distressed her to no end.

And it was not Minnie alone who was worried about Gaston's decision. Heirs are, by their very definition, interested parties in the dissolution of an estate, and it did not escape anyone in Gaston's family that the sale of the company for a fraction of its worth meant that there would necessarily be less money to disburse in the event of Gaston's death (and given that he was ninety-five years old at the time of the sale, that inevitable death was an any-day-now kind of event). Because his was a large family, reactions ran the gamut: For some, the matter was of little concern—fodder for humor more than anything else. For others, the sale was a direct affront—and proof to those looking for it that Gaston had lost the ability to think rationally.

In general, the members of the Gardner family—who, since they had no blood relation to Gaston also had no obvious claim to his estate—were concerned with seeing that Minnie would be well compensated for her more than fifty years of marriage (whether that concern was ever fully satisfied, again, depends on whom you ask). Gaston's direct heirs, however, may have perceived themselves as standing to lose a great deal as a result of Gaston's bargain basement sale. In response to what they saw as uncharacteristic and bizarre behavior on A. G.'s part, the children of A. G. Gaston Jr. brought a competency suit against A. G. Gaston Sr. and took him to court, seeking to block the sale of the companies. In the end, however, Gaston was able to retain control and complete the sale as he wished. Thus in 1987, the profits from nearly seventy years of hard work were turned over to the employees of the Booker T. Washington Insurance Company.

Whatever the effect at home, in the public imagination, the sale had made Gaston into a hero of sorts. Newspaper reports were uniformly full of praise, and Gaston's image as a big-league philanthropist spread nationwide, culminating with *Black Enterprise* choosing him as their entrepreneur of the century in 1992 and placing him on the cover of the magazine. Employees of the companies were, needless to say, quite happy with Gaston's decision. It removed the element of insecurity that had been attached to the possibility of Gaston selling to an outside source, and put them, to some extent, in control of their own destinies.

If we believe that "competition is the name, and moving up—often by any means necessary—is the game" in this "so called free enterprise society" of ours, then in his last act of business management Arthur Gaston had played his hand badly. No textbook on business management would ever advise making a move like Gaston did in 1987—and for good reason. Undercutting yourself in the marketplace just isn't "good business." But at ninety-five years of age, after a lifetime spent accumulating wealth, Gaston had no doubt that what he was doing was the best business of all: He was taking riches from the hands of the few and placing them in the hands of the many. He was creating wealth in the black community by fostering an expansion of the black middle class in very real and measurable terms. He was putting others first. His mother, he was fairly certain, would have been proud.

On the morning of January 18, 1996, Arthur Gaston lifted his head from his pillow to stare out the window at the approaching day. There was the threat of a chill in the air, the sky steel gray if, as ever, snowless. He called to his nurse to help him out of bed; together they shifted his body, minus one amputated leg, into his wheelchair. It was time to get ready for work.

Though the companies had been sold years before, Gaston continued to make himself a presence at the bank, often showing up every day of the week to greet his employees and keep an eye on where things were headed. The daily trips downtown helped fill some of the space that had been left by Minnie's departure. After the failure of Minnée in the late 1980s, Minnie had returned to her life as Mrs. A. G. Gaston—except that, with the closing of the business college, that life had changed dramatically. Though she still had her many charitable interests to attend to, and her ever growing extended family to keep tabs on, none of this could provide the kind of stimulation that had kept Minnie vibrant from her earliest days. She was, in all truth, heartbroken over the closure of the business college, and that pain was redoubled by the loss of both Minnée and the companies A. G. had sold in 1987. Despite her deteriorating state, Minnie had guessed correctly that the continued influence her husband had been promised in selling the companies would be short lived. Before long it was clear that though A. G. could continue to turn up every day, the new ownership had ideas of its own about where the business should be headed. If Gaston suffered as a result, he never admitted it, but it was impossible not to read the slight in his wife's more emotional aspect.

The new quiet of relative retirement did not bode well for Minnie Gaston, a woman who had been on the move and in charge since her early days on her family farm. As weeks turned into months, it became clear to members of the Gardner family that what had started out as a quirky kind of forgetfulness in their aunt's character was growing into a bona fide crisis. Appointments were missed, names forgotten, and soon enough the discombobulation and frustration that are now diagnostic markers of Alzheimer's disease were everywhere evident. A home care nurse was initially brought in to care for Mrs. Gaston in her own residence, but as her condition worsened, placement in a nursing care facility was the only option.

In 1990 arrangements were made to transfer Minnie Gaston to the care of St. Vincent's Nursing Home. She was a celebrity from her first moments there—everyone on the staff knew who she was. Her nieces and nephews were frequent visitors, along with the family friends, former employees, and students who remembered Mrs. Gaston's kindness to them over the years. But no one turned up to visit Minnie more often than A. G. Gaston. He visited her each and every day, after he concluded his "appointments" at the bank.

January 18th, Gaston imagined, would be a day no different than any other. The stroke he had suffered a few years before had slowed him down considerably, but he was still on the move. He was tired, but he had been tired before. There was no excuse for spending any day curled up in bed, and Gaston brought himself encouragement by remembering how Dad Smith had worked right up to the very end.

He intended to be the same kind of man. So he sat in his wheelchair that gray morning, and waited for his nurse to return from the closet with a suit and one of his favorite broad-patterned ties. He liked to look good for his employees.

———————

At 2 A.M. the following day, Gaston was pronounced dead by his doctors. On his way to the office, he had suffered yet another stroke. He was 103 years old.

CODA: BOTH SIDES NOW

You couldn't appreciate what I have seen.
You couldn't believe it.

On a crisp January day in 1996, the flags were flying low all over Birmingham. They had been pulled down from their usual heights above the city's buildings to honor the passing of A. G. Gaston, Birmingham's most famous black entrepreneur. The boy who had ridden into town ninety years earlier on a segregated train, coughing from the cinders in the air, was now being saluted by the city he had dedicated much of his life to improving. Nothing would have made him happier.

Richard Arrington, Birmingham's mayor at the time of Gaston's death, and a friend and confidant of the recently deceased businessman, called Gaston "a model citizen, whose monument was the life he lived. . . ." His epitaph, Arrington suggested, "must be what he achieved in life and what he loved in life." And among the things he loved the most was the city of Birmingham, Alabama. No matter how bad it got in the city, he was always a believer. "None of us had the talent or wisdom he had," Arrington would offer in 2002. "He had his finger on the pulse of this city."

"Birmingham, Alabama is my home," Gaston had written in his autobiography, "and I am among those who are not only fighting for our rights in the Constitution of America as first class citizens, but who have also elected to remain in Birmingham in the South and fight to preserve our democracy." Gaston had, in his own way and according to his own ideals, helped preserve that democracy during the civil rights era—and in return had been insulted for not being "radical enough." Forty years after the 1963 protests, the Reverend Wyatt T. Walker opined that Gaston was "the unsung hero of the civil rights movement." Gaston's insistence on fiscal as well as social responsibility had been the unwelcome caution of the time. But in retrospect, people realized, the counsel of the elder man had been wise. As the Reverend Fred Shuttlesworth put it in a recent interview, "What was that he always said—a part of what you earn is yours to keep? He was sure right about that."

As reward for his decision to stay in the South and focus on ameliorating life in Birmingham, Gaston got a first-row seat to watch from as the political landscape of his hometown shifted dramatically. A. G. Gaston had lived to see Arrington, a black man, be elected mayor of Birmingham, which pleased him greatly. There were still things amiss—for example, Gaston believed, well into his nineties, that the reason so many white people called him "Dr. Gaston" was that they still had a hard time referring to any black man as "Mr."—but America, and specifically Birmingham, was a different place than it once had been. Gaston's own climb up the ladder of success proved it.

Earl Graves, the publisher of *Black Enterprise* magazine, who had idolized Gaston in his youth, delivered the eulogy at Gaston's funeral. Gaston, Graves said, was one of the giants. It was on certain elements of the model of Gaston's success that Graves had crafted his own multimillion-dollar empire of communications and bottling companies. He had used Gaston as the centerpiece of his pitch materials when trying to sell his magazine idea to investors thirty years before. Gaston, he told them, was the epitome of the kind of successful black businesspeople *Black Enterprise* would be profiling. Gaston and Graves would later wind up serving on the Tuskegee University Board of Trustees together. Though they became good friends, Graves never allowed his familiarity with A. G. Gaston, the man, obscure the import of what A. G. Gaston, the legend, had accomplished, and in 1992 *Black Enterprise* selected Gaston as the Entrepreneur of the Century. He was, in the magazine's estimation, "the consummate entrepreneur."

Gaston died too soon to witness America's first black billionaires cross the line into the next economic threshold, but he obviously would have been pleased with their success. Robert Johnson was first to gain billionaire status, with the sale of his Black Entertainment Network to Viacom in 2001. Oprah Winfrey and her Harpo Productions were to be next. Not only would Gaston have been proud to see black faces at the top of the economic scale, he would have been thrilled to be vindicated in his prediction that the communications industry would become the country's next gold mine. He had always been entranced by radio and television, and regretted that he hadn't had time to add television and cable interests to his roster of companies.

Gaston would also have been immeasurably proud of the men—and women—who made it onto *Fortune* magazine's most powerful African Americans list in 2002 (and proud, too, that such a list could even exist in a mainstream white magazine). Among them: Stanley O'Neal, like Gaston the grandson of a slave, and head of Merrill Lynch; Ken Chenault, CEO of American Express; Richard Parsons, CEO of AOL Time Warner; and Cathy Hughes, the black woman and single mother who spent many nights sleeping in her office when she started with RadioOne, only to wind up owning sixty-five radio stations and becoming the first black woman to trade her company on a major American stock exchange. And he would have been satisfied, too, to see that the Executive Leadership Council, comprising black executives situated three steps or less from the top positions in their companies, currently boasts nearly three hundred members nationwide. The organization had given Gaston its very first award, back when there were only a handful of blacks who qualified for membership.

———

However proud Gaston would be of many of the gains blacks have made to date, he would nevertheless still be disturbed by the gap that continues to exist between the money African Americans have to spend and the amount of it they spend with black businesses. Throughout his business life he had been dismayed by the lack of foresight in the black community on this issue and always hoped that blacks would come to have a better understanding of the economic power at their fingertips. After integration arrived in Birmingham, Gaston's motel became a victim of precisely this lack of thoughtfulness on the part of blacks about where they were spending their money. His former guests now availed themselves of the (white-owned) Tutweiler Hotel and Parliament House . . . and the Gaston Motel languished.

To his dying day Gaston's greatest regret was his lack of education—although he could kid about it, often declaring, "It's better to say 'I are rich,' rather than 'I am poor.' " Perhaps, then, the Gastons' immense contributions to education were a way of making up for that lack. Together, Minnie and Arthur set up multiple scholarship and loan programs across the state. Tuskegee University received particular generosity; the school meant much to them both. It was Booker T. Washington's creation, Minnie's alma mater, and A. G. had served a nearly thirty-year tenure on the university's board of directors. So in 1988 the Gastons established the A. G. & Minnie Gaston Foundation at Tuskegee, begun with a hundred-thousand-dollar endowment. It was only one among many financial contributions the Gastons would make to the school through the years.

Tuskegee was not alone in receiving the Gastons' generosity, however: Miles College, Daniel Payne College, and the University of Alabama Law School (along with too many other institutions to mention) were recipients of their largesse. At Lawson State, the A. G. Gaston Building stands as a testament to Gaston's memory and spirit of giving.

Hundreds of students received their college, law, and business degrees because of A. G. and Minnie Gaston—and Birmingham businessman Jesse Lewis was one of them. In his opinion, the Gastons had "saved the town" through their charity. Lewis knew their generosity firsthand: He had personally reaped the benefits of their kindness. When he didn't have the money to pay the business college for his courses, Minnie Gaston had let him attend for free. Lewis went on to become the president of Lawson State College, and to own the region's first and largest black advertising agency—as well as the *Birmingham Times,* a hugely successful black newspaper. And he got his start through the Gastons.

A reflection of their legacy of institutional giving can be seen on the facades of the schools in Birmingham that bear Gaston's name: the A. G. Gaston Junior High School and the A. G. Gaston Elementary School carry on the tradition of Gaston's commitment to education. One of Minnie Gaston's nephews, Carson Gardner, is the principal of that elementary school; A. G. Gaston's great-granddaughter Rochelle Melton teaches kindergarten there.

Education was not the couple's only interest: In their later years the Gastons stayed politically active. They were invited back to the White House many times, and A. G. particularly liked to tell the story of President Johnson's informality ("Gaston," he had cried, "have a drink!"). Presidents Nixon, Carter, Reagan, and Clinton corresponded with the couple. Back in Birmingham, the Gastons took up political causes of their own. In 1979, they held a solemn candlelight vigil on the grounds of their home in support of President Carter's (controversial) policy on Iran. More than 150 people turned up for the event, despite the fact that Mrs. Gaston had only conceived of the vigil the night before. Even on such short notice, the lieutenant governor of the state and the mayor of Birmingham made sure they were there, to stand beside the Gastons and offer their prayers for the hostages' safe return.

Minnie and A. G. Gaston's partnership lasted fifty-three years; together they built businesses, helped their families, and traveled the world. They visited Batista's Cuba, witnessed riots in Guatemala, and survived Soviet Union surveillance, the traffic in Japan, and a return to the slave holds in Ghana. Their interest in life and people was inexhaustible. He called her "Mrs. G." and she called him "Darlin'," and it was only near the very end that they were separated at all. When Minnie was diagnosed with Alzheimer's and living in a nursing home, A. G.—his leg amputated, wheelchair-bound—visited her daily. She expected him every day, too, putting on her makeup, awaiting his arrival. And when he died, she continued to wait, because there was no way to make her understand that her "Darlin' " was gone.

On Friday, June 30, 2000, Minnie Gaston passed away in her sleep at Fairview Nursing Home (where she had moved in the mid-1990s), bringing to a close two remarkable lives, and an amazing journey.

In an assessment of his life written seventy-six years into it, Gaston remarked "I had managed to overcome poverty, limited education, segregation and discrimination to become a contributor to society with some national recognition. There ought to be plenty young people of today who could achieve far more than I had."

Given the scope of Gaston's life and the America in which he lived it, that's a risky bet indeed. But it is a bet we should all be willing to take.

The Companies Today

THE BOOKER T. WASHINGTON INSURANCE COMPANY: According to *Black Enterprise* magazine, in 2003 BTW was ranked the fourth largest black insurance company in the nation, with $1.5 billion of insurance in force and assets of $55 million. The company is still owned by its employees. It divested itself of the radio stations WAGG and WENN; purchased for about $600,000 in the 1970s, the stations eventually sold for a combined $15 million. Having merged with Thatcher Engineering, Inc. (a black owned interest based in Atlanta) in 1995, the A. G. Gaston Construction Company is now a multi-million-dollar enterprise working on municipal, airport, and university projects throughout the South.

CFSBANCSHARES (FORMERLY CITIZENS FEDERAL SAVINGS AND LOAN): Ranked as the seventeenth largest black bank in America, with assets of $108.5 million and $77.5 million in deposits. In 2003 it was bought by Citizens Trust of Atlanta, a black bank founded in 1921. Citizens Trust's aim was "to become the country's first billion dollar black bank," and together the merged banks moved within striking distance of becoming the largest black bank in the country. Kirkwood Balton, who spent forty years in the Gaston fold, believes A. G. would have approved of the merger. "He, above all, knew that times change and people have to move along with the changes. He would have been proud that it was another black bank that enhanced the growth."

THE A. G. GASTON MOTEL: Sold to the city of Birmingham, plans are now in place for the building to become part of the Birmingham Civil Rights Institute. That museum sits on the spot where Gaston's mansion facing Kelly Ingram Park—the first Birmingham home of the Booker T. Washington Insurance Company—once stood. After the old building was torn down, the land was used for a parking lot until the construction of the institute (dedicated in November 1992).

THE A. G. GASTON BUILDING: Built in 1960 for $1.5 million ("cash," as A. G. liked to say), the structure was bought from the insurance company by the Gastons for their own use, then sold to a local doctor in 1996. It will retain the name *A. G. Gaston Building*. Its forty-three thousand square feet of office space have been taken over by the Birmingham Housing Authority and a technology center for inner-city youth. Its six-thousand-square-foot auditorium is used by the Civil Rights Institute for gatherings.

BOOKER T. WASHINGTON BUSINESS COLLEGE closed in 1988, having given an employment boost to the nearly fifteen thousand Birmingham residents who took classes there. Its graduates are employed all over the world.

THE A. G. GASTON BOYS AND GIRLS CLUB continues to provide a haven for hundreds of Birmingham youngsters. It offers afternoon and weekend activities for students from thirty-two local schools. One hundred and forty students a day can use computers, get tutoring, or play basketball on the premises. There are eight football teams that practice on the eighteen-acre grounds. The Gaston Boys and Girls Club is now part of the United Way family.

THE FAMILY

Four of Gaston's five grandchildren (who declined to be interviewed for this book) are, at the time of this printing, still alive. The eldest, Arthur-Jean, passed away in 2002; she spent her working life as a teacher in Birmingham. A. G. "Brother" Gaston III is an attorney and resident of Houston, Texas. Creola Gaston made her living in the real estate field (though not in her grandfather's companies), and Rachel and Patricia Gaston both established successful careers in education. While the majority of Gaston's estate was donated to charity at the time of his death, each of his grandchildren was awarded a modest inheritance.

The Gardner family continues its exponential growth across Alabama and throughout the United States. As of 2003, six of Minnie's fourteen siblings are still alive: Roberta, Susie, Helen, Elizabeth, Clint, and Dixie. With the exception of Elizabeth (who moved to New York in the 1940s), all still reside in Alabama. The more than forty first cousins have gone on to produce more than one hundred second cousins, all of whose accomplishments would have made their aunt Minnie and uncle Arthur proud.

AND IN BIRMINGHAM . . .

Kelly Ingram Park, scene of the calamitous events that defined the civil rights movement, is now a memorial site dotted with commemorative sculptures and plaques. Among them is a sculpture dedicated to Carrie Tuggle at the behest of her former student, A. G. Gaston. Tuggle's grandson, Oscar Adams, went on to become the first black man to sit on the Alabama Supreme Court.

In 2003 a black woman, Annetta Nunn, was appointed Birmingham's chief of police—a fitting conclusion to an era initiated by the violent tactics of former police chief "Bull" Connor.

A. G. GASTON'S
TEN RULES FOR SUCCESS

1. Save a part of all you earn. Pay yourself first. Take it off the top and bank it. You'll be surprised how fast the money builds up. If you have two or three thousand dollars in the bank, sooner or later somebody will come along and show you how to double it. Money doesn't spoil. It keeps.

2. Establish a reputation at a bank or savings and loan association. Save at an established institution and borrow there. Stay away from loan sharks.

3. Take no chances with your money. Play the safe number, the good one. A man who can't afford to lose has no business gambling.

4. Never borrow anything that, if forced to it, you can't pay back.

5. Don't get bigheaded with the little fellows. That's where the money is. If you stick with the little fellows, give them your devotion, they'll make you big.

6. Don't have so much pride. Wear the same suit for a year or two. It doesn't make any difference what kind of suit the pocket is in if there is money in the pocket.

7. Find a need and fill it. Successful businesses are founded on the needs of the people. Once in business, keep good books. Also, hire the best people you can find.

8. Stay in your own class. Never run around with people you can't compete with.

9. Once you get money or a reputation for having money, people will give you money.

10. Once you reach a certain bracket, it is very difficult not to make more money.

EPILOGUE

. . . if you are ready to come to grips
with the inevitable slipperiness of most
available facts, you come to realize that realism
is not a direct approach to the truth
so much as it is the most
concentrated form of fantasy.

—Norman Mailer

Did you know him? It is inevitably the first question people ask when they hear I have written this book. Did you know him? He was born in 1892, I, eighty-three years later. We could just as easily not have known each other at all. But the truth is, we did. Though I grew up far from Birmingham, I saw Uncle Arthur frequently in my childhood years. He and Auntie always traveled to New York on their way to their exotic vacations, and I have vivid memories of Uncle Arthur sitting in my grandparents' apartment off Union Square, talking business with my grandfather, his pipe gripped tightly between his teeth. He called me Princess and let me play with his dark wooden cane, and he left in his wake a stream of sugary smoke that lingered in the house for days after his departure. These are the things I remember.

But if knowledge is information, an accrual of facts and figures and critical events, then my knowledge of Uncle Arthur, before writing this book, was severely limited. I knew things about him that I had never been told, certainly. From listening surreptitiously to the adults around me and by observing their behavior around him, I had gleaned that there was something that made Uncle Arthur different from the rest of them—that somehow he was special. I learned that there was a deference required in talking to or being with him that was never necessary with any of my other great-uncles. I knew that if you were too loud when you were at the big white house in the country, you would inevitably be collared by one of a thousand relatives and reminded, in a hiss, that, "Dr. Gaston would not be pleased." He was a figure of authority for all of us, adults and children alike—even if we children were never directly told *why* that was so.

I was twenty-one years old when Uncle Arthur died, and by then some of the more tangible of his accomplishments has been impressed upon me. Walking around downtown Birmingham, it was impossible not to notice his name clinging in bold letters to the side of so many buildings, impossible not to recognize that it was not just the members of my family who deferred to him but people all over the city. I learned that he had built businesses, and that he owned a bank, that he had known Martin Luther King Jr. and had shaken President Kennedy's hand more than once. Though his climb up from the bottom of society was never discussed per se, I began to understand why Uncle Arthur's expectations of us were always so high—sometimes, it seemed, impossibly so. There were no excuses in his house (or when he was in yours). He and Auntie both made it clear that excellence was the only option. And though their methods could have had precisely the opposite effect, the fact of the matter was that you wanted to be better when you were around them; they made you want to measure up. None of this was accomplished with threats (though intimidation was definitely a factor) or rewards. It was simply the case that you looked at Uncle Arthur and knew, just knew, that this was a man who had done something big—and it made you want to be big someday, too.

It is this, I have realized—his ability to challenge and inspire— that remains Uncle Arthur's greatest legacy. This, I believe, is part of what Uncle Arthur would have wanted you to take away from his story: that role models—whether you are looking for one or acting as one—are as essential to building success as any single other thing. "The best thing I can be is an inspiration," he often said, and he took that charge seriously, not only with his family, but with the thousands of boys and girls, women and men, with whom he came into contact through his charitable works. It was the example of his own role models that had allowed him to believe that his life could be something other than what his context demanded, and he strove through his own example to provide all of us—and all of you—with similar inspiration.

This imperative to find and be models of excellence should be of particular concern to those of us who care about black communities, where too many children and adults continue to feel trapped by hopelessness and, patently, lack of inspiration. Athletes and musicians who have made millions in their industries deserve our respect, but it is critical that blacks understand that our history, and our (often neglected) successes, run deeper than that. Black children *and* white children need to be made familiar with images and stories of blacks who have found success in the boardroom and the classroom, along with those who have found it on the court and in the clubs. Every child should have the privilege of believing, as I did growing up, that skin color does not determine success—dedication does.

The process of writing this book has made it clear to me that "knowing" is a complicated business—but it is a business we cannot do without. Coming to know the details of my uncle Arthur's life and trying to construct a viable history out of those details has been the greatest challenge of my (admittedly short) life—but it has also, as most great challenges do, proved the most satisfying. That famous line about history being the nightmare from which we cannot awake has stuck around for so long because it is essentially true, but to my mind it gives "history" a pretty bad rap. Knowing our histories (and they are as multiple as we are) is necessary because it is prophylactic (that is, when we know better, we do better). But history is not merely a nightmare—it is a dream, one that contains within it all the possibilities of human greatness and achievement. History should give us hope, and for me, that is precisely what A. G. Gaston meant for us to understand, and what I hope you will understand, after reading this book.

My uncle taught me a great lesson in hope one day, when I was not more than seven years old. Though my immediate family are transplanted Northerners, we are Southerners at heart, and in part this means that when we die, we are buried in the South. It would not be overstating the case to say that my grandfather was, in the period before his death, my best friend. We adored each other and we both knew it. By the time he actually died, my grandfather had been sick for many years, and in order to help look after him my mother and I had moved in with him and my grandmother when I was not more than four years old. I had seen him every morning and night for over half my life, and his death, when it came, mystified me. I didn't get it, and didn't want to; all I knew was that I felt alone without him.

Until that particular trip to Birmingham to bury my grandfather, showing up in town had always simply meant fun. I had more cousins to play with than I could count, and my great-aunts always indulged me. This time, though, I wasn't precisely in the mood. Not only had I lost my grandfather, but on the plane ride down I had developed a case of the chicken pox, and thus had spent the better part of my first two nights in Birmingham wide awake and bristling with pain.

Nevertheless, the day after the funeral, I was ordered by Auntie to put on my bathing suit and sit by the pool (contagion, apparently, didn't much concern her). I did as I was told because there was no other option, and made my way down to the backyard as instructed. Uncle Arthur was there, as usual, swimming his laps.

When he saw me, he called to me, inviting me to join him. I shook my head; I didn't want to, I said—and I really didn't. I was still not well and as sad as I could ever remember being. I would have rather been inside with my books to begin with. In any case, Auntie had only said I had to *sit* by the pool, and I meant to follow her instructions to the letter without extending myself any farther. Uncle Arthur, though, had other plans.

He called me to him again, this time instructing, not inviting, me to come to the edge of the pool. I thought about saying no, might have even tried it, but somehow those lessons about authority had sunk in: Before I knew it I was standing not merely at the pool's edge but on its first step.

I remember seeing Uncle Arthur moving toward me, then, and I remember knowing he was going to lift me up; I also remember pleading frantically for him not to do it, not to dump me in. I knew how to swim, but didn't want to, and I was so sad and overwrought that I think I became I little hysterical in the moments between when I felt Uncle Arthur's strong, bony hands grab my waist and when I felt my body take flight. I remember the water rushing up beneath me, and feeling its iciness wrap around my still prickly skin. It was, unexpectedly, a relief. After a moment, I shot up and out of the water to catch my breath, sucked in the already warming morning air and paddled my way to the side of the pool. I looked around to find my uncle, as yet unsure whether I was cross with him or elated. By then, however, he had already gone back to swimming his laps.

It was not an act of cruelty my uncle perpetrated on me that day—it was one of infinite kindness. He had tossed me in the water, despite my protestations, to teach me a lesson about life that I have never forgotten, and one that has come back to me every time in my life I have come up against disappointment. Arthur Gaston was a man who lived in the moment, always, and took nothing for granted. What he taught me by throwing me in the pool—and what he demonstrated by the example of his life—was that every day is a chance to do better, every moment of every day an opportunity to experience the fullness of life in a new and startling way. The important part, he would tell you, is not how many days you have—it's what you do with the ones you've got.

I understood what he was saying that day, even though I was only seven and could not have articulated it so precisely. To make it easier on me, Uncle Arthur had made sure to whisper something in my ear before he launched me in the air: *You're going to be okay,* he'd said. And I was. What I understood then was that you can't simply sit by the pool and wait for something to save you. You've got to just jump in. And you've got to believe.

—Elizabeth Gardner Hines

ACKNOWLEDGMENTS

First-order thanks go to our wonderful editor, Elisabeth Kallick Dyssegaard, for her diligence and patience in working with two first-time authors. Our agent, Charlotte Sheedy, has been indispensable to us for many years now as both friend and mentor; we thank her tremendously for her support. Julia Cheiffetz and Carolyn Kim made our days inestimably easier, and Dreu Pennington-MacNeil gifted us with a most beautiful cover—thanks to you all.

It was Anita Diggs who first knew enough about A. G. Gaston to want to know more; without her this project would not have been, and we thank her for her inspiration. Patricia Thompson Stelts compiled a persuasive master's thesis on A. G. Gaston, and we are indebted to her for her early research on his businesses.

Thanks to Professor Manning Marable, the Reverend Wyatt T. Walker, Earl Graves, Autherine Lucy, Richard Arrington, the Reverend Fred Shuttlesworth, David Garrow, Bruce Llewellyn, Kirkwood Balton, and Jesse Lewis for their insights on the times.

Many thanks to the Gardner family: Edna Gardner for keeping the family history, Billy and Nancy Gardner for their research on the Gardner-Carson genealogy, Cheryl Davis at Tuskegee, Paul Gardner,

Minnie and Richard Finley, Kaye Underwood, Cecil Shorte, Helen Washington, Roberta Shorte, Dixie Harris, Susie Lowe, and Clint Gardner.

For research assistance, thanks to John Taylor and Walter Hill at the National Archives and Sharon Howard at the Schomburg Library. Dr. Jeanette Greaves Brown and her daughter Leah Brown were of marvelous assistance down in Virginia.

And to our animals Jackson, Stanley, Timmy, and Tricks, who kept us laughing every moment.

Carol Jenkins

Thanks to Dr. Lennette Benjamin and Jeff Madrick for daily encouragement and exceptional friendship through many years and many things.

A special thank you to Sandy Lerner, a patron and a saint and a pretty cool person; and to Diane Heath, friend and optimist extraordinaire. To Janet Jacobs, Norma Quarles, Delores Harvin, Yvonne Somers, and Carole Owens, thanks for keeping tabs on us.

To my coven: Gloria Steinem, Marilyn French, and Esther Broner. After fifteen years of talking, I finally joined the writers' circle.

Gus Heningburg, Charles Howard, Dr. Reggie Gardner, Kaye Underwood, and Jayne Sherman deserve special appreciation for being there.

To the Hunter's Head crowd, especially Don Roden for time, and Mike Gannon for getting our computers running again.

To my sister, Holly Low, nephew Andy Low, and Ruby Dallas Young, for all your help.

To Mike Hines, my wonderful son: Thank you for taking such good care of us. I'm so proud of you. We know you're the next A. G. Gaston.

And to my daughter, Elizabeth Hines: It has been so wonderful to work beside such a gifted and perceptive writer. People predicted we'd stop speaking, but it was a joyous time. For the love and the laughter, I thank you from the bottom of my heart.

Elizabeth Gardner Hines

Much love and appreciation go out to Niki Benjamin, Fred Benjamin, Heidi Gilchrist, Dr. Phoebe Dann, Abby Durden, Nina Morrison, Maurice Wallace, Gwen Urdang-Brown at Harvard University, Molly Breen, Kathryn Parsons Hoek, Jennifer Farrington, Cameron Hyzer, Laura D'Anca, and Elisabeth Barbiero for their friendship and support throughout this process. Thanks also to Sarah MacArthur and the MacArthur family for, among other things, the gift of Maine in the summer of 2002.

My godparents, Lennette Benjamin and Jeff Madrick, have taught me much about the twin virtues of fortitude and compassion through their living example. I am blessed to call them mine.

And speaking of blessings . . . Many people never stumble upon one great friend in the course of a lifetime; I am privileged to have found *four* particularly extraordinary ones: Jennifer Feeley, whose grand sense of humor and unwavering belief in me has lit up the darkest of places; Elizabeth Wallace, whose kindness, generosity, and general hilarity have kept me buoyant all these many days; Ingrid Eberly, *la mariposa màs hermosa,* possessor of razor-sharp wit and eternally steadying hand; and my soul mate Nicholas Boggs, who has, from the first, inspired me with his unparalleled brilliance and sustained me by way of his love. Without you all, I don't know where I'd be.

Finally, thanks to my brother and best friend Michael Hines, who over the last year has taught me, yet again, what life is really about. And to my mother, as always and as ever, who has made everything—*everything*—possible.

THE LIFE OF A. G. GASTON

1892

On the Fourth of July, Arthur George Gaston is born in Demopolis, Alabama. He lives in a log cabin with his mother and sharecropper grandparents, who were former slaves. Frederick Douglass, Harriet Tubman, Booker T. Washington, W. E. B. DuBois are all alive.

1905

Art moves to Birmingham with his mother, who is the cook for the Loveman family, owners of the largest department store in the city. Art and his mother live above the stable.

Attends Tuggle Institute where Booker T. Washington lectures regularly. The first book he owns is Washington's *Up From Slavery*.

1910–1913

Art works as bellhop at the famous Battlehouse Hotel in Mobile, Alabama, among other jobs.

Fathers a son, Arthur George Gaston Jr.

1914–1919

A. G. Gaston purchases his first plot of Birmingham land—a lot he held until his death—for $200.00. He paid it off in monthly installments of $15.00.

Joins army, serves with distinction in France in segregated unit during World War I. Falls in love with Paris and traveling.

1919

Unable to find work upon return from the war, he drives a delivery truck for the OK Dry Cleaning Company. For the first and last time, he is fired from a job.

1920

Works in the iron mines and railroad car workshop for the Tennessee Coal & Iron Company (TCI). Begins first Gaston commercial enterprise: selling lunches and peanuts and lending money to fellow workers.

1923–1937

Marries Creola Smith, his childhood sweetheart from Demopolis.

Forms Booker T. Washington Insurance Company with father-in-law Dad Smith, selling and collecting small premiums door-to-door: becomes the largest black owned insurance company in Alabama.

Forms Smith and Gaston Funeral Home. Expands burial insurance into funeral business: becomes the largest black owned chain in Alabama.

Continuing vertical integration of businesses, buys Mt. Zion Cemetery. Businesses flourish, even during Depression.

1938

Insurance company moves into mansion on Kelly Ingram Park in Birmingham, former home of Birmingham coal baron.

Dad Smith and Creola Smith die.

1939

Unable to find trained personnel for businesses, opens Booker T. Washington Business College, which provides hundreds of staff members for government and businesses during World War II.

1943

Marries his second wife, Minnie Gardner, who would become director of BTW Business College, in New York.

1950

Shutters his only unsuccessful business venture, the Brown Belle Bottling Company, manufacturer of a soda called The Joe Louis Punch. Gaston said it was his only business built on greed instead of filling a need.

1954

The A. G. Gaston Motel opens to great fanfare. Known as one of the finest in the South, hosted guests like boxing champ Joe Louis and baseball great Willie Mays and many a black traveler through the South.

1957

Gaston raises nearly $500,000 to secure the charter for the Citizens Federal Savings and Loan, the first black bank in Birmingham since 1915. Black residents and churches are able to get loans without being discriminated against because of race.

1962
The imposing $1.5 million A. G. Gaston Building opens, featuring offices for Gaston's businesses, and a large auditorium. From his third floor office facing Kelly Ingram Park, Gaston had a unique view of the civil rights protests of the 1960s.

1963
A. G. Gaston Motel becomes headquarters for Martin Luther King Jr. Gaston participates in negotiations, meets with President John Kennedy, bails MLK Jr. and protestors out of jail. Both his house and motel are bombed.

1965
In famed Selma to Montgomery march, protestors spend one of the nights on the family farm in Lowndes County, just outside of Montgomery.

Minnie Gaston testifies before Congress on the need for vocational student loans. Millions of students get vocational training through loan program.

1966
Gaston builds a new Birmingham affiliate of the Boys Club of America—now known as the A. G. Gaston Boys and Girls Club. A. G. and Minnie begin setting up scholarships at colleges, most prominently the Gaston Fund at Tuskegee University.

1968
A. G. Gaston publishes autobiography, *Green Power*, reminding readers that "part of what you earn is yours to keep." Introduces his Ten Rules of Wealth Building.

1969
Inducted into the Alabama Academy of Honor. Among its other famous inductees: Governor George Wallace.

1975
Acquires WAGG and WENN radio stations and forms the Booker T. Washington Broadcasting Company. The stations become number one in their market.

1976
A. G. and Minnie are kidnapped. Both are seriously injured and hospitalized. Their attacker is apprehended and sent to jail.

1977
For their contributions to the city, A. G. and Minnie Gaston are inducted into the Birmingham Hall of Fame.

1984

A. G. Gaston Construction Company becomes largest black owned construction company in Alabama.

1987

In a historic move for black business, turns his Booker T. Washington Insurance Company, which controlled several other companies, over to his employees in an ESOP (employee stock option program). Nine companies worth approximately $35 million are transferred to 350 staff members for just $3.4 million.

1992

Black Enterprise magazine names Gaston "Entrepreneur of the Century."

January 19, 1996

At age 103, A. G. Gaston dies in Birmingham Medical Center East at 2 A.M. from complications of a stroke. Flags in the city of Birmingham fly at half-mast in honor of the great leader-citizen.

ENDNOTES

Chapter 1

5 **"Not all who had come"** Lefebvre-Desnouettes was by far the wealthiest of the new French residents, and ever loyal to Napoléon. He is said to have had a log cabin on his property, his sanctuary, "in the center of which stood a bronze statue of Napoleon." Albert James Pickett, *History of Alabama: And Incidentally of Georgia and Mississippi.* Harper Lee, 2001.

6 **"Indeed the country"** Robert L. Heilbroner, and Aaron Singer, *The Economic Transformation of America: 1600–the Present.* Harcourt Brace Jovanovich, 1984, p. 155.
Ibid. **"Thousands, known as"** Harold Evans, Gail Buckland, and Kevin Baker, *The American Century.* Alfred A. Knopf, 1998, p. 33.

8 **"Prior to this"** Gavin Wright, *The Political Economy of the Cotton South.* W. W. Norton, 1978.
Ibid. **"But the increasing demand"** Ibid., p. 14.

9 **"Historian Gavin Wright"** Ibid., p. 35.
Ibid. **"Slavery had turned"** W. E. B. DuBois, *Black Reconstruction in America, 1860–1880.* Atheneum, 1985, p. 47.
Ibid. **"For all its moral"** Ibid., p. 12.
Ibid. **"Influenced by the shift"** Ibid., p. 14.
Ibid. **"Its growth dictating"** This Black Belt Prairie (in the middle of which Demopolis sits) represents a piece of one of the five major landscapes that make up the agricultural geography of the Cotton State. Though cotton was certainly grown all over the state, it tended to meet with its greatest success in those parts of the region that offered the

dark, loamy soil whose stickiness and potency seemed heaven sent for cotton production. It is in these regions—across the Black Belt—that the vast majority of cotton plantations were established.

10   **"When Alabama had been"** In fact, the Supreme Court of the United States had agreed with this basic assessment. In the *Dred Scott* decision of 1857, the Court determined that blacks were not citizens of the United States, and held no rights.

Ibid. **"Its corner stone rests upon"** The Cornerstone Speech was delivered extemporaneously by Vice President Alexander H. Stephens, and no official printed version exists. The text was taken from a newspaper article in the *Savannah Republican*, as reprinted in Henry Cleveland, *Alexander H. Stephens, in Public and Private: With Letters and Speeches, before, during, and since the War, Philadelphia,* 1886, pp. 717–29.

11   **"Perhaps Joe and Idella"** This is where the phrase *forty acres and a mule* originated.

12   **"These codes"** So egregious were the crimes against blacks that in 1867 the government stepped in and created military zones to protect black interests. The period became known as Radical Reconstruction, for a brief moment in southern history blacks did have rights, including the vote.

13   **"As the primary cook"** T. G. and Louisa Jane Cornish were merchants who owned a store in town called Cornish and Sharpe.

14   **"Not once did a penny"** A. G. Gaston, *Green Power: The Successful Way of A. G. Gaston.* Troy State University Press, 1968, p. 9.

15   Trudier Harris, "Sharecropping." In *The Oxford Companion to Women's Writing in the United States,* Oxford University Press, 1995, p. 797.

Ibid. **"The average wage"** Howard Zinn, *A People's History of the United States, 1492–Present,* HarperPerennial, 1995, p. 209.

16   **"Like just about every other"** Gaston, *Green Power,* p. 6.

17   **"The railroads were coming"** Ibid., p. 3.

18   **"Demopolis had been chosen"** John Osborne, "Railroad Yesterdays: The Frisco Comes to Demopolis, Alabama." http://www.frisco.freewebspace.com/. 800 Pinhook Road. Demopolis, AL 36732-5702.

Ibid. **"The Lovemans were"** John Hood, "Capitalism: Discrimination's Implacable Enemy." *The Freeman* (a publication of the Foundation for Economic Education, Inc.), 48, no. 8 (August 1998).

19   **"With the relocation"** Gaston, *Green Power,* p. 18.

Ibid. **"The soil was anything but"** Edward Shannon LaMonte, *Politics & Welfare in Birmingham 1900–1975.* The University of Alabama Press, Tuscaloosa, 1995.

Ibid. **"The city quickly grew"** Ibid., p. 4.

Ibid. **"The vaults"** Ibid., p. 4.

Ibid. **"The tax rate"** Ibid., p. 5.

20 "Most often he found" Gaston, *Green Power*, p. 4.
Ibid. "The possibility of such" Ibid., p. 3.
Ibid. "His most frequent" By Gaston's account, Martin "remained in the slums and inevitably ended up in prison." Ibid., p. 5.
Ibid. "I was nobody's hero" Ibid., p. 5.
23 "Any nigger who did not" Gaston, *Green Power*, p. 6.
24 "A. G. reached in" Ibid., p. 13.

Chapter 2

26 "Alabama's 1901 constitution" Lynne B. Feldman, *A Sense of Place: Birmingham's Black Middle Class Community, 1890–1930*. University of Alabama Press, 1999, p. 10.
27 "Despite it all" Ibid. p. 11.
Ibid. "Beyond the buildings" Arthur George Gaston, *Green Power: The Successful Way of A. G. Gaston*. Troy State University Press, 1968, p. 16.
Ibid. "At the turn of the century" Mark H. Elovitz. *A Century of Jewish Life in Dixie: The Birmingham Experience*. University of Alabama Press, 1974, pp. 25, 26.
28 "There was already a small" Ibid., p. 23.
29 "Black and white parishioners" Gaston, *Green Power*, p. 19.
Ibid. "Berney poked me" Ibid., p. 20.
30 "She explained to him" Ibid.
31 "As recently as 1890" Robert A. Margo, *Race and Schooling in the South, 1880–1950*. University of Chicago Press, 1990, p. 8.
Ibid. "In 1880" Ibid., p. 6.
Ibid. "Seventy-six percent of blacks" Ibid.
Ibid. "The literacy gap" Ibid., p. 8.
32 "Between 1891 and 1907" Edward Shannon LaMonte. *Politics & Welfare in Birmingham 1900–1975*. University of Alabama Press, 1995, p. 10.
Ibid. "Moreover, one of the most important" *Birmingham News*, September 4, 1901.
Ibid. "In this same year" LaMonte, *Politics & Welfare*, p. 11.
33 "Criminals are generally" Gaston, *Green Power*, p. 22.
Ibid. "In Gaston's own words" Ibid.
34 "Leaving Birmingham proper" Ibid., p. 21.
Ibid. "As for the boys" Ibid., p. 21.
35 "Arthur remembered him as" Ibid., p. 24.
Ibid. "Washington's life story" Washington's autobiography tells of the extraordinary steps that took him from slavery to being asked to serve as Tuskegee Institute's first president.
36 "But Washington was equally" Robin D. G. Kelley and Earl Lewis, *To Make Our World Anew: A History of African Americans*. Oxford University Press, 2000, p. 315.

Ibid. **"President Roosevelt, admiring"** Mark Sullivan, *Our Times III: Pre-war America, 1900–1925.* Charles Scribner's Sons, 1930, p. 133.

37   **"Was there ever a nation"** W. E. B. DuBois, "The Talented Tenth" (1903) in *African American Social and Political Thought: 1850–1920.* Howard Brotz, ed. Transaction Publishers, 1992, p. 522.

38   **"Unlike any other blacks"** Gaston, *Green Power*, p. 23.
       Ibid. **"Like its larger"** Feldman, *A Sense of Place*, p. 3.
       Ibid. **"Residents belonged to elite"** By and large, Enon Ridge residents (like many in the black middle class) were not generally interested in mixing socially with blacks from the lower classes. Tuggle students may have fallen into their good graces because work with them was clearly charity and probably qualified as a nod in the direction of "uplifting the race."

39   **"I mowed and raked lawns"** Gaston, *Green Power*, p. 24.

40   **"He burned no bridges"** Ibid., p. 25.

41   **"Every persecuted individual"** Booker T. Washington, *Up From Slavery*, Carol Publishing Group, 1997, pp. 40–41.

42   **"Though his intention was"** Though in his autobiography Gaston claims to have forged his mother's signature and enlisted in the service right away, he would later admit that he had spent time in Mobile after leaving Tuggle.

43   **"The summer was unusually hot"** Gaston, *Green Power*, pp. 35.
       Ibid. **"There Gaston served"** Ibid.
       Ibid. **"The punch—delivered"** Ibid., p. 37.

44   **"By 1917, after years on the base"** Ibid., p. 33.

45   **"Though the American government"** Howard Zinn, *A People's History of the United States: 1492–Present.* HarperPerennial, 1995, p. 355.
       Ibid. **"Nevertheless, one month after"** Emmett J. Scott, *Official History of the American Negro in the World War.* Arno Press, 1919, p. 118.

46   **"White troops lived"** Gail Buckley, *American Patriots: The Story of Blacks in the Military from the Revolution to Desert Storm.* Random House, 2001, p. 179.
       Ibid. **"At another camp"** Ibid.
       Ibid. **"It had been raining"** Gaston, *Green Power*, p. 39.
       "The steady 'bombardment' " Ibid., p. 39.

47   **"Organized and trained in five"** Buckley, *American Patriots*, p. 180.
       Ibid. **"As Gaston said of his time"** Gaston, *Green Power*, p. 32.

49   **"While in Kansas"** Ibid., p. 37.

50   **"Instead, he had sent"** Ibid., p. 35.
       Ibid. **"He attended performances"** In 1918 General John J. Pershing issued a directive to dissuade French military officers from "spoiling" Negro soldiers, stating that the "vices of the Negro are a constant menace to the American." Pershing warned the French that they "must not eat with them, must not shake hands or seek to talk or meet with them outside the requirements of military service." Similar propaganda was disseminated to the civilian population of France; it was largely ignored. *The Crisis*, May 1919, pp. 16–17.

Chapter 3

52　**"More than ten million"** Howard Zinn, *A People's History of the United States: 1492–Present.* HarperPerennial, 1995, p. 359.
Ibid. **"Indeed, the year 1914"** Ibid., p. 362.

53　**"Within the first two years"** Ibid.
Ibid. **"As Lieutenant Colonel David A. Lane"** John P. Davis, ed., *The American Negro Reference Book.* Prentice-Hall, 1966, p. 616.

54　**"In going to war"** Lynne B. Feldman, *A Sense of Place: Birmingham's Black Middle-Class Community, 1890–1930.* University of Alabama Press, 1999, p. 21.
Ibid. **"In 1917, race riots"** Tom Cowan and Jack Maguire, eds., *Timelines of African American History.* Roundtable Press, New York, 1994, pp. 149–153.
Ibid. **"In 1918, W. E. B. DuBois"** W. E. B. DuBois, "The Black Soldier." *The Crisis,* June 1918. As cited in Feldman, *A Sense of Place,* p. 179.
Ibid. **"Indeed, in at least one well-documented"** Gail Buckley, *American Patriots: The Story of Blacks in the Military from the Revolution to Desert Storm.* Random House, 2001, p. 219.

55　**"The world seemed fresh"** Gaston, *Green Power: The Successful Way of A. G. Gaston.* Troy State University Press, 1968, p. 44.
Ibid. **"In one instance, a member"** Buckley, *American Patriots,* p. 219.

56　**"One black private wrote"** Ibid., p. 221.
Ibid. **"More than twenty-five race riots"** Cowan and Maguire, *Timelines,* p. 156.
Ibid. **"The Ku Klux Klan"** Zinn, *A People's History,* p. 382.

59　**"Don't give up your dreams"** Gaston, *Green Power,* p. 45.
Ibid. **"She rented herself a house"** Ibid., p. 46.

60　**" 'After all,' he wrote"** Ibid.
Ibid. **"It paid five dollars"** Ibid., p. 46.

61　**"I wanted to go to Tuskegee"** Ann Elizabeth Adams, interview with A. G. Gaston, November 17, 1976. Property of the University of Alabama at Birmingham, Mervyn H. Stern Library.

62　**"World War I had"** Buckley, *American Patriots,* p. 224.

63　**"I am not sure whether"** Gaston, *Green Power,* p. 47.

65　**"After a financial crisis"** Morgan only unwittingly made a contribution to black America: In 1905 he hired Belle da Costa Greene to curate his extensive art and book collections at the Morgan Library in New York City. She became an indispensable part of his life. What he didn't know was that she was black, but "passing." According to Morgan biographer Jean Strouse, Greene was the daughter of the first black man to graduate from Harvard, Richard Greener. Morgan died in 1913, leaving da Costa Greene $50,000 in his will. She remained head of the library for the next thirty-five years.
Ibid. **"U.S. Steel's discriminatory pricing"** Feldman, *A Sense of Place,* p. 7.

66　**"In Birmingham, a staggering"** Mitch Menzer and Mike Williams, "Images of Work: Birmingham 1894–1937" in *The Journal of the Birmingham Historical Society*. Vol. 7, no. 1 (June 1981).

Ibid. **"Typically, each miner"** Mary Ellen Curtin, *Black Prisoners and Their World, Alabama, 1865–1900*. The University Press of Virginia, 2000, p. 2.

67 **"Eighty percent of the convicts"** Menzer and Williams.

Ibid. **"Not only did this system"** Ibid.

68 **"He watched a house"** Gaston, *Green Power*, p. 48.

69 **"In 1901 Carnegie sold"** Jean Strouse, *Morgan: American Financier*. New York: Random House, 1999. p. 403.

Ibid. **"Believing that 'the man who dies rich' "** Frederick D. D. Lynch, *Personal Recollections of Andrew Carnegie*, 1920; as cited in *The Naked Word* (electronic edition: xooqi.com/iboox/xo_0074_lynch_andrew-carnegie.html).

Ibid. **"We cannot afford to lose"** Andrew Carnegie, *The Gospel of Wealth, 1889*. Bedford, MA: Applewood Books, 1998, p. 18.

71 **"The paint, it seemed"** Ibid., p. 49.

Ibid. **"He had, he wrote, 'vacillated' "** Ibid.

72 **"He began selling peanuts"** A. G. Gaston, "How to Make a Million." *Ebony Magazine*, January 1963.

Ibid. **"Once he had secured"** Ibid.

73 **"In fact, the interest was"** Gaston, *Green Power*, p. 53.

75 **"Solicitors carried lists"** Ibid., p. 52.

76 **"It was a racket"** Ibid.

Ibid. **"It seemed logical to him"** Ibid., p. 54.

77 **"However, he was absolutely"** Ibid.

78 **"His rate was twenty-five cents"** Ibid., p. 55.

79 **"Without hesitation"** Ibid., p. 58.

80 **"The deceased, he said"** Ibid., p. 59.

Chapter 4

82 **"What happens to us *just* after"** Witness the fact that this year, the television show that garnered the most Emmy nominations was *Six Feet Under*—HBO's hugely popular series about a family of undertakers. *Time* magazine and *People* both recently featured full-color stories about the ever-widening variety of choices available to us to commemorate this final event in our lives.

83 **"From 1922 to 1929"** Howard Zinn, *A People's History of the United States: 1492–Present*. HarperPerennial, 1995, p. 382.

Ibid. **"Critically, one-tenth of one percent"** Ibid.

84 **"Funeral homes and service directors"** Karla F. C. Holloway, *Passed On: African American Mourning Stories*. Duke University Press, 2002, p. 18.

85 **" 'Memorialization is love' "** Jessica Mitford, *The American Way of Death, Revisited*. Vintage, 1998, p. 79.

86 **"Washington's statement that"** Booker T. Washington, "Atlanta Exposi-

tion Address," as reprinted in *African American Social and Political Thought, 1850–1920*. Howard Brotz, ed. Transaction Publishers, 1992, p. 359.

Ibid. **"In 1899, under the auspices of"** W. E. B. DuBois, ed., *The Negro in Business*, Atlanta University Publications, No. 4, 1899, as reprinted in Lynne B. Feldman, *A Sense of Place: Birmingham's Black Middle-Class Community, 1890–1930*. University of Alabama Press, 1999, p. 85.

87   **"After moving from Montgomery"** Feldman, *A Sense of Place*, p. 105.

88   **"Pettiford had come to Alabama"** Ibid., p. 90.

Ibid. **"He proved a master"** Ibid., p. 91.

89   **"The idea for building"** Ibid., p. 93.

Ibid. **"Formed in 1890"** *Montgomery Colored Alabamian*, June 28, 1913.

90   **"Though his experiences"** Arthur George Gaston, *Green Power: The Successful Way of A. G. Gaston*. Troy State University Press, 1968, p. 48.

91   **"To do so he began to hire"** Ibid., p. 62.

92   **"What Creola Smith actually"** Dad Smith was clearly against marrying his daughter off in any instance. If she had rejected Gaston's proposal, it therefore seems highly unlikely that he would have pushed her into it.

93   **"Arthur went back to Alabama"** Gaston, *Green Power*, p. 64.

Ibid. **"She had, in Gaston's words"** Ibid.

94   **"He was assigned to work"** Ibid., p. 65.

97   **"The frock coat"** William C. Nelson, private interview of August 9, 1972, conducted by Patricia Thompson Stelts (p. 6 of *Black Midas* thesis).

Ibid. **"He was never shy"** Gaston, *Green Power*, p. 169.

99   **"They withdrew all the money"** Ibid., p. 70.

100   **"Government regulation"** Suzi Parker, "Get Your Laws Off My Coffin." *Salon Magazine*, January 12, 2001.

Ibid. **"He did not spare himself"** Gaston, *Green Power*, p. 70.

102   **"Most economists agree"** Zinn, *A People's History*, p. 386.

103   **"According to economist John Kenneth Galbraith"** Galbraith, *The Great Crash: 1929*. Houghton Mifflin, 1972, as quoted in Zinn, *A People's History*. p. 386.

Ibid. **"Those [businesses] that continued"** Ibid., p. 387.

104   **"The available examples"** Fredrick M. Binder and David M. Reimers, *The Way We Lived—Essays and Documents in American Social History, Volume II: 1865–Present*. D.C. Heath and Company, 1996, p. 186.

Ibid. **"Nationally, the rates rose"** Ibid.

Ibid. **"Fewer jobs meant"** Ibid., p. 185.

105   **"And it was not the Klan alone"** Ibid., p. 150.

106   **"Only a year after the crash"** Steven Mintz, Susan Kellogg. "America's Families Face the Great Depression," in Binder and Reimers, p. 192.

Ibid. **"The situation in Texas"** Ibid., p. 193.

107   **"It was this municipality"** Edward Shannon LaMonte, *Politics & Welfare in Birmingham 1900–1975*. University of Alabama Press, 1995, pp. 90–91.

Ibid. "By 1932 the city's situation" Ibid., p. 90.

Ibid. "Demands on the Community Chest" Feldman, *A Sense of Place*, p. 182.

Ibid. "Before the crash" Juliet E. K. Walker, *The History of Black Business in America: Capitalism, Race, Entrepreneurship.* Twayne Publishers, 1998, p. 226.

Ibid. "Though the Red Cross" LaMonte, p. 90.

108   "My father-in-law" Ann Elizabeth Adams, interview with A. G. Gaston, June 1, 1977. Property of the University of Alabama at Birmingham, Mervyn H. Stern Library.

Chapter 5

112   "We were constantly plagued" Arthur George Gaston, *Green Power: The Successful Way of A. G. Gaston.* Troy State University Press, 1968, p. 73.

Ibid. "As Supreme Court Justice Hugo Black" Ann Elizabeth Adams, interview with A. G. Gaston, November 17, 1976. Property of the University of Alabama at Birmingham, Mervyn H. Stern Library.

118   "Minnie Louise Gardner" Billy Gardner had fathered two other children, Joseph and Nancy, prior to his marriage to Roberta.

121   "Arthur Gaston was unwaveringly" Gaston, *Green Power*, p. 73.

125   "The primary accusation" Ibid., p. 77.

126   "A. G. instructed his employees" Ibid., p. 78.

127   "Word of the program got out" Booker T. Washington Business College Brochure, 1946.

Ibid. "Its expanded classes" Gaston, *Green Power*, p. 80.

128   "Some two and a half million" Harold Evans, et al., *The American Century.* Knopf, 1988, p. 247.

Ibid. "Roosevelt had courted" Harvard Sitkoff, "Blacks and the New Deal" in *Civil Rights Since 1787: A Reader on the Black Struggle.* Jonathan Birnbaum and Clarence Taylor, eds. University Press, 2000, p. 284.

129   "Direct federal relief" Edward LaMonte, *Politics & Welfare in Birmingham 1900–1975.* University of Alabama Press, p. 130.

Ibid. "Whereas in the past" Robin D. G. Kelley and Earl Lewis, *To Make Our World Anew: A History of African Americans.* Oxford University Press, 2000, p. 414.

134   "Billy and Roberta certainly had" Patricia Thompson Stelts, *Black Midas: Arthur George Gaston.* Master's thesis, Georgia Southern College, Department of History, August 1973, p. 11.

135   "The business college continued" Ibid., p. 36.

136   "If financial crises hit" Gaston, *Green Power*, p. 81.

Ibid. "Becoming the very best" Ibid., p. 79.

Chapter 6

138   **"Moriarty and Gaston"** Arthur George Gaston, *Green Power: The Successful Way of A. G. Gaston.* Troy State University Press, 1968, p. 71.
      Ibid. **"No, A. G. Gaston"** Ibid., p. 72.

139   **"I'll make you"** Ibid., p. 72.

140   **"These representatives still"** BTW Insurance would continue to operate on an "in person" basis well into the 1990s: sales were still done door to door, though customers could mail in their monthly payments.

141   **"When we talk"** Philip Dray, *At the Hands of Persons Unknown.* Random House, 2002, p. 363.
      Ibid. **"The poet Langston Hughes"** Langston Hughes, "Nazi and Dixie Nordics," *The Chicago Defender.* March 10, 1945.

142   **"Moreover, the same government"** It was not until 1948, under President Harry S. Truman, that the armed forces were finally fully desegregated.
      Ibid. **"According to Zinn"** Howard Zinn, *On History.* Seven Stories Press, 2000, p. 419.

143   **"He had set up"** "Finding Place for the Negro: Stalking Robert C. Weaver Through the Federal Bureaucracy" by Walter B. Hill Jr., Senior Archivist, National Archives and Records Administration, College Park, MD (unpublished) and Walker, p. 242.
      Ibid. **"Nevertheless, three-quarters"** Gail Buckley, *American Patriots: The Story of Blacks in the Military from the Revolution to Desert Storm.* Random House, 2001, p. 279.
      Ibid. **"It was a segregation"** Benjamin O. Davis Jr., *Benjamin O. Davis, Jr.: An Autobiography.* Penguin Books, 1991, pp. 73–74.
      Ibid. **"The 99th Fighter Squadron"** Letters of Robert C. Weaver, National Archive Entry 188, Box 179.
      Ibid. **"Booker T. Washington Business College"** Gaston, *Green Power*, p. 81.

144   **"In addition, Gaston chaired"** Ibid., pp. 81, 82.
      Ibid. **"By this point"** Gaston Enterprises advertisement brochure, 1941.

146   **"In addition to offering"** *Birmingham World*, August 8, 1947, as quoted in Patricia Thompson Stelts. *Black Midas*, thesis, p. 86.
      Ibid. **"By 1965"** Minnie Gaston testimony: National Vocational Student Loan Insurance Act of 1965, hearings before the Select Subcommittee on Education of the Committee on Education and Labor, House of Representatives, Eighty-ninth Congress, First Session on HR 6468, Adam C. Powell, Chair. Washington, DC, April 5–7, 1965, p. 98.

147   **"At the league's inaugural"** Juliet E. K. Walker, *The History of Black Business in America: Capitalism, Race, Entrepreneurship.* Twayne Publishers, 1998, p. 184.
      Ibid. **"I am now putting"** Private letter of A. G. Gaston to W. D. Morison, September 12, 1947. Files of Emmer M. Lancaster, Negro Advisor to Secretary of Commerce. National Archives II, College Park, MD.

Ibid. **"I think this is"** Letter of W. D. Morison, President, National Real Estate Brokers to general membership, October 1947. Files of Emmer M. Lancaster. Ibid.

149 **"He advertised anyhow"** Gaston, *Green Power*, p. 83.

150 **"In Gaston's 1946 speech"** A. G. Gaston, address to Second Conference on the Negro in Business, October 17, 1946, Washington, D.C. Files of Emmer M. Lancaster.

151 **" '. . . we had not' "** Gaston, *Green Power*, p. 83.

152 **"I'm afraid we will not"** Private letter of A. G. Gaston to Emmer M. Lancaster, March 15, 1950. Files of Emmer M. Lancaster.

153 **"Though he glosses"** Gaston, *Green Power*, p. 84.

155 **"He bought lots"** Ibid., p. 84.

156 **"In acquiring the"** Stelts, *Black Midas*, p. 22.
Ibid. **"Even in his younger, struggling"** Ibid., p. 59.

157 **"In 1951, Gaston was selected"** Gaston, *Green Power*, p. 93.
Ibid. **"Renamed the World Methodist"** umns.umc.org/wmc/wmcfacts.htm.

158 **"Their departure was"** The *Queen Elizabeth* had served as a troopship in World War II, ferrying more than 750,000 troops overseas. It was decommissioned in 1945 and in October 1946 departed on its first public voyage.

159 Ibid. **"Their stateroom cabin"** Ibid., p. 95.

160 **"I began to consider"** Ibid., p. 98.

161 **"Though a 1943 survey"** Walker, *The History of Black Business in America*, p. 254.

162 **"In Monaco"** Gaston, *Green Power*, p. 103.

163 **"It was with pride"** *Birmingham News*, November 17, 1982, p. 10A.
Ibid. **"After their August 25, 1962, marriage"** Powell, p. 70—see note on text.

164 **"It must have been divine"** Gaston, *Green Power*, p. 35.
Ibid. **"Accordingly, Gaston formed"** *Birmingham World*, May 13, 1959.

165 **"Famously, robber baron"** Walker, p. 164.
Ibid. **"The Depression and"** Ibid., 188.

166 **"Citizens Federal became known"** Author interview with Kirkwood Balton, July 2003.
Ibid. **"Why should I be greedy"** Gaston, *Green Power*, p. 114.

Chapter 7

172 **"The group's spokesmen"** William Warren Rogers, Robert David Ward, Leah Rawls Atkins, and Wayne Flynt, *Alabama: The History of a Deep Southern State*. University of Alabama Press, 1994, p. 548.

173 **"In Anniston"** John Lewis, *Walking with the Wind: A Memoir of the Movement*. Harcourt Brace & Company, 1998, p. 156.
Ibid. **"They carried every makeshift"** Ibid.

174 **"A more conservative organization"** The organization would take any number of hits as an accommodationist enterprise throughout the civil rights era.

174 **"As Carl Rowan writes"** Carl T. Rowan, *Dream Makers, Dream Breakers: The World of Justice Thurgood Marshall.* Little, Brown, 1993, p. 252.

Ibid. **"There, she was given a job"** Stelts, p. 105.

175 **"They did not like"** E. Culpepper Clark, *The Schoolhouse Door: Segregation's Last Stand at the University of Alabama.* Oxford University Press, 1993, p. 59.

Ibid. **"At one point . . ."** Ibid., p. 64.

Ibid. **"Many from the staff"** Arthur George Gaston, *Green Power: The Successful Way of A. G. Gaston.* Troy State University Press, 1968, p. 117.

176 **"Speaking before the angry"** Ibid., p. 118.

Ibid. **"As a part of this commitment"** Ibid.

177 **"It was in this role"** Glenn T. Eskew, *But for Birmingham: The Local and National Movements in the Civil Rights Struggle.* University of North Carolina Press, 1997, p. 196.

Ibid. **"Despite the committee's efforts"** Ibid., pp. 178–179.

Ibid. **"On a trip to Tokyo"** Andrew M. Manis, *A Fire You Can't Put Out: The Civil Rights Life of Birmingham's Reverend Fred Shuttlesworth.* University of Alabama Press, 1999, p. 304.

178 **"According to historian Barbara Ransby"** Barbara Ransby, *Ella Baker and the Black Freedom Movement: A Racial Democratic Vision.* University of North Carolina Press, 2003, p. 218.

179 **"In one instance"** Diane McWhorter, *Carry Me Home: Birmingham, Alabama, the Climactic Battle of the Civil Rights Revolution.* Simon & Schuster, 2001, p. 264.

184 **"He worked with the students"** Eskew, *But for Birmingham*, p. 196.

Ibid. **"According to Diane McWhorter"** McWhorter, p. 264.

Ibid. **"Working with the students"** Manis, *Fire You Can't Put Out*, p. 307.

185 **"It soon became"** Clayborne Carson, ed., *The Autobiography of Martin Luther King, Jr.* Warner Books, 1998, p. 173.

Ibid. **"Over the years"** Ibid.

186 **"On March 29"** Manis, *Fire You Can't Put Out*, p. 307.

Ibid. **"With near total support"** Eskew, *But for Birmingham*, p. 200.

Ibid. **"The boycott was effective"** Ibid., p. 200.

188 **"Kennedy had other"** McWhorter, *Carry Me Home*, p. 288.

Ibid. **"Fred's the man"** Howell Raines, *My Soul Is Rested: Movement Days in the Deep South Remembered.* Viking, 1983, p. 169, and author interview with Shuttlesworth, November 2002.

189 Ibid. **"Rising swiftly"** McWhorter, p. 291.

Ibid. **"Shuttlesworth warned"** Manis, *Fire You Can't Put Out*, p. 325.

Ibid. **"Shuttlesworth, flush with"** Ibid.

190 "The Birmingham police" David J. Garrow, *Bearing the Cross: Martin Luther King, Jr. and the Southern Christian Leadership Conference.* Vintage, 1993, p. 221.
Ibid. "In a 1975 interview" Stelts, *Black Midas* thesis, p. 105.

191 "The whole city" Garrow, *Bearing the Cross*, p. 223.
Ibid. "Speaking in bold" McWhorter, p. 311.

192 "When the election was held" Eskew, pp. 187–188.

193 "Voters cast a historic" Ibid., p. 190.

194 "As Birmingham edged" Harold Evans, Gail Buckland, and Kevin Baker, *American Century*, 1998, p. 557.

195 "The Gaston Motel" Ralph D. Abernathy, *And the Walls Came Tumbling Down: An Autobiography.* HarperPerennial, 1990, p. 240.
Ibid. "The gatherings" Andrew Young, *An Easy Burden: The Civil Rights Movement and the Transformation of America.* HarperCollins Publishers, 1996, p. 231.

196 "And according to Wyatt Walker" Interview with author, April 2002.
Ibid. "Gaston was one of" Abernathy, *And the Walls*, p. 240.

197 "According to eyewitnesses" Eskew, *But for Birmingham*, p. 226.
Ibid. "Back at the A. G. Gaston Motel" Garrow, *Bearing the Cross*, p. 239.

198 "He told his audience" McWhorter, pp. 331–332.
Ibid. "I regret the absence" Gaston, *Green Power*, p. 120.

199 "That last line" McWhorter, *Carry Me Home*, p. 336.
Ibid. "If you picket Gaston" Ibid., p. 336.
Ibid. "Instead of acknowledging" Ibid., p. 337.

200 "We believe in a system" Clayborne Carson, *In Struggle: SNCC and the Black Awakening of the 1960s.* Harvard University Press, 1981, p. 181.

201 "Ralph Abernathy said" Abernathy, *And the Walls*, p. 248.
Ibid. "We recognized the line" Ibid.
Ibid. "Addressing the pillars" King himself, however, remembered the closing scene a little differently: "As Ralph stood up, unquestioningly, without hesitation, we all linked hands involuntarily, almost as if there had been some divine signal, and twenty five voices in Room 30 at the Gaston Motel in Birmingham, Alabama, chanted the battle hymn of our movement, 'We Shall Overcome.' " Carson, *MLK*, p. 183.

202 "By this point" Edward Shannon LaMonte, *Politics & Welfare in Birmingham 1900–1975.* University of Alabama Press, 1995, p. 178.
Ibid. "But King would answer" Carson, *Autobiography of MLK*, p. 190.
Ibid. "It is Young's theory" Young, *An Easy Burden*, p. 229.

203 "But even Young" Ibid., p. 230.
Ibid. "King is said to have told" Garrow, *Bearing the Cross*, p. 247.
Ibid. "As Taylor Branch put it" Branch, *Parting the Waters*, p. 728.

204 "She never forgot" Antonia Felix, *Condi: The Condoleeza Rice Story.* Newmarket Press, 2002, p. 55.

205 "An injured, maimed or" Manis, *Fire You Can't Put Out*, p. 370.

Ibid. **"When asked about"** Gaston, *Green Power*, pp. 132–134. The term *responsible Negro* would become one of derision, used against Gaston as a synonym for *Uncle Tom.*

Ibid. **"At the motel"** McWhorter, p. 368.

Ibid. **"As Andy Young remembered"** Young, *An Easy Burden*, p. 239.

206 **"Lawyer Vann"** McWhorter, p. 371.

Chapter 8

208 **"Even though the idea"** David J. Garrow, *Bearing the Cross: Martin Luther King, Jr. and the Southern Christian Leadership Conference.* Vintage, 1993, p. 252.

Ibid. **"Emerging from the building"** Clayborne Carson, *In Struggle: SNCC and the Black Awakening of the 1960s.* Harvard University Press, 1981, p. 213.

209 **"If the events"** Arthur George Gaston, *Green Power: The Successful Way of A. G. Gaston.* Troy State University Press, 1968, p. 119.

Ibid. **"The bank he had founded"** Glenn T. Eskew, *But for Birmingham: The Local and National Movements in the Civil Rights Struggle.* University of North Carolina Press, 1997, p. 207.

210 **"In his memoir of the era"** Andrew Young, *An Easy Burden: The Civil Rights Movement and the Transformation of America.* HarperCollins Publishers, 1996, p. 207.

Ibid. **"A 1957 survey"** Gaston, *Green Power*, p. 118.

Ibid. **"Gaston was outspoken"** Ibid., p. 127.

Ibid. **"While Martin Luther"** Ibid., p. 123.

212 **"Bond for their release"** Ibid.

213 **"I am happy to report"** Carson, *In Struggle*, p. 215.

Ibid. **"Fortunately, no one"** The question of who planted the bomb would never be answered, but we do know that in Bessemer (a short thirteen miles from Birmingham), a full-regalia, cross-burning gathering of twenty-five hundred Klansmen preceded the attack.

214 **"Claude Sitton"** Taylor Branch, *Parting the Waters: America in the King Years, 1954–63.* Simon & Schuster, 1988, p. 796.

Ibid. **"By dawn"** Ibid.

Ibid. **"In a live broadcast"** Ibid., p. 800.

215 **"Arthur Shores's home"** Ibid., p. 868.

216 **"He recalls reading"** Gaston, *Green Power*, p. 131.

Ibid. **"The invitation reinforced"** Ibid., p. 130.

217 **"I started running"** Ibid., p. 131.

218 **"He used the occasion"** Carson, *In Struggle*, p. 231.

219 **"What murdered"** Branch, *Parting the Waters*, p. 893.

Ibid. **"As the session began"** Gaston, *Green Power*, p. 135.

Ibid. **"I don't want to invade"** Branch describes the president as somber and distracted during much of the discussion: "President Kennedy said nothing until A. G. Gaston interrupted King to complain that insurance companies were canceling commercial policies on Negro businesses. . . . At this Kennedy perked up to say here was a problem they could take care of." Branch, *Parting the Waters*, p. 894.

220 **"Indeed, Gaston *had* written"** Andrew M. Manis, *A Fire You Can't Put Out: The Civil Rights Life of Birmingham's Reverend Fred Shuttlesworth.* University of Alabama Press, 1999, pp. 410, 414.

221 **"We have talked long enough"** Taylor Branch, *Pillar of Fire: America in the King Years 1963–65.* Touchstone, Simon & Schuster, 1998, p. 178.

222 **"I conclude that this award"** Martin Luther King Jr. Nobel Prize acceptance speech, Oslo, Norway. December 10, 1964.

223 **"Their cause must be"** Special message to the congress, "The American Promise," March 15, 1965. Public Papers of the Presidents of the United States, Lyndon B. Johnson, 1965.

224 **"He commented that"** As printed in *The New York Times*, March 22, 1965, pp. 1–2.

225 **"What Mary remembered"** Author interview with Mary Gardner, June 2003.

226 **"Hearings for the"** National Vocational Student Loan Insurance Act of 1965, hearings before the Select Subcommittee on Education of the Committee on Education and Labor, House of Representatives. Eighty-ninth Congress, First Session on HR 6468, Adam C. Powell, Chair. Washington, DC, April 5–7, 1965, p. 98.

227 **"The vast need"** Ibid., p. 101.
Ibid. **"During the academic year"** Ibid., p. 103.
Ibid. **"When she had finished"** Ibid., p. 107.

228 **"On August 6, 1965"** Sanford Wexler, *The Civil Rights Movement: An Eyewitness History.* Checkmark Books, 1999, p. 227.

230 **"Birmingham newspaperman"** Jesse Lewis, interviewed by author, May 2003.

Chapter 9

232 **"The numbers in the middle years"** Howard Zinn, *On History.* Seven Stories Press, 2000, pp. 458, 466.
Ibid. **"As of 1977"** Ibid., p. 466.
Ibid. **"Very few civil rights leaders"** Robin D. G. Kelley, *Race Rebels: Culture, Politics & The Black Working Class.* The Free Press, 1996, p. 78.
Ibid. **"Formed, it would seem"** Ibid., pp. 84–85.

233 **"The argument here"** Moreover, the absence of issues relating to poverty (not to mention poor people) from the front lines of civil rights agitation in itself betrays a crucial historical evasion on the part of the black community when it comes to the question of economic stability. It is only more recently, as certain advances on the racial landscape have come to fruition, that many blacks have come to take seriously the need to ask questions related to class and the economics of power. Yet for any

number of reasons, those questions fell out of the picture while "civil rights" were being legislated.

233 **"Yet, as Jay R. Mandle reveals"** Jay R. Mandle, *The Roots of Black Poverty*. Duke University Press, 1978, p. 119.

234 **"The mines, which"** Kelley, *Race Rebels,* p. 79.

236 **"McWhorter's repetition of the characterization"** Diane McWhorter, *Carry Me Home, Birmingham, Alabama: The Climactic Battle of the Civil Rights Revolution.* Simon & Schuster, 2001, p. 335.

239 **"If wanting to spare"** Arthur George Gaston, *Green Power: The Successful Way of A. G. Gaston.* Troy State University Press, 1968, p. 125.

240 **"Though there was already"** Furthermore, the existent Boys Club originally had been established for use by the white community in Birmingham. Though the passage of civil rights legislation meant that it was now incumbent upon the club to admit black members, Gaston was hesitant to push for such inclusion given the relatively new peace that had been reached in the city.
Ibid. **"By the time the doors"** Gaston, *Green Power*, p. 155.

242 **"Gaston also offered"** *Birmingham World*, August 8, 1947, as quoted in Patricia Thompson Stelts, *Black Midas*, thesis, p. 87.
Ibid. **"So dedicated was he"** Stelts, *Black Midas*, p. 88.

243 **"If we believe"** James Carville, *We're Right, They're Wrong: A Handbook for Spirited Progressives.* Random House, 1996, p. xvi.

244 **"As of 1972"** Stelts, *Black Midas*, appendix A, p. 140.
Ibid. **"The bank held"** Juliet E. K. Walker, *The History of Black Business in America: Capitalism, Race, Entrepreneurship.* Twayne Publishers, 1998, p. 299.

245 Ibid. **"The insurance company had continued"** "Financial Statement of Negro Insurance Companies," U.S. Department of Commerce, Emmer Marin Lancaster, Special Advisor to the Secretary of Commerce (1941, 1949, and 1951, respectively). Property of National Archives II, College Park, MD.
Ibid. **"As of 1951"** Also *Black Enterprise* magazine, June–July 1982.
Ibid. **"One version"** Author interview with Jesse Lewis, June 2003.

247 **"I've got a fine"** Ingrid Kindred, "A. G. Gaston," *Birmingham News*, July 4, 1982, p. B1.

248 **"Downstairs, at the"** Garland Reeves, Andrew Kilpatrick, Walter Bryant, and Dale Short, "Gaston Kidnapped from His Home, Rescued by Deputies; Man Held," *Birmingham News*, January 24, 1976, p. 1.

249 **"Whoever was working"** Edna Gardner, interview by the author, July 2003.
Ibid. **"Both Arthur and Minnie"** Paul Gardner, interview by the author, July 2003.

250 **"And though Clayborn"** Frances Spotswood, "Clayborn Guilty, Receives Life in Gaston Burglary," *Birmingham News*, May 27, 1976.

250 **"Her nephew Paul"** Paul Gardner, interview by the author, July 2003.

251 **"I forgot about"** Kindred, "A. G. Gaston," p. B1.

Ibid. **"My name is not"** Ibid.

252 **"The publicity surrounding"** Gaston was also implicitly criticizing how his race was playing a factor in the media's representation of him, his status as a "millionaire" perceived as a bigger accomplishment than his role as a successful businessman.

Ibid. **"The only thing the black people"** Stelts, *Black Midas*. Emory Jackson, interview. Birmingham, Alabama, August 10, 1972, p. 126.

258 **"Grasping the knife"** Gaston, *Green Power*, p. 10.

Ibid. **"This is the way"** Ibid., p. 11.

"I didn't get into business" Rick Harmon, "Gaston Story Offers Students Inspiration," *Birmingham News*, February 17, 1982.

259 **"In 1987"** Walker, p. 299.

262 **"If we believe that"** Derek Bell, *Ethical Ambition: Living a Life of Meaning and Worth*. Bloomsbury, 2002, p. 7.

Chapter 10

265 **"A model citizen"** *Birmingham News*, January 20, 1996, p. 1.

Ibid. **"He had his finger"** Richard Arrington, interview with the author, November 2002.

Ibid. **"Birmingham, Alabama is my home"** Arthur George Gaston, *Green Power: The Successful Way of A. G. Gaston*, Troy State University Press, 1968, p. 172.

266 **"What was that"** Fred Shuttlesworth, interview by the author, November 2002.

Ibid. **"He had used Gaston as"** Graves still keeps a copy of those promotional tools, featuring Gaston, proudly displayed in his New York City office.

268 **"Throughout his business life"** In 2003 blacks controlled $588.7 billion in spending power; by 2007 that figure is likely to reach $900 billion. "The Multicultural Economy 2003" published by The Selig Center for Economic Growth, University of Georgia: GBEC, Vol. 63, No. 1, Second Quarter 2003, p. 2.

Ibid. **"A. G. had served a nearly"** One of Gaston's favorite activities during his time on the board was his monthly lunch with Dr. George Washington Carver, the brilliant Tuskegee scientist who had taught Alabama farmers how to rotate their devastated crops—and whose experiments with peanuts and sweet potatoes resulted in the development of many modern-day products.

269 **"Gaston, he had cried,"** *Birmingham News*, October 2, 1978.

Ibid. **"Back in Birmingham"** Al Fox, "Demos Assemble at Gaston Home to Show Support of Carter on Iran" in *The Birmingham News*, December 12, 1979.

270 **"There ought to be plenty"** Gaston, *Green Power*, p. 174.

Ibid. **"He, above all,"** Kirkwood Balton, interview with the author, July 2003.

SELECTED BIBLIOGRAPHY

Abernathy, Ralph D. *And the Walls Came Tumbling Down: An Autobiography*. New York: HarperPerennial, 1990.

Allport, Gordon W. *The Nature of Prejudice: A Comprehensive and Penetrating Study of the Origin and Nature of Prejudice*. New York: Anchor Books, 1958.

Bell, Gregory S. *In the Black: A History of African Americans on Wall Street*. New York: John Wiley & Sons, 2002.

Bennett, Lerone Jr. *Before the Mayflower: A History of Black America*. New York: Penguin Books, USA, 1984.

Binder, Frederick M., and David M. Reimers. *The Way We Lived—Volume II: 1865–Present*. Boston: D. C. Heath and Company, 1996.

Birnbaum, Jonathan, and Clarence Taylor, eds. *Civil Rights Since 1787: A Reader on the Black Struggle*. New York: New York University Press, 2000.

Borstelmann, Thomas. *The Cold War and The Color Line: American Race Relations in the Global Arena*. Cambridge, MA: Harvard University Press, 2001.

Bowden, Witt. *Industrial History of the United States*. New York: Augustus M. Kelley, Publishers, 1967.

Branch, Taylor. *Pillar of Fire: America in the King Years 1963–65*. New York: Touchstone, Simon and Schuster, 1998.

———. *Parting the Waters: America in the King Years 1954–63*. New York: Simon and Schuster, 1988.

Brotz, Howard, ed. *African-American Social & Political Thought 1850–1920*. Somerset, NJ: Transaction Publishers, 1991.

Bruchey, Stuart. *The Wealth of the Nation: An Economic History of the United States.* New York: Harper & Row, 1988.

Buckley, Gail. *American Patriots: The Story of Blacks in the Military from the Revolution to Desert Storm.* New York: Random House, 2001.

Butgereit, Betsy. "A. G. Gaston Dies." *Birmingham News,* January 19, 1996, pp. 21, 2A.

Butgereit, Betsy, Robert Gordon, and Patricia Dedrick. "Blacks, Whites Mourn Loss of 'Leader-Citizen.' " *Birmingham News,* January 19, 1996.

Cantor, Milton, ed. *Black Labor in America.* Westport, CT: Negro Universities Press, 1969.

Carnegie, Andrew. *The Gospel of Wealth.* Bedford, MA: Applewood Books, 1998.

Carson, Clayborne. *In Struggle: SNCC and the Black Awakening of the 1960s.* Cambridge, MA: Harvard University Press, 1981.

Carson, Clayborne, ed. *The Autobiography of Martin Luther King, Jr.* New York: Warner Books, 1998.

Chamblee, Leonard, "Gaston Cites Negro Leadership Change," *Birmingham Post-Herald,* August 30, 1963.

Clark, E. Culpepper. *The Schoolhouse Door: Segregation's Last Stand at the University of Alabama.* New York: Oxford University Press, 1993.

Cowan, Tom, and Jack Maguire. *Timelines of African-American History: 500 Years of Black Achievement.* New York: HarperCollins Publishers, 1994.

Curtin, Mary Ellen. *Black Prisoners and Their World, Alabama, 1865–1900.* Charlottesville: The University Press of Virginia, 2000.

Davis, Benjamin O. Jr. *Benjamin O. Davis, Jr., American: An Autobiography.* New York: Penguin Books, USA, 1991.

Davis, John P., ed. *The American Negro Reference Book.* Englewood Cliffs, NJ: Prentice Hall, 1966.

de Tocqueville, Alexis. *Democracy in America: Volume I.* New York: Random House, 1990 (first published in 1835).

Dray, Philip. *At the Hands of Persons Unknown: The Lynching of Black America.* New York: Random House, 2002.

DuBois, W. E. B. *Black Reconstruction in America, 1860–1880.* New York: Atheneum, 1985 (first published in 1935).

——— *The Souls of Black Folks.* New York: Dover, 1994.

Dyson, Michael E. *I May Not Get There with You: The True Martin Luther King, Jr.* New York: The Free Press, Simon & Schuster, 2000.

Eskew, Glenn T. *But for Birmingham: The Local and National Movements in the Civil Rights Struggle.* Chapel Hill, NC: University of Chapel Hill Press, 1997.

Evans, Harold, Gail Buckland, and Kevin Baker. *The American Century.* New York: Alfred A. Knopf, 1998.

Feldman, Lynne B., and John N. Ingham, eds. *African-American Business Leaders: A Biographical Dictionary.* Westport: Greenwood Press, 1994.

Feldman, Lynne B. *A Sense of Place: Birmingham's Black Middle Class Community, 1890–1930.* Tuscaloosa: University of Alabama Press, 1999.

Fitch, John A. *The Steel Workers.* Pittsburgh: University of Pittsburgh Press, 1989.

Fitzhugh, H. Naylor, and Jesse O. Walker. *Howard University: Social Science Conference 1945.* Washington, DC: Howard University Press, 1946.

Foner, Eric. *Reconstruction: America's Unfinished Revolution 1863–1877.* Baton Rouge: Louisiana State University Press, 1989.

Foner, Philip S., and Ronald L. Lewis. *The Black Worker to 1869: Volume 1.* Philadelphia: Temple University Press, 1978.

Fowlkes, Ben F. *Cooperation: The Solution to the So-Called Negro Problem.* Birmingham: Birmingham Novelty Book Concern, 1908.

Fox, Al. "Demos Assemble at Gaston Home to Show Support of Carter on Iran." *Birmingham News,* December 12, 1979.

Franklin, John Hope, and Isidore Starr, eds. *The Negro in Twentieth Century America: A Reader on the Struggle for Civil Rights.* New York: Vintage, 1967.

Franklin, John Hope. *Race and History: Selected Essays 1938–1988.* Baton Rouge: Louisiana State University Press, 1989.

Gaines, Kevin K. *Uplifting the Race.* Chapel Hill: University of North Carolina Press, 1996.

Garraty, John. *The Great Depression.* New York: Bantam Doubleday Dell, 1987.

Garrow, David J. *Bearing the Cross: Martin Luther King, Jr. and the Southern Christian Leadership Conference.* United Kingdom: Vintage Random House, 1993.

———. *Protest at Selma: Martin Luther King, Jr., and the Voting Rights Act of 1965.* New Haven, CT: Yale University Press, 1978.

Gaston, Arthur George. *Green Power: The Successful Way of A. G. Gaston.* Troy, AL: Troy State University Press, 1968.

Genovese, Eugene D. *Roll Jordan Roll: The World The Slaves Made.* New York: Random House, 1976.

———. *The Political Economy of Slavery: Studies in the Economy and Society of the Slave South.* New York: Random House, 1965.

Gutman, Herbert H. *The Black Family in Slavery and Freedom, 1750–1925.* New York: Pantheon Books, 1976.

Harmon, Rick. "Gaston Story Offers Students Inspiration." *Birmingham News,* November 17, 1982.

Harris, Jacqueline, L. *History and Achievement of the NAACP.* New York: Franklin Watts, 1992.

Haws, Robert, ed. *The Age of Segregation: Race Relations in the South, 1890–1945.* Jackson: University Press of Mississippi, 1978.

Heilbroner, Robert L., and Aaron Singer. *The Economic Transformation of America: 1600–the Present.* New York: Harcourt Brace Jovanovich, 1984.

Hemphill, Paul. *Leaving Birmingham: Notes of a Native Son.* New York: Penguin Books, USA, 1993.

Henderson, Alexa Benson. *Atlanta Life Insurance Company: Guardian of Black Economic Dignity.* Tuscaloosa: University of Alabama Press, 1990.

Higginson, Thomas Wentworth. *Army Life in a Black Regiment and Other Writings*. New York: Penguin Books, 1997 (first published in 1870).

Hine, Delores Clark, and Kathleen Thompson. *A Shining Thread of Hope: The History of Black Women in America*. New York: Broadway Books, 1998.

Holt, Rackham. *George Washington Carver: An American Biography*. New York: Doubleday, Doran & Company, 1943.

Hood, John. "Capitalism: Discrimination's Implacable Enemy." *The Freeman*, a publication of The Foundation for Economic Education, Inc., Vol. 48, No. 8 (August 1998).

Images of America: Birmingham and Jefferson County Alabama. Mount Pleasant, SC: Arcadia Publishing, 1998.

Kelley, Robin D. G., and Earl Lewis. *To Make Our World Anew: A History of African Americans*. Oxford: Oxford University Press, 2000.

Kelley, Robin D. G. *Race Rebels: Culture, Politics, and the Black Working Class*. New York: The Free Press, 1996.

Kennedy, William J. Jr. *The North Carolina Mutual Story*. Durham, NC: The North Carolina Mutual Life Insurance Company, 1970.

Kilpatrick, Andrew. "Fear of Law Sparked Gaston's Climb to Top—Dedicated to Hard Work." *Birmingham News*, October 2, 1978, p. 10A.

Kindred, Ingrid. "A. G. Gaston—He's Lived Through Nine Decades." *Birmingham News*, July 4, 1982, p. 1B.

LaMonte, Edward Shannon. *Politics & Welfare in Birmingham 1900–1975*. Tuscaloosa: University of Alabama Press, 1995.

Larson, Erik. *The Devil in the White City: Murder, Magic, and Madness at the Fair that Changed America*. New York: Crown, 2003.

Lemann, Nicholas. *The Promised Land: The Great Black Migration and How It Changed America*. New York: Random House, 1992.

Levi, Primo. *The Drowned and The Saved*. New York: Random House, 1988.

Lewis, David L. *W. E. B. DuBois: Biography of a Race—1868–1919*. New York: Henry Holt and Company, 1993.

———. *King: A Biography*. Chicago: University of Illinois Press, 1978.

Lewis, John, and Michael D'orso. *Walking with the Wind: A Memoir of the Movement*. New York: Harcourt Brace & Company, 1999.

Long, Richard A., and Eugenia W. Collier, eds. *Afro-American Writing: An Anthology of Prose and Poetry*. University Park: Pennsylvania State University Press, 1985.

Mandle, Jay R. *The Roots of Black Poverty: The Southern Plantation Economy After the Civil War*. Durham: Duke University Press, 1978.

Manis, Andrew, M. *A Fire You Can't Put Out: The Civil Rights Life of Birmingham's Reverend Fred Shuttlesworth*. Tuscaloosa: University of Alabama Press, 1999.

Marable, Manning. *How Capitalism Underdeveloped Black America: Problems in Race, Political Economy and Society*. South End Press, 1983.

———. *Black Leadership: Four Great American Leaders and the Struggle for Civil Rights*. New York: Penguin Putnam, 1998.

Margo, Robert A. *Race and Schooling in the South, 1880–1950: An Economic History.* Chicago: University of Chicago Press, 1990.

McWhorter, Diane. *Carry Me Home: Birmingham, Alabama, the Climactic Battle of the Civil Rights Revolution.* New York: Simon and Schuster, 2001.

Meltzer, Milton. *The Black Americans: A History in Their Own Words 1619–1983.* New York: Harper & Row Publishers, 1984.

Menand, Louis. *The Metaphysical Club: A Story of Ideas in America.* New York: Farrar, Straus and Giroux, 2001.

Menzer, Mitch, and Mike Williams, "Images of Work: Birmingham 1894–1937." *The Journal of the Birmingham Historical Society.* Vol. 7, No. 1 (June 1981).

Mitford, Jessica. *The American Way of Death, Revisited.* New York: Random House, 1998.

Morris, Aldon D. *The Origins of the Civil Rights Movement: Black Communities Organizing for Change.* New York: The Free Press, 1984.

Moore, Geraldine H. "A. G. Gaston Paid National Honor," *Birmingham News,* March 13, 1960.

Motley, Constance Baker. *Equal Justice Under Law: An Autobiography.* New York: Farrar, Straus and Giroux, 1998.

Motley, Mary P. *The Invisible Soldier: The Experience of the Black Soldier, World War II.* Detroit: Wayne State University Press, 1987.

Murray, Pauli. *Pauli Marray: The Autobiography of a Black Activist, Feminist, Lawyer, Priest, and Poet.* Knoxville: University of Tennessee Press, 1989.

Newman, Debra L. *Black History: A Guide to Civilian Records in the National Archives.* Washington, DC: National Archives Trust Fund Board, 1984.

Olson, Lynne. *Freedom's Daughters: The Unsung Heroines of the Civil Rights Movement from 1830–1970.* New York: Simon & Schuster, 2001.

Osborne, John. "Railroad Yesterdays: The Frisco Comes to Demopolis, Alabama." http://www.frisco.freewebspace.com/. 800 Pinhook Road, Demopolis, AL 36732-5702.

Pickett, Albert James, and Harper Lee. *Pickett's History of Alabama: And Incidentally of Georgia and Mississippi.* River City Press, 2003.

Ploski, Harry, A., and Roscoe C. Brown. *The Negro Almanac.* New York: Bellwether Publishing Company, 1967.

Powell, Colin and Joseph E. Persico. *My American Journey.* New York: Random House, 1995.

Ragan, Larry. *True Tales of Birmingham: Birmingham Historical Society.* Birmingham: Birmingham Historical Society, 1992.

Ransby, Barbara. *Ella Baker and the Black Freedom Movement: A Radical Democratic Vision.* Chapel Hill: University of North Carolina Press, 2003.

Ravitch, Diane, ed. *The American Reader: Words That Moved a Nation.* New York: HarperCollins Publishers, 1990.

Reeves, Garland, Andrew Kilpatrick, Walter Brant, Dale Short, and Frances Spotswood. "Gaston Kidnapped from his Home, Rescued by Deputies, Man Held." *The Birmingham News,* January 24, 1976.

Robertson, Peggy. "Gastons Glad To Be Back from Russia," *The Birmingham News,* January 1, 1972.

Roediger, David R. *The Wages of Whiteness: Race and the Making of the American Working Class.* New York: Verso, 1991.

Rogers, William, W., Robert D. Ward, Leah R. Atkins, and Wayne Flint. *Alabama: The History of a Deep South State.* Tuscaloosa: University of Alabama Press, 1994.

Rowan, Carl T. *Dream Makers, Dream Breakers: The World of Justice Thurgood Marshall.* Boston: Little, Brown and Company, 1993.

Schlesinger, Arthur M., Jr. *The Coming of the New Deal.* Boston: Houghton Mifflin, 1958.

Schulke, Flip, and Penelope McPhee. *King Remembered.* New York: Simon & Schuster, 1986.

Scott, Emmett J. *Official History of the American Negro in the World War.* New York: Arno Press, 1919.

Spotswood, Frances. "Clayborn Guilty, Receives Life in Gaston Burglary," *The Birmingham News,* May 27, 1976.

Stein, Judith. *The World of Marcus Garvey: Race and Class in Modern Society.* Baton Rouge: Louisiana State University Press, 1986.

Stelts, Patricia Thompson. *Black Midas: Arthur George Gaston.* Master's thesis, Georgia Southern College, Department of History, August, 1973.

Strouse, Jean. *Morgan: American Financier.* New York: HarperCollins Publishers, 2000.

Sullivan, Mark. *Our Times III: Prewar America, 1900–1925.* New York: Charles Scribner's Sons, 1930.

Swygert, Dorothy. *The Biography of A. G. Gaston—Birmingham's Self-Made Millionaire.* New York: Rekindling the Heart Publications, 1999.

Walker, Juliet E.K., ed. *Encyclopedia of African American Business History.* Westport: Greenwood Press, 1999.

———. *The History of Black Business in America: Capitalism, Race, Entrepreneurship.* New York: Twayne Publishers, 1998.

Walker, Wyatt T. *Millennium End Papers: The Walker File '98–99.* New York: Martin Luther King Fellows Press, 2000.

Ward, Robert David, and William Warren Rogers. *Convicts, Coal and the Banner Mine Tragedy.* Tuscaloosa: University of Alabama Press, 1987.

Washburn, Dennis. "Filling Needs Opened Doors for Dr. Gaston," *The Birmingham News,* February 15, 1970.

Washington, Booker T. *Up From Slavery: The Autobiography of Booker T. Washington.* Secaucus, NJ: Carol Publishing Group, 1997.

Washington, Booker T., and the Reverend W. R. Pettiford. *The Negro in Business.* Boston: Hertel, Jenkins and Co., 1907.

Watson, Denton, L. *Lion in the Lobby: Clarence Mitchell, Jr.'s Struggle for the Passage of Civil Rights Laws.* New York: William Morrow and Company, 1990.

Weeks, J. D. *Birmingham: A Postcard Tour.* Mount Pleasant, SC: Arcadia Publishing, 1999.

Wexler, Sanford. *The Civil Rights Movement: An Eyewitness History.* New York: Checkmark Books, 1999.

Wheeler, Mark, ed. *The Economics of the Great Depression.* Kalamazoo, MI: W. E. UpJohn Institute, 1998.

White, Marjorie L. *A Walk to Freedom: The Rev. Fred Shuttlesworth and the Alabama Christian Movement for Human Rights, 1956–1964.* Birmingham: Birmingham Historical Society, 1998.

———. *The Birmingham District: An Industrial History and Guide.* Birmingham: Birmingham Historical Society and the First National Bank of Birmingham, Publishers, 1981.

———. *Downtown Birmingham: Architectural and Historical Walking Tour Guide.* Birmingham: Birmingham Historical Society, the First National Bank of Birmingham, and the Junior League of Birmingham, Publishers, 1980.

Williams, Juan. *Eyes on the Prize: America's Civil Rights Years 1945–1965.* New York: Penguin Books, USA, 1987.

Winkler, Allan M. *The Recent Past: Readings on America Since World War II.* New York: HarperCollins Publishers, 1989.

Work, Monroe N. *Negro Year Book: An Annual Encyclopedia of the Negro 1931–1932.* Tuskegee, AL: Tuskegee Institute Press, 1931.

Wormley, Stanton L., and Lewis H. Fenderson, eds. *Many Shades of Black.* New York: William Morrow, 1969.

Wormser, Richard. *The Rise and Fall of Jim Crow.* New York: St. Martin's Press, 2003.

Wright, Gavin. *The Political Economy of the Cotton South: Households, Markets and Wealth in the Nineteenth Century.* New York: W. W. Norton & Company, 1978.

———. *Old South, New South: Revolutions in the Southern Economy Since the Civil War.* New York: Basic Books, 1986.

Wright, Kai. *The African-American Archive: The History of the Black Experience Through Documents.* New York: Back Dog & Levnthal Publishers, 2001.

Young, Andrew. *An Easy Burden: The Civil Rights Movement and the Transformation of America.* New York: HarperCollins Publishers, 1996.

Zinn, Howard. *A People's History of the United States: 1492–Present.* New York: HarperPerennial, 1995.

———. *On History.* New York: Seven Stories Press, 2000.

INDEX

Page numbers in *italics* refer to illustrations.

Index